| Table of Contents | Page |
|---|---|
| Introduction | 2 |
| Proverbs | 5 |
| Yorùbá Alphabets & Pronunciation Guide | 231 |
| Personal Pronouns | 233 |
| Yorùbá words used in this book that have synonyms | 235 |
| About the Author | 236 |

## Introduction

The author, Táiyé Amọ́lẹ̀sẹ̀, is a descendant of the Yorùbá tribe in South-Western Nigeria.

The Yorùbá tribe is the largest tribe in Africa with approximately 60 million people within Nigeria alone. They are a group of people steeped in millennia of traditions, customs and beliefs.

The Yorùbá language is one of the principal languages spoken in Nigeria and in some surrounding West African countries. The Yorùbá language, culture and religions are still prominent in Brazil, Cuba, Haiti and the Caribbean to this day.

Moreover, first and second generations of the Yorùbá people can be found in North America, United Kingdom and parts of Europe. They are an ever evolving and migrating people. According to the BBC and a London daily (either the Daily Mail or the Daily Mirror) published in the summer of 1990, a Yorùbá king was the LAST ruler of Egypt circa 3,500 B.C., making Yorùbá the oldest race in all of Africa.

The Yorubas' migrating tendencies and far flung descendants are one of the inspirations for this book. While they've adapted to the various cultures in the Diaspora, their hearts and souls are still tied to their Yorùbá roots. The author is obliged to help preserve the treasured culture and beliefs for generations to come.

One thing that is common among most cultures, if not all, is idioms and proverbs. Rarely will a Yorùbá person speak without invoking a proverb or two to drive their point home. The use of proverbs is applied to every life situation. If there is a problem, concern, or happy occasion there is an accompanying proverb to underscore the issue.

The author is well versed in Yorùbá language and has painstakingly compiled 1,500 proverbs. The proverbs all have correct accent marks to help with pronunciation and understanding. The accent marks are important because in the Yorùbá language one word can have multiple meanings. It is the accent marks that unambiguously guide the reader to the correct pronunciation of homonyms. Each proverb is accompanied by a direct [literal] translation and explanation. Same as a Yorùbá word, one proverb can apply to multiple situations.

The book will be useful to Yorùbá speakers within Nigeria proper in general, as well as being beneficial for students of Yorùbá language in Nigeria's primary, secondary and tertiary institutions. Additionally, the book aims to be helpful to those learning the Yorùbá language in West Africa, Brazil, Cuba, Haiti and the Caribbean.

As a matter of fact, the Yorùbá language is currently being taught in some universities in the United States, viz.:

- University of Texas at Austin (Dept. of African & African Diaspora Studies);
- Harvard University (African Language Program);
- University of Florida (College of Liberal Arts and Sciences).

In England, the language is a popular program at the

- University College London;
- University of London (SOAS);
- University of Cambridge.

Finally, it is the author's desire to help preserve the Yorùbá culture and the language they love so much. The author also wishes to share his gift of words and help Yorùbá people in the Diaspora rekindle their connection to their culture and more importantly pass on to coming generations a sense of pride and belonging.

This Glossary of Yorùbá Proverbs, each with its own humorous literal interpretation as well as actual meaning, has a target audience of circa 300m world-wide, when the Yorùbá peoples of Nigeria, Benin Republic, Burkina Faso, Gambia, Ghana, Ivory Coast, Sierra Leone, Togo, Brazil, Cuba, Haiti, The West Indies, Europe, and North America are factored in.

Copyright © 2024 Taiye Amolese. All Rights Reserved

| Òwe l'ẹṣin Ọ̀rọ̀, Ọ̀rọ̀ l'ẹṣin Òwe; b'ọ́rọ̀ọ́ bá s'ọnù, Òwe l'a fi ń wa | A Proverb is the horse of Words, a Word is the horse of Proverbs; if a Word gets lost, we use a Proverb to find it. |
|---|---|

|   | Yorùbá Proverb | English Literal Translation and Meaning |
|---|---|---|
| 1. | Áá b'ẹ́kùn mi ní Bùba<br>Wàá b'ẹ́kùn mi ní Bùba | He/she will meet my leopard in the den<br>You will meet my leopard in the den<br>- I shall be ready for him/her!<br>- I shall be ready for you! [This is a sort of battle cry expressed in defiance of an adversary]. |
| 2. | A bẹ́'gi Ìrèké tútù kò ṣ'omi; ṣé gbígbẹ è ní ó m'ómi wá? | We cut fresh sugarcane and no juice came out of it; is the dry one going to produce juice?<br>- We tried an expensive/top-of-the-range version, it produced nothing; is a used older version going to do anything? |
| 3. | À dé'gbó àì fọ'hùn ún máa ń mú k'ẹiyẹ ṣu lé'ni l'órí ni | Arriving silently in the forest makes a bird shit on one's head<br>- If someone was insolent to a powerful person with authority to punish at will and went unpunished, this could lead to more disrespect from others. An example has to be made. |
| 4. | A dùn ún ṣe bọ̀rọ̀, Ohun t'Ọlọ́un l'ọ́wọ́ sí; a ṣòro ó ṣe, Ohun t'Ọlọ́un ò l'ọ́wọ́ sí | Effortless like child's play, what God Has a hand in; difficult to do, what God Has no hand in<br>- This might be a muse of someone who is embarking on a personal project. |
| 5. | A dúró l'ókèèrè t'ó ń wò'ṣe Ẹiyẹ | Standing at a distance while observing the shenanigans of a bird<br>- If someone is acting funny or behaving strangely, you stand and watch them or pretend like you don't notice their improper behavior. |
| 6. | A f'àparò s'ábẹ́, à ń gbin'kà | We place a bush-fowl under us while we plant seeds<br>- You're entrusting the wrong individual with an important duty; be ready for a probable betrayal;<br>- Resolve the nagging issue on the ground |

| | | |
|---|---|---|
| | | before embarking on another effort. |
| 7. | A fẹ́ á jẹ, má jẹ́ á yó | Doesn't mind us eating, but does not want us to be filled<br>- This adage is said of someone who [apparently] doesn't wish another success. |
| 8. | A fẹ́ á jẹ, má jẹ́ á yó, t'ó ń fún'ni n'ílẹ̀ n'ídī Ọ̀pẹ | Someone who wants us to feed but not be full, that gives another 'free' land by the palm trees [knowing the portion of land surrounding a palm tree is not easy to till due to the perennial thorns that wither and fall off of the tree and spread at the base]<br>- A selfish individual who doesn't have the interests of others at heart. |
| 9. | A fi ẹ́ jo'yè Àwòdì, oò lè gb'ádìẹ | You have been coronated with the chieftaincy of the eagle, you cannot even grab a chicken<br>- You are not worthy of your position. |
| 10. | A fi Jàgùdà s'ílé Owó, ẹ ní ò níí k'ówó ná | We put a robber in charge of a bank and you all said in his favor that he'd never take any money<br>- You all voted for the new leader and welcomed his government with open arms, now the country is in economic ruin. |
| 11. | A fi Òjé bọ Ọwọ́ Olórìṣà; Ìgbà tí wọn ó fi bọ̀ọ́ l'ọ́wọ́, a máa ni'ra. Ìgbàt'ọ́n bá wọ̀ọ́ tán, kìí ṣeé yọ bọ̀rọ̀ | We put a gold bangle on the messenger-god priest; when they were putting it on his wrist, it did not snap on with ease. Though the bangle has finally entered, pulling it out is now a colossal problem<br>- Building someone up might have been a tremendous task; however, to get him down from the pedestal on which you have placed him is now an uphill task. Extreme caution needs to be exercised. |
| 12. | A gbà l'ọ́wọ́ọ Mẹ́èrí, Baálẹ̀ẹ Jòntolo | One who takes from those who have nothing, overseer of Jòntolo<br>- A selfish taker who asks for a pound of flesh from defaulters of his loans. |
| 13. | A gb'ẹ̀hìn b'ẹbọ jẹ́ | Someone who goes behind to destroy a ritualistic pot containing food (offering) of |

|  |  | appeasement to some god<br>- This is an accusative adage to someone who has betrayed a secret that they were privy to. |
|---|---|---|
| 14. | A ì ń p'àrọwà f'ẹni tí Wèrè é lù'yá ẹ pa | We do not plead with someone whose mother has been beaten to death by a mental patient<br>- It would be hard to dissuade [this person] from exacting revenge. |
| 15. | A ìí bá'ni n'ídï Ẹ̀rọ̀, k'á má bù yí'wọ́ | We don't find someone at the base of Ẹ̀rọ̀ [harmony] and we don't scoop some and splash our hands with it<br>- We don't find a great opportunity and pass it up;<br>- We don't find some freebie and we look down on it and be snobbish. |
| 16. | A ìí bu Omi k'ó l'ójú | We don't scoop water and it has eyes [scar, sore, mark]<br>- Whatever you do to me will not have any effect. |
| 17. | A ìí dá'gbó ṣe l'ẹ́hìn Apènà | We can't do anything in the woods without the pathfinder<br>- We have to do things according to custom so things will work out accordingly. |
| 18. | A ìí j'ọba k'a l'ójo; t'énìà bá j'ọba t'ó l'ójo, Ṣàngó níí pa'rúu wọn | We don't ascend to the throne and have fear; if a man becomes the king and is timid, it is Ṣàngó that kills his kind<br>- If you knew you weren't an able man, why did you contest to be king in the first place? Now whom do you want your citizens to rely on in times of war, etc.? |
| 19. | A ìí m'awo tán, k'á tún wá fi p'ọmọ Emèrè jẹ | We don't master the knowledge of divinity and use it to kill a reincarnated child<br>- We don't acquire power from someone and use it to harm his family and loved ones. |
| 20. | A ìí ri k'á láà ri mọ́n | We don't see [it] and unsee [it] again<br>- You cannot say you were a witness to something and say you didn't see it again. |

| | | |
|---|---|---|
| 21. | A ìí sh'òwò Ọ̀pẹ̀lẹ̀ k'a maa n'íwà méjì | We do not practice the trade of divination and have two entirely different personalities<br>- Always speak the truth [about your findings];<br>- Your word should be your bond. |
| 22. | À ìí tó'nií bá rìn k'á má t'ọ̀rọ̀ ọ́ bá'ni sọ | We can't be worthy of walking together and be less worthy of the standard of someone to have a discussion with<br>- Somebody cannot be your playmate and yet you find them beneath you when it comes to advising you. |
| 23. | A ìí wí s'íbẹ̀, k'á kú s'íbẹ̀ | We don't talk there and die there<br>- You don't have to be afraid - speak your mind! |
| 24. | A kì ń bá Oníṣẹ́ Ọba rìn | We do not walk in tandem with the king's messenger<br>- After a bearer delivers a message, the recipient will respond in their own good time without the bearer waiting for an immediate response. |
| 25. | A kì ń bá'ni í tan, k'á fa'ni n'ítan ya | We can't, on account of being related, tear apart someone's thigh<br>- This is a pun on "tan" which means "to be related" and "itan" which means "thigh";<br>- It really means "I can't put myself out on a limb, do you a great favor, and regret helping you out."<br>- "I can't shield you from the law, and end up in jail for obstruction, perjury or worse."<br>- Another example: "I can't give a vagrant shelter and end up being the one who becomes homeless." |
| 26. | A kì ń f'ọlá j'iyọ̀ | We don't eat salt as much to reflect our wealth<br>- We do things in moderation and not engage in unnecessary activity because of who we are, however rich or however connected we think we are; |

| | | |
|---|---|---|
| | | - Another example: We do not leave all the lights and ACs in our house on and go on holiday and say 'what the heck, we have money to pay for the bill when we return'. |
| 27. | A kì ń f'ọmọ Ọbà f'ọ́ṣun | We don't pass off the son of Ọbà to Ọ̀ṣun<br>- Render unto Caesar the things that are Caesar's; and unto God the things that are God's. |
| 28. | A kì ń f'ìkánjù l'ábẹ̀ t'ó gbó'ná | We don't hastily lick soup that is hot<br>- We don't eat hot soup in haste;<br>- We handle a sensitive matter with care. |
| 29. | A kì ń f'ikú wé'run | We don't compare death to sleep<br>- You can't compare one to the other<br>- This situation is like comparing chalk to cheese; there's a glaring contrast. |
| 30. | A kì ń gb'ókèèrè m'adùn Ọbẹ̀ | We don't stay at a considerable distance and appreciate the taste of a stew<br>- To be part of the event, you need to be there in person. |
| 31. | A kì ń gbọ́ burúkú l'ẹnu | We don't hear 'terrible' in the mouth<br>- Delightful thoughts are what people really want their minds to retain. |
| 32. | A kì ń jẹ méjì l'ábà Àlàdé | We don't eat two [twice] at Àlàdé's hut<br>- We don't eat two different kinds of food at someone else's house, i.e. we can't be choosy;<br>- Someone offering us free meal in their home is not a right but a privilege;<br>- Don't be greedy. |
| 33. | A kì ń júbà Afòògùn s'ínú kú | We don't bow down to he who keeps the secret formula of a juju in the stomach until he/she dies<br>- The nasty character [in this allegory] is or was of no benefit to anyone;<br>- Can even be said of a wealthy individual who helped no one rise up from poverty with their riches. |
| 34. | A kì ń l'ọ́kọ́ ńlé k'á f'ọwọ́ kó'mí | We do not have a hoe in our yard and use our bare hands to scoop up faeces<br>- We do not have an army, government or |

| | | |
|---|---|---|
| | | an established authority and fight our own battles or face our challenges alone. |
| 35. | A kì ń ní Ilé Ìyá, k'á má ní ti Baba | We do not have a mother's home and not have a father's<br>- Whoever the rival group sends as emissary, we send a secret spy to investigate the emissary without their knowledge. |
| 36. | A kì ń r'éwú l'ọ́sãn | We don't often see a giant pouched rat in the afternoon<br>- This adage is expressed when something unusual has just taken place, i.e. an unexpected visitor suddenly turns up at your residence or an event where he/she was hitherto unexpected;<br>- When you notice something unexpected in another person; for example, a young man of circa 30 years of age having grey hair. However, you only state this proverb because this young man is someone you knew before and are just seeing for the first time in years and you are shocked to see his grey. |
| 37. | A kì ń s'òòṣà l'ódò kí Làbẹlàbẹ má mọ̀n | We don't worship an Òòṣà (messenger-god) in the river that Làbẹlàbẹ will be unaware of it<br>- Nothing gets past the state secret service. |
| 38. | A kì ń ṣ'íwájú Ẹléẹ̀dẹ́ | No one precedes Ẹléẹ̀dẹ́ [the accused person]<br>- We don't speak for the man who has just been caught with his hand in the cookie jar;<br>- Let the man speak first; don't interrupt! |
| 39. | A kì ń ṣ'oore fún'ni k'a tún l'ọ́ṣọ̀ tìí | We don't do someone a favor and we 'crouch on' the assistance, i.e. making him never to forget the help rendered<br>- This idiom is telling off someone who helps another out of dire straits but never lets them forget it. |
| 40. | A kì ń t'ẹnu Òkùnrùn-ún j'oògùn | We don't swallow medicine through the |

| | | |
|---|---|---|
| | | mouth of the sick<br>- The man is right here; let him speak for himself. |
| 41. | A kì ń t'ojú Ẹlẹ́sẹ̀ Mẹ́sãn kàá | We don't stand before someone with nine toes and start counting them<br>- We should be careful and mindful of what we say within the earshot of whomsoever we're gossiping about. |
| 42. | A kì ń t'orí Àwíjàre k'ítọ́ gbẹ l'ẹ́nu | We don't because of speaking and being exonerated [and let] saliva dry up in the mouth<br>- I can't explain and explain more than I have done already!<br>- What's the big deal...so what? |
| 43. | À kì ń tó b'ẹni í bá gbé'lé k'á má t'ọ̀rọ̀ ọ́ bá'ni í sọ | We can't be worthy of sharing a house together and be less worthy of having a dialogue with<br>- If someone has been of great influence in your life, they should be worthy of being listened to, even if you eventually disagree with them;<br>- Regardless of the position of one's spouse in public life, their partner should be able to talk to them. |
| 44. | A kì ń tó'níí fẹ́ k'á má lè tó'níí bá s'ọ̀rọ̀ | We can't be worthy of being betrothed and not be up to the standard of someone to have a dialogue with<br>- If someone has been a great ally to you, they should be worthy of being listened to;<br>- Regardless of the position of one's spouse in public life, their partner should be able to talk to them. |
| 45. | A kì ńbá'ni rìn k'á má mọn'lé Ẹni | We don't walk along with someone [as buddies] and don't know where they live<br>- We can't be friends with someone and not know where they live with their family. |
| 46. | A kì ńgbọ́ Wuyẹ-wuyẹ n'ílé Àgbà lẹ́ẹ̀mejì | We don't hear whispers in an elder's house twice<br>- If you have to hear it twice, you're not |

| | | |
|---|---|---|
| | | welcome in the house, i.e. it's not a place you should be visiting. |
| 47. | A kìí l'énìà n'ídī Ọsàn k'ó fún'ni l'éyī tí ò dáa ẹ̀ | We don't have someone [friend, companion] at the bottom of an orange [tree] and he/she gives us the rotten ones<br>- It's not what you know; it's who you know. |
| 48. | A kìí n'ígi l'ógbà k'á má m'èso è | We do not have a tree in the garden [orchard] and not know its fruit<br>- It's quite clear who is responsible;<br>- I know what he/she is capable of (in the case of friends and family). |
| 49. | À kú sọ'rínù nii t'ọ̀gẹ̀dẹ̀ | In death, head slumped and leaning forwards is the appearance of dead banana trees<br>- One might say this to express their glee that something they found odious is now as dead as a dodo. The adage is not really of any importance. |
| 50. | A lè mú Ẹṣin lọ Odò ni, a ò lè fi Ipá mú Ẹṣin m'omi | We may lead a horse to the stream, but we cannot force a horse to drink water<br>- We may show you a way out of the situation you are in, but we cannot force you to take up the counsel. |
| 51. | À ń b'ẹ̀rù Alájá, Ajá rò'pé òun l'à ń b'ẹ̀rù | We exhibit our fear of the dog owner, the dog thinks it's him we're afraid of<br>- This is a derisive saying, like<br>- "Who is afraid of you?"<br>- "Who do you think you are?" |
| 52. | À ń gb'òròmọndìẹ l'ọ́wọ́ Ikú, ó ní nwọn ò jẹ́ k'óun lọ s'áàtàn k'óun lọ jẹ | We are trying to preserve a chick from death, it complains they don't allow it to go and play on the refuse dump<br>- This allegory is warning someone for their own good. |
| 53. | À ń jà nítorí Ọ̀jà, Ọ̀jà ní taló ńjà L'éhìnkùnlé òun? | We are fighting in defence of the hermit, the ungrateful recluse cries out "who are those fighting in my backyard?"<br>- We are doing all we can to restitute the wealth and dignity of someone who hardly deserves it, and here he is, complaining of us disturbing him. |

| | | |
|---|---|---|
| 54. | À ń kìí, À ń sàá, o l'ó ò m'ẹni t'ó kú | We have been praising him/her, we have been offering tributes and panegyrics, you claim you don't know who died<br>- With evidence and activity surrounding the current events, how can you turn around and claim ignorance? |
| 55. | A ń l'éku sí wọn, nwọ́n ń l'éjò sí wa | We are driving mice toward them, they're driving snakes toward us<br>- We are doing things to uplift or assist someone; the same person rewards us by plotting bad things against us in return. |
| 56. | À ń péé gbọ́n ni; a kì ń péé gọ̀ | We 'complete' [gather together] to get wiser; we don't 'complete' to get dumber<br>- We put heads together to reach a mutually-beneficial solution;<br>- Two heads are better than one. |
| 57. | À ń pọ́n Jẹ̀bẹ̀ l'ákīsà | We are wrapping raggedy tatters fit for recycling in Àkísà shreds of old clothing [fit for garbage]<br>- You're belittling the importance;<br>- Someone is just flattering another by not calling him out for what he truly is. Unfortunately, the person being flattered does not really merit the adulation. |
| 58. | À ń pọ́n Jẹ̀bẹ̀ lé l'a fi ń pèé ní Àkísà | We are honoring Jẹ̀bẹ̀ [raggedy tatters fit for recycling] by calling them Àkísà [rags]<br>- Someone is just flattering another but the person in the narrative does not really merit any honor. |
| 59. | À ń pọ́n'kú lé l'à ń p'ófọ̀ ọ́ ṣẹ | We are euphemizing Ikú [death] by saying Òfọ̀ [passing] has occurred instead<br>- We are just being nice and courteous to someone out of politeness or respect and so we are not showing how we really feel. |
| 60. | À ń rọ́'jú j'ẹ̀kọ Ọ̀bùn, ó tún ń pọn kéré | We are managing to eat Ẹ̀kọ [hardened corn-pap] of Ọ̀bùn [slovenly person], she portions it out in smaller wraps [than the competition]<br>- This is directed at someone [or entity] whose business people are being magnanimous enough to patronize [to |

| | | |
|---|---|---|
| | | keep them afloat] and yet lacks enviable customer service. |
| 61. | A ní k'á j'èkuru k'ó tán, a tún ń gbọn'wọ́ ẹ s'áwo | We said let's eat and finish Èkuru till there's none left, and yet here we are, shaking the crumbs in the plate<br>- We agreed to let bygones be bygones yet some members of the accord are still bringing up unnecessary issues that could add more fuel. |
| 62. | A ní k'a sò'lèkè m'ọmọ Ẹranko l'ọ́rùn k'ọmọ Ẹranko ó má wulẹ̀ s'áré ká'gbó mọ́n. Ẹranko ò m'ẹ̀ṣọ́, kò m'àrà; ó gb'ọ́ṣọ́ lù'gbẹ́ | We decided to put beads on the neck of a baby animal so the baby animal would cease to run around in the bush any more. The animal neither understands jewelry nor how to look decent; it entered the bush with all the jewelry<br>- The person in question does things with impunity and without regard or appreciation, as might an animal;<br>- You can't put lipstick on a pig. |
| 63. | A n'íṣú ṣe dín'kan, ó l'ójò Ọdún yī ò rọ̀ dēdē | We demanded how one of the yams is missing, he retorted that this year's rain was not regular<br>- Is that what you're being asked?<br>- Stop hedging and answer the question! |
| 64. | À ò níí b'ínú Orí k'a fi filà dé'dodo | We can't be mad with the head and put the hat on the navel<br>- We can't be angry with someone enough that we would give what is rightfully theirs to someone else. |
| 65. | A p'orí Àparò, ó já'ko | We call the bush-fowl's spirit, and out from the bush it pops out<br>- The very moment we start to discuss someone who is not present, a knock comes on the door and the person appears;<br>- Sort of "talk of the devil". |
| 66. | A rí Igi gbogbo n'ínú Igbó k'a tó fi Ọ̀mọ̀ gbẹ́ Gbẹ̀du | We saw all trees in the forest before we chose to use Ọ̀mọ̀ to sculpture Gbẹ̀du drums<br>- We knew what we got before we elected to go this route. |

| 67. | A rí t'ẹni mọ̀n-ọ́n wí, a f'àpáàdì bàǹtà bo ti ẹ̀ mọ́n'lẹ̀ | The observant of someone else's faults that makes remarks, uses a large earthenware vessel to conceal their own<br>- This proverb is said to accuse someone of hypocrisy. |
|---|---|---|
| 68. | A rí t'ẹni mọ̀n-ọ́n wí, A f'àpáàdì bààrà-baara bo ti ẹ̀ mọ́n'lẹ̀ | Has a lot to say about someone else's business, uses a large broken clay-pot to cover his/her own<br>- The poke-noser always has something to say about everyone's affairs, but never their own. |
| 69. | A s'ọ̀rọ̀ ṣẹ kìí s'ọ̀rọ̀ọ́ dànù | He who says something and it comes to pass never speaks for nothing<br>- What someone just hinted might happen has just happened;<br>- "See, what did I just say?!" Or, "Wow! Didn't she say so?". |
| 70. | À t'owó Olówó, à t'owó Ẹni, k'ọlọ́un má f'ìkan wọ́n'ni | Money belonging to someone else, the money that belongs to us, may God never let us lack either<br>- This idiom is a nonchalant attitude to usurp something that doesn't belong to you, regardless of who owns it. |
| 71. | À ta dànù ò ní k'óbì má pèé | The unevenness in the growth of some kola nuts does not [have to] result in its incompleteness or shortfall<br>- The current development does not have to require deviating from the original course of action. |
| 72. | A ti fi Òjé bọ Olóòṣà l'ọ́wọ́, ó ku Baba Ẹni tí ó bọ́ọ | We have put the gold bangle on the messenger-god priest, let's see whose father would dare to attempt to remove it<br>- You have helped create a monster and placed him on the throne; to unseat him will be almost an impossible endeavour. |
| 73. | À ti j'ẹlẹ́dẹ̀ yùngbà-yungba, àti san'wó ẹ̀ tìkọ̀tikọ | To eat pig [pork] is finger-licking delicious, but to pay for it is teeth-gnashing unsavory<br>- Obliging an expensive taste has its unsavory payback. |
| 74. | À ti kékeré lati ńp'ẹkan Ìrókó; | From young we nip the Ìrókó tree in the |

|  |  | t'ó bá d'igi ńlá, á máa gb'ẹbọ | bud, otherwise, when it becomes big, it will demand sacrifices continually<br>- It's from young you inculcate a child to have good character; when he grows it may be more difficult to bend him the right way;<br>- If we don't put a check on a nascent concern, it will take more than a concerted effort to deal with the problem it will create. |
|---|---|---|---|
| 75. | A ti m'ójú olóko k'onísọ̀ |  | We have arranged a meeting between the farmer and the seller of his/her produce<br>- We have already forged a meeting between the adversaries [in view to a resolution]. |
| 76. | À ti rán'múu Gángan kìí ṣe Ẹ̀hìn Èékánná |  | The Gángan's (talking drum's) capability to vary its tone is not behind [i.e. independent of] the drummer's nails<br>- You didn't get to where you are without the groundwork having been laid nicely by the very person being discussed. |
| 77. | À ti ṣ'ẹbọ, à ti ṣ'òògùn, báa ti wá'yé pé aá rĩ nã l'àá rí |  | Whether we offer sacrificial food to the gods or consult the oracle is irrelevant, what we had chosen to be before we were born is what we will be<br>- Do not seek wealth through shortcuts or maneuverings. |
| 78. | A wí fún'ni k'ó tó da'ni, òun ni Àgbà Ìjàkadì |  | He who apprises someone before he betrays them is the winner of a wrestling bout<br>- The penalty for breaking rules has been announced, so let no one complain;<br>- In other words, to be forewarned is to be forearmed. |
| 79. | Aà kì ń m'ọkọ Ọmọ Ẹni k'á tún m'àlè e ẹ̀ |  | We do not know the husband of one's daughter and at the same time know her secret lover<br>- We cannot be two-faced;<br>- We can't be disloyal and acknowledge another entity [in this situation]. |
| 80. | Aà kì ńsọ fún Onígbègbè k'ó gbé |  | We don't tell a laryngeal cancer sufferer |

|  |  |  |
|---|---|---|
|  | t'ọrũn è mì | to swallow the tumor [goiter] in his neck<br>- We don't tell someone with an obvious problem not to seek remedy but to just shut up or go and die. |
| 81. | Aá kọ́kọ́ lé Akátá lọ ná k'a tó wá f'àbọ̀ b'ádìẹ | We should first chase away the fox before we return to admonish the fowl/chicken<br>- We gather together to fight he who has done a loved one a wrong, then put our heads together to chastise the person we're defending for having initiated or drawn first blood that had caused the ire of the person we're complaining about. |
| 82. | Aá kọ́kọ́ lé Ewúrẹ́ lọ k'a t'ó f'àbọ̀ b'ádìẹ | We first chase away the goat before we shoo away the chicken<br>- We first confront the issue at hand and resolve it before we confront the instigator of the problem. |
| 83. | Aá l'ẹ́lẹ́yọ́rọ́ jìnà k'á tó f'àbọ̀ b'adìẹ | We first chase away the fox before we return to the chicken<br>- We first confront the issue at hand and resolve it before we confront the instigator of the problem. |
| 84. | Aà lè fá'rí l'ẹ̀hìn Olórí | We can't shave a head behind the owner of the head<br>- The party cannot go on when the celebrant is not around;<br>- The proceedings cannot hold without the accused being present in court. |
| 85. | Aà lè fi Ikú w'órun | We can't compare death to sleep<br>- The issue is simply incomparable, like chalk and cheese basically. |
| 86. | Aà lè máa bọ Òrìṣà k'a tún máa bọ Obì | We can't worship Òrìṣà god and worship the kolanut as well (the latter is used to worship/appease the former)<br>- We can't pay both ways; it's either we pay for one and the concerned person takes responsibility for the other. |
| 87. | Aà ń ṣípẹ̀ẹ̀ nọ̀n'ró f'ábuké | We don't tell a hunchback to stand upright<br>- If you won't take heed and protect yourself or do something that's going to |

| | | |
|---|---|---|
| | | be beneficial to your wellbeing, it's your problem and all eyes will see and you'll bear the consequence. |
| 88. | Aà ní k'ọmọdé má wun'yín Ganganran, ìgbàt'ó bá ti lè r'ẹnu bòó | We don't plead with the little kid to not grow buck teeth, as long as he's got the lips to cover them<br>- You may break any law or do something intolerable as long as you're prepared for the consequences of your action. |
| 89. | Aà r'írú eléyī rí; A fi ń d'ẹru b'ọlọ́rọ̀ ni | We have never seen this kind of thing before; we use it [only say it] to frighten the subject of the conversation<br>- There is nothing new under the sun. |
| 90. | Aá ti ṣe t'ibi Irin-ẹsẹ̀ mọn Olòṣì? | How do we know a mentally-indigent man from [his] manacles?<br>- You have to excuse us for not recognizing a worthless man when we see one. |
| 91. | Aà tíì kó'fá ń'lẹ̀, Ifá ti ń ṣe | We haven't removed the shells of Ifá oracle from the floor [divination mat], the divination is already manifesting<br>- We have hardly spoken, what we just talked about is already beginning to take place. |
| 92. | Àá wẹ̀ k'á jàre Ọyẹ́ ni | We bathe to 'subdue' or 'beat' the Harmattan<br>- We do what is necessary to placate a thorny issue. |
| 93. | Ààbọ̀ Ọ̀rọ̀ l'à ńsọ f'ọmọlúwàbí, t'ó bá dé'nú ẹ́ á d'odi-ñdi | The little narrative we tell a wellborn & intelligent child, when he absorbs it, it becomes whole<br>- You have only to suggest or give a hint to someone, and if he is wise enough, he'd get the whole picture. |
| 94. | Ààfã ń jó'ná, ẹ ńbèèrè Irùgbọ̀n | A priest is ablaze and you're asking whither is his beard?<br>- Only a fool would ask the obvious;<br>- The issue at hand is illogical or a non-sequitur. |
| 95. | Aájòó j'òwó | Showing consideration and compassion trumps giving someone money |

| | | |
|---|---|---|
| | | - Concern and empathy is way better than sending money to someone who would rather have your quality time. |
| 96. | Àánú Ojú ì í jẹ́ á t'ọwọ́ b'ojú | The compassion we feel towards eyes precludes us from sticking fingers in eyes<br>- If a blind person or a physically challenged person offends us, we wouldn't raise our hand and strike them, so we let them be;<br>- Because of our inbuilt empathy we don't beat someone who is down and out. |
| 97. | Ààrò mẹ́ta ò gbọdọ̀ d'ọbẹ̀ nù | A three-stone fire pit must not tip over a pot of soup<br>- With the three (or more) of us, the support for our collective goal would be much stronger. |
| 98. | Ààrò ó ti d'ilẹ̀ l'ẹ́hìn Amùkòkò | The fire pit has turned to sand after the pipe smoker<br>- There is rehabilitation after the fire and brimstone [of the troublemakers] |
| 99. | Ààrò t'ó bá tutù l'ẹdìẹ ń yé sí | A fire pit that is cold is where a chicken hatches in<br>- Where things are cool and calm is where a woman births. |
| 100. | Ààyé gb'ebòlò, ó ń rán'ni s'ódũ; Ààyé gb'ẹlẹ́dẹ̀, ó wá fẹ́ máa sun Àsùnhọn'run | Exploiting the occasion, the Ebòlò spinach sent someone an errand to the Òdú spinach; the pig made the most of the privilege, it wanted to sleep the snoring-sleep<br>- You were given a chance, see how you have been using it for the wrong purpose;<br>- Someone is misusing an opportunity given to them, though undeserved, in a dishonest or destructive way. |
| 101. | Àbá n'ikán ń dá, Ikán kan ò le j'òkúta | It's only a proposal [idea], no termite can eat stone<br>- It's only a boast, he wouldn't dare try what he's bragging he's capable of doing;<br>- He's only threatening, he won't kill himself [over that];<br>- It's only a campaign promise [plan], no |

| | | |
|---|---|---|
| | | third world leader or politician can be honest enough and not loot his country's treasury and then relinquish power at the end of his term. It's their stock in trade. |
| 102. | Àbàtá ta kété bí Ẹni tíò b'ódò tan | The mud stands at an arm's length like it's not related to the brook<br>- In time of trouble some close friends or colleagues may desert you and act like they don't know you. |
| 103. | Abẹ gé'mọ l'ọ́wọ́, Ọmọ́ s'abẹ nù; ṣé Abẹ ò ti ṣe'hun t'ó fẹ́ ṣe ni? | A blade accidentally cut a child's finger, the child throws the blade away; has the blade not accomplished its mission?<br>- The damage is already done. |
| 104. | Abẹ́rẹ́ á lọ k'ọ̀nà Okùn t'ó dí | The needle will pass before the thread's path closes<br>- I'll get safely out of town before the trouble, earthquake, disaster etc. begins. |
| 105. | Abẹ́rẹ́ sọ nù, o lọ gbé Ṣàngó<br>Abẹ́rẹ́ sọ nù, nwọ́n lọ́ gbé Ṣàngó | A needle is missing, you went to summon Ṣàngó<br>A needle is missing, they went to summon Ṣàngó<br>- Is the situation so serious or dire [that summoning the god of thunder is the solution]? |
| 106. | Abìnrìnbẹ̀rẹ̀ ní ó m'óyè dé'lé | He who crouch-walks is the one that returns home with a chieftaincy title<br>- He who is diligent, careful, not confrontational, avoids stepping on toes and ruffling feathers but works quietly in the background unseen, unnoticed, like a fly on the wall, is the one that succeeds and comes away with something tangible out of the commotion. |
| 107. | Àbọ̀ábá l'ọ̀rọ̀ ẹ | Return to later is your matter<br>- I shall deal with you later. |
| 108. | Àbòtán ni Òòṣà ń bò'dí Ìgbín; táa bá d'áṣọ f'ọ́lẹ, aá paá l'áró ni | It is with full shield that messenger-gods protect the snail; if we buy clothes for a lazy person, we tie-dye them before giving the dresses to him<br>- The speaker is pleading for full help and assistance for someone (could be himself), |

| | | |
|---|---|---|
| | | even for the smallest thing so that he'll not have to spend a penny or invest the least effort at all. |
| 109. | Àdàbá ń p'òwe bí ẹni p'ẹiyẹlé ò gbọ́; títiiri l'ó ń tiri | The dove speaks in parables like the pigeon cannot figure out what it's saying; it continues to ramble on<br>- The rival continues to carry on his/her business activity in hostile fashion, encroaching on rival territories without as much as a care in the world, like his/her competitors do not exist; he/she is only compounding issues for himself/herself for the showdown that's sure to come. |
| 110. | Adákẹ́-máfọhùn, aà mọn t'ẹni t'ó ńṣe | The reticent man, we don't know whose side he's on<br>- A habitually quiet stakeholder that gives no one a clue as to what he's thinking. |
| 111. | Àdán d'orí k'odò, ó ń wò'ṣe Ẹiyẹ | The bat perches and faces downwards while watching the shenanigans of birds<br>- The citizens are watching the wanton irresponsible behaviors of their corrupt leaders. |
| 112. | Adánilóró f'agbára kọ́'ni | The psychopath has [inadvertently] taught someone strength<br>- Surviving an evil act makes one develop inner toughness, self-belief, and strength, which was not the intention of the wicked felon;<br>- Once bitten, twice shy. |
| 113. | Àdàpèmòn l'ọmọ mí ń fẹ́'wó; Olè l'olè ńjẹ́ | Denial is "my child borrows things without the permission of the owners and forgets to return them"; a thief is what a thief is<br>- Call a spade a spade; don't shy away from the truth that is right before you. |
| 114. | Adé Orí l'a fi ń m'ọba, Ìrùkẹ̀rẹ̀ l'a fi ń mọn'jòyè | The crown on the head symbolizes a king; the horsetail fly-whisk is how we recognize a chief<br>- With certain peculiarities and qualities we know who's in charge or who's got the balls. |
| 115. | Adìẹ funfun tí 'ò m'ara ẹ̀ l'ágbà | The white hen that does not recognize |

| | | |
|---|---|---|
| | | itself as the 'adult'<br>- This is said to someone who is held in higher regard than the behavior they are exhibiting;<br>- The issue you are arguing about is beneath you. |
| 116. | Adìẹ ìí t'ẹsẹ̀ ẹ́ kú | A fowl [hen] never dies from its leg or foot [injury]<br>- This is an inspirational adage to someone who is enduring some great distress or pain. |
| 117. | Adìẹ tí ó bã kọ, Àṣá ìí gbe l'óròmọndìyẹ | A chicken [hen] that would crow, a hawk would not snatch it when it is young<br>- A child that is going to be someone someday will listen to its parents' guidance [and not join bad company]. |
| 118. | Adìẹ t'ó bà l'ókùn; Ara ò rọ'kùn, Ara ò r'ẹdìẹ | The chicken that lands and perches on a rope; the rope is not settled and neither is the chicken<br>- A vexatious bothersome person who keeps stirring up trouble wherever he goes, yet he's not at peace himself. |
| 119. | Adìyẹ ìrà'nà ìí ṣe'hun Àjẹ̀gbé | The 'passage' fowl [to the great beyond] is not something one eats and disregards<br>- You've got to pay what you owe, no matter what. |
| 120. | Aféfé kan ò níí fẹ́ k'ó má kan Igi Oko l'ára | No wind will blow and not touch the body of trees in the forest<br>- Repercussions of a major governmental decision will be felt by every citizen in the Diaspora. |
| 121. | Aféfé ti fẹ́, a ti rí fùrọ̀ Adìẹ | The wind has blown; we have seen the anus of the chicken<br>- The cat has been let out of the bag! |
| 122. | Aféfé t'ó fẹ́ t'ó ń dààmú Ológì, k'élélùbọ́ má ṣ'àfira | The wind that blew that was unsettling the seller of corn-pap, let the yam-flour seller [observe] and not take things for granted [herself]<br>- If whatever is currently happening has affected the rich and the powerful that they are feeling the pinch, the |

| | | |
|---|---|---|
| | | underclasses and those caught in a poverty trap had better double their vigilance;<br>- You'd better pay attention so you too don't meet the same fate! |
| 123. | Afetísáròyé, kò ní ǹkankan-án ṣe ni | A listener who just listens and doesn't offer any advice with regard to the matter someone is narrating to him really has no clue what should be done. |
| 124. | Àfi tí Olúwá bá kọ́ Ilé nã, Ẹ̀dá ńṣe l'ásán ni | Except God builds the house, human beings are only "making" in vain<br>- If you are trying hard to achieve something important, except it be given you from above, you're only wasting your time. |
| 125. | Àgàn t'ó ń gb'ọ́mọ Ẹgbẹ́ ẹ̀ jó, ó ń rọ́'jú ni | A barren woman who is dancing with the children of her peers, she's just grinning and bearing it.<br>- The person being referred to in this expression is just accepting a difficult or unpleasant situation without complaining because they know there is nothing they can do to change things. |
| 126. | Agb'éjọ́ Ẹnìkan dá, Àgbà Òṣìkà ni | The mediator that listens only to one side of a story is the elder statesman of the Evil Ones<br>- Usually uttered by someone who feels he needs to hear the two sides of a story before rendering his judgment. |
| 127. | Àgbà (Àgbàlagbà) ìí ṣ'orò bí Èwe | The elders don't celebrate festive periods like the youth<br>- You don't expect elders or those in authority to behave in an unexpected manner that is unbefitting of their position in society. |
| 128. | Àgbà Ajá ìí b'awọ jẹ́ | The 'elderly' dog does not ruin leather hide [its own leather may have to be used to make a new one]<br>- He who has succeeded in defying the odds to get to where he is in life would appreciate the suffering and challenges |

| | | that he went through, and would not want to misuse his office;<br>- He who has been given a special privilege will not want to misuse it, knowing that it can be taken away by those in authority who originally gave him the opportunity, and given to someone else;<br>- Being fully aware of the fate of the previous occupant [of an office] due to bad governance, it is now incumbent on the current office holder to learn from the mistake(s) of his predecessor, as he too may lose his job [for the same type of reason];<br>- You should know better than to involve yourself in such activity. |
|---|---|---|
| 129. | Àgbà ìí wà l'ójà, k'órí Ọmọ tuntún wó | Elders cannot be in the market and a toddler's head is lopsided<br>- There should be no disorder when there is a power/leader or council that can control the situation and dowse the flames. |
| 130. | Àgbà l'ó ń gb'èkọ tíò l'éwé | It is the elder that accepts the hardened corn-pap that has not been properly dished out in leaves<br>- This is a plea to someone to try and accept the situation at it currently stands. |
| 131. | Àgbà níí gba'ni l'ójọ́ Ìṣòro, òun l'ó mú kí Alákàrà mí sá ti Ẹlẹ́kọ ọ rẹ | The elders are those that rescue someone at a time of distress, that's what made my Àkàrà seller chase after your Ẹ̀kọ seller. [The Àkàrà and Ẹ̀kọ both complement one another]<br>- The speaker is crying out for help from the listener. |
| 132. | Àgbá Òfìfo níí p'ariwo | An empty barrel makes the most noise<br>- Those who are given to boasting about their accomplishments are often the worst underachievers;<br>- If you know your own self-worth and you're a fantastic individual, you do not |

| | | |
|---|---|---|
| | | need to beat your own drum. |
| 133. | Àgbà tí ò bá gbó'jú-gbó'nu, òun ní ńta Màrìwò | The elder who lacks genuine power is the one that wears palm fronds<br>- He who lacks real influential power puts on the façade of importance when the real power-movers are not around. |
| 134. | Àgbà tíò b'ínú òun l'ọmọ ẹ ń pọ̀ jọjọ | The elder who is not angry is the one whose children number a lot<br>- Don't be quick to anger;<br>- Accept what is going on as "it is what it is" and endeavor to control your temper;<br>- Endeavor pain or hardship in a stoical manner;<br>- Grin and bear it;<br>- Count your losses and move on. |
| 135. | Àgbà t'ó bá jẹ Àjẹ Ìgbẹ̀hìn, fún'ra Alára ẹ̀ l'ó máa ru Igbá ẹ̀ dé'lé | The elder who relishes eating leftovers, by himself will he carry its calabash-container home [when everyone has left him to it]<br>- An upright member of the community who does not respect himself but dishonors himself by his actions should be ready to bear the humiliation all by himself. |
| 136. | Àgbà wá bú'ra b'éwe ò bá ṣe ẹ́ rí | Elders should come and swear that they'd never been young once<br>- Let he who is without sin come and cast the first stone. Something like that. |
| 137. | Àgbà, Ikúù rẹ rèé; ó sàn ju Àgbà, Ojúù rẹ rèé lọ | Senior citizen, here's your death; this is better than "elderly one, this is your eyes!" (You did this [evil deed]?!) (This is your handwork?!)<br>- Death with honor is better than life with dishonor. |
| 138. | Agbààwẹ̀ má dã'tọ́ mì, Ọlọ́run l'ẹlẹ́rï Ọfun | A faster who swears he never swallows spittle during a fast, God is the only witness<br>- What someone says may be factual, only God Knows if it is the truth. |
| 139. | Àgbájọ Ọwọ́ l'a fi ń sọ'yà | With supportive hands [in unison] do we beat our chest<br>- United we stand, divided we fall. |

| 140. | Àgbàlagbà t'ó bá san Yangan mọ́n'dī ó ti di Alámũṣeré Ẹdìẹ | The elder who ties a belt of corn [grains] to his waist makes himself the chicken's clown<br>- Whoever attempts to do what you have in mind will shame himself. Better perish the thought. |
|---|---|---|
| 141. | Àgbàrá máa ń k'ẹrù ni, kìí kóo dé'lé | A flood carries loads and belongings, it never drops them off at home<br>- A flood carries a lot of debris and, when the velocity of the flash flood slows, it begins depositing this debris along the way;<br>- A vindictive person would not think twice to destroy their opponents. |
| 142. | Àgbàrá Òjò ni ẹ, oò l'óò n'ílé é wó | You're flood water, you can't say you're not ready to bring down a house<br>- For example, the hyperbole could rebuke someone thought to expose secrets going on in a business, and the revelation could make the company lose patronage and fold up as a result of everyone knowing secrets of how they're making their profit;<br>- To judge from your lack of respect for money, you're ready to ruin someone, spending anyhow the way you do. |
| 143. | Àgbàrá Òjò ò l'óun ò n'ílée wó, Onílé ni ò níí gbà fun | Flash flood [after a rainfall] wouldn't decline to destroy a house, it's the homeowner that should not permit it<br>- You need to be security-cautious about your personal information and stuff. |
| 144. | Àgbàrá t'ó ń kọjá l'ójúde Ọba tí ò k'ọ́ba | Flood water that flows past the king's palace but doesn't stop to salute the king<br>- Passing right in front of the house of someone you know and not saluting them;<br>- Imagine the Russian president coming to America on private business without paying a visit to the US president. |
| 145. | Àgbàtán l'à ń gb'ọ̀lẹ; táa bá d'áṣọ f'ọ́lẹ, aá pã l'áró ni | It is with total support we assist the lazy; if we wish to clothe a lazy person, we tie-dye the clothes before giving them to him |

| | | |
|---|---|---|
| | | - Give a man a piece of fish, and you feed him for a day; show him how to catch fish, and you feed him for a lifetime. |
| 146. | Àgbébọ̀ ń ràgà b'ọmọ ẹ̀ nítorí Àwòdì-òkè; Òròmọndìẹ wá ń wẹ́yì pé Àwòdì-òkè é ti ń ṣ'àṣejù | A hen covers her hatchlings because of the bush-eagle in the sky; meanwhile, the baby chickens are moaning that the bush-eagle is overdoing it.<br>- Be content that the situation is not worse than it is! |
| 147. | Agbèf'ọ́ba kan ìí j'ẹ̀bi | No royal announcer is ever guilty<br>- The pronouncements he makes are given to him by the ruler or the chiefs. |
| 148. | Àgbò t'ó tà'dí m'ẹ́hìn, Agbára l'ó lọọ mú wá | The ram that appears to withdraw or retreat has gone to bring might<br>- He who retreats has probably gone to bring reinforcement;<br>- He who fights and runs away lives to fight another day. |
| 149. | Agbójú l'ógún, ó fi'ra ẹ̀ f'óṣì ta | Anyone dependent on bequeathed property [beneficiary] leaves themselves open to penury<br>- Don't place your hopes on what may or may not happen. |
| 150. | Agbọ́n ń sẹ́, Oyín ń sẹ́, Ojú Olóko dẹ reé kùdùrù-kuduru ni | The wasp is refuting, the bee is also denying [knowledge of what might have caused it], yet the farmer's face looks so puffed-up with blotchy welts<br>- The case is clear-cut as to what happened and who is responsible. |
| 151. | Àgbọ̀nrín Èṣí l'ò ńjẹ l'ọ́bẹ̀ | The deer you killed last year is what you're still eating in stews<br>- New things are in vogue;<br>- The world has evolved and moved beyond your thinking. |
| 152. | Àgékù Ejò ìí ṣ'oro bí Agbọ́n | An almost-hacked-to-death snake is not as lethal as a swarm of wasps<br>- A man who has been unjustifiably wronged without recompense is an angry man. |
| 153. | Àgékù Ejò ò ṣeé fi s'ílẹ̀ | An almost-hacked-to-death snake cannot be left alive |

| | | |
|---|---|---|
| | | - The son of an assassinated king, leader or warrior cannot be spared because when he comes of age, he may seek retribution, just like a decimated force cannot be allowed to regroup and wreak havoc in a later skirmish. |
| 154. | Agídí Ọkàn-án lè sọ'hun gbogbo d'òfo | Stubbornness of the mind could turn all things to nothingness<br>- Learn to calm down and take things easier;<br>- Unchecked stress can wreak havoc on your well-being. |
| 155. | Àgò t'ó bá d'ilẹ̀ l'ẹdìẹ́ ń yéé sí | The coop that has turned to sand [is vulnerable or unlocked] is where hens lay their eggs<br>- People will tread on you if you allow them. |
| 156. | Agódó-ńgbó Ẹsin ni, kò tíì t'éréé sá | He is a colt; he is not yet fit to run<br>- He's a kid in the scheme of things; he can't defend himself, let alone a whole town/community;<br>- He's not up to someone I can pick a fight with; I guess I'll pick someone my own size. |
| 157. | Àgùtán ti g'òkè tán k'á tó máa ké Kàì m'ágùtàn | The sheep had already climbed up before we began shouting "káì" [like 'shoo'] at the sheep<br>- We had already let our guards down [or inadvertently allowed the thieves in] before we started looking for [a non-existent] security |
| 158. | Àgùtàn t'ó bá b'ájá rìn á jẹ'gbẹ́ | A sheep that is friends with a dog will eat faeces<br>- An upright individual who mixes with a bad crowd will commit crimes. |
| 159. | Àgùtàn t'ó bá da'fá nù, Ẹ̀jẹ̀ ẹ̀ẹ́ l'ó yẹ k'ọ́n fi ko | The sheep that upended Ifá [and the shells], it's its blood they should use [as sacrifice] to pick up the pieces of the Ifá<br>- The offender is the one that ought to be punished, not the unlucky individual who is suffering the repercussion. |

| | | |
|---|---|---|
| 160. | Àì bá wọn dé'lé Arọ́ kò jẹ́ k'a mọ̀n pé Ìdààmú ń ṣẹ'lẹ̀ l'ágbẹ̀dẹ, nítorí nwọ́n ń lu Irin l'ójõjúmọ́n; a ṣe bí ojõjúmọ́n l'ó fi ń dáa fún wọn | Not accompanying them to the workshop of the smith did not accord us the opportunity to realize that commotion was happening at the smithy because they forged metal every day; everyone thought everyday was a good day for them<br>- It's just you and your assumptions;<br>- Be sure of your facts; don't jump to conclusions. |
| 161. | Àì dúró n'ijó; Ìbẹ̀rẹ̀ n'íṣẹ́ | Perpetual motion is dancing; starting is working<br>- Get a move on; don't tarry;<br>- Could be said as a mantra to associates in a group [or protest]: let's do this! |
| 162. | Àì fi'ni pe'ni, àì f'ènìà p'ènìà tí ńmú Ará Oko sán Bàǹtẹ́ wọ̀'lú | Not having regard for someone, not having respect for a human that makes bush folks enter a town with only a loin cloth on the waist<br>- A rebuke for a flagrant disrespect shown by someone or group to some higher person such as a chief or a king. |
| 163. | Àì jẹun ká'nú Ológbò kọ́ niò jẹ́ 'ó t'ájá | It is not the lack of enough food that made the cat smaller than a dog<br>- It is the way it is; can't do anything about that. |
| 164. | Àì lè jà níí jẹ́ Oko Babaà mi ò dé'bíyï | It's the lack of ability to fight that makes someone say "my father's farm does not extend up to here"<br>- I have proof of what I'm saying, so let's go to court;<br>- It's cowardly to utter such words when it's really the fear of your opponent's power or influence that made you say it. |
| 165. | Àì l'ówó l'ọ́wọ́ ò pa'ni l'órúkọ dà; ẹ kàn lè má fi 'Ògbẹ́ni' si ni | Being not wealthy does not change a man's name; only thing is you may not precede the name with 'Mr.'<br>- Not having a particular thing or being part of a group does not negate the legitimacy or right of an individual. |
| 166. | Àì mọ Iṣẹ́ ẹ́ kọ̀ l'ó mú Ọmọ Orogùn ki Orí b'omi gbígbóná | The lack of ability to refuse errands is what makes the wooden spatula stick its |

| | | |
|---|---|---|
| | | head into boiling water<br>- If someone sends you to do some evil deed, it behooves you to refuse or proceed. |
| 167. | Àì ṣ'àlàyé Ọ̀rọ̀ l'ó p'eléte Ìṣáájú | Not explaining and clarifying "what you said" was what killed the forerunner of traitors<br>- You need to make yourself unambiguously clear when in a serious dialogue; if people misinterpret your statement, this could create irreparable division in the nation or community;<br>- "So that we are clear - are you thinking what I'm thinking..?" |
| 168. | Àìd'óko Baba Ẹlòmîìn rí l'a fi ńrò'pé Oko Baba Ẹni nìkan l'ó tóbi jù | Not having had the privilege to visit the farm of someone else's father makes us believe that our father's farm alone is the largest in the world<br>- If you are cocooned by the belief that what you have is one of a kind, that may be because you're only aware of yours and no one else's. |
| 169. | Àìgbọ́'fá l'à ń wò'kè; Ifá kan ò sí ní Bárá | Not adhering to Ifá oracle's divinations is why we keep staring into empty sky; there's no revelation in Bárá<br>- In gullibility we look up to someone or entity to feed us when there's no manna from anywhere. |
| 170. | Àìjiná Ọ̀ọ̀lẹ̀ kò ní k'á kan'ra m'éwé | The undercooking of Ọ̀ọ̀lẹ̀ [bean cake baked in broad leaves] does not make us short-tempered with the leaves<br>- Don't punish the messenger. |
| 171. | Àìrìn k'á pọ̀ l'ó ńj'ọmọ Ejò ń'yà | Not walking together in unison results in the suffering of hatchling snakes<br>- There's safety in numbers;<br>- Not having agreement and understanding with your own folks exposes a man to unnecessary suffering as a result of going it alone. |
| 172. | Àìrìnjìnà l'a ò kan Abuké Ọ̀kẹ́rẹ́ | It's because you haven't walked far enough that you haven't encountered a |

| | | |
|---|---|---|
| | | hunch-backed squirrel<br>- If you think you are the best/greatest at one thing, that's probably because you haven't heard of anyone else who might have accomplished the same 'feat'. There is always something greater and more amazing than what you do know. |
| 173. | Àìrírárá l'à ń j'ẹ̀kọ | Due to scarcity is why we eat Ẹ̀kọ [hardened corn-pap]<br>- I'm accepting this [whatever] because there's no alternative anywhere. |
| 174. | Àìsàn l'ó ṣeé wò; a ò rí t'ọlójọ́ ṣe | Illness is what's curable; we can't do anything about death<br>- Everything else can be looked at and resolved; as for the issue at hand, it's totally beyond the scope of debate. |
| 175. | Àìsí ènìà l'óko l'a fi ńpe Ajá l'áwē | It's the lack of humans in the farm [wood] that we call a dog "buddy"<br>- The speaker is suggesting this is the best one can do under the circumstances. |
| 176. | Àìsí ńbẹ̀ l'àì dá si | Not being there is not participating in it<br>- You can't be at the event and not give a helping hand. |
| 177. | Àìsọ̀rọ̀ Ẹ̀là l'ó pa Baálẹ̀ Atẹ̀gúnsí; ó ní "Ibi tí mo bá f'iṣu sí, Ibẹ̀ ni k'ẹ gún l'ódó." Ńgbàt'ó dẹ f'iṣu s'ẹ́nu, nwọ́n gún Ẹnu ẹ̀ l'ódó ni | Not speaking common-speak [vernacular] was what killed the overseer of Atẹ̀gúnsí; he had instructed that "wherever I place the boiled yam is exactly where you should pound [with a pestle]", and when he placed the yam in his mouth, they pounded his mouth<br>- This is a hilarious metaphorical take on someone telling another to do something they please when he's not around, when he really means the opposite;<br>- This is a lesson to always make yourself clear and always say what you mean. |
| 178. | Àìt'éyín í ká l'à ń f'ọwọ́ bòó | Not being up to the age of losing teeth is why we cover them<br>- Not being certain of one's own innocence is why anyone would not readily deny what they've been accused |

|     |     | of;<br>- Not being confident of one's own ability (or conviction) is why one might not venture to do something, not speak out and/or why one would rather keep [a truth] out of public knowledge and "keep it in the closet." |
| --- | --- | --- |
| 179. | Àìtètè m'ólè, Olè ń m'ólóko | If a farm thief is not apprehended in time, he may turn out and accuse the farm owner of stealing<br>- You're accusing me of what you're actually guilty of yourself. |
| 180. | Aiyé ò fẹ́ k'á r'ẹrù k'á sọ̀ | The world does not want us to carry a load and be able to put it down<br>- No one truly wishes us success except perhaps our parents;<br>- Take care of yourself as no one else will. |
| 181. | Ajá ìí rorò tàbí gbó'ná k'ó ṣọ́ ojú'lé méjì | A dog is not brutal or ferocious so much that it guards two houses at once<br>- No matter how strong you might be, you cannot fight two battles at the same time;<br>- No matter how rich you are, you cannot drive two cars at the same time, sleep in two beds in two houses in one night or eat the food of many people at one sitting. |
| 182. | Ajá Ìwòyí l'ó mọn Ehoro Ìwòyí í lé | Only the dogs of today know how to chase the rabbits of today<br>- It's only the modern youth that can deal with modern issues;<br>- It's only the crime fighters of today that can catch today's criminals;<br>- The old ideas have been revamped and upgraded to meet today's needs. |
| 183. | Ajá l'óṣõ, a reé k'ówó r'ọ̀bọ | A dog squatts idly, we decided to put money on acquiring a monkey or invest scarce resources on acquiring destructive monkeys<br>- There is an obvious [easier] option sitting in plain sight! |
| 184. | Ajá m'ọmọ tiẹ̀ ẹ́ fún l'ọ́mú; ó mọ t'ọmọ Ẹlòmîn í bù jẹ | A dog knows how to breast-feed her own puppy; she knows how to bite the puppy |

| | | |
|---|---|---|
| | | of another<br>- Rather like having one set of laws for a group and another set for others (one nation, two justice systems). |
| 185. | Ajá tí ń yọ'rù kí'ni tẹ́lẹ̀ ò gbọdọ̀ rí'ni gbó | The dog that used to wag its tail to greet someone should not [now] see one and start barking<br>- Something must be off here; something is not right. |
| 186. | Ajá t'ó bá ma sọ'nù kìí gbọ́ Fèrè Ọlọ́dẹ | The dog that is going to go astray will never hear the whistle of the communal night guard<br>- He who is destined to suffer the loss of something valuable to him will not heed any dissuading advice contrary to his own decision. |
| 187. | Ajá t'ó bá re'lé Ẹkùn t'ó bọ̀ l'áyọ̀, ńṣe l'ó yẹ k'a kíí kú Orí Ire | The dog that visits the tiger and returns with joy unscathed, we should congratulate it<br>- Who has gone through this sort of trial and tribulation and lives to tell the tale should be able to face any challenges and adversities, so congratulate them. |
| 188. | Ajá t'ó bá tó, k'ó dú'bũ Ẹkun l'ọ́nà | A dog that is sure of himself, let him waylay a tiger on the path<br>- The speaker is challenging an adversary to meet him force with force if he would dare. |
| 189. | Ajá t'ó f'orí sọ̀'gún ò lọ mọ́n | The dog that headbutts Ògún [or an iron or metal, which is a representation of Ògún] will not go again [escape]. Ògún was the god of iron in Yorùbá religious folklore. The dog would be beheaded in sacrifice to Ògún<br>- Whoever is guilty of this kind of deed will not go scot-free. |
| 190. | Àjànàkú kọ'jáa mo rí ǹkan firí | An elephant is beyond "I just glimpsed something in a twinkle of an eye"<br>- A huge event or a noteworthy object cannot be discarded as insignificant. |
| 191. | Àjé ké l'ánã̄, Ọmọ kú l'énî; tani | A witch howled last night, a child suddenly |

|     |     |     |
| --- | --- | --- |
|     | ò mọ̀n pé Àjẹ́ t'ó ké l'ánã ló p'ọmọ jẹ? | drops dead the next morning; who doesn't know that it was the witch that screeched yesterday that killed the child [to eat] spiritually?<br>- What problem you may be experiencing was probably set in motion by betrayal from someone you foolishly confided in. |
| 192. | Àjẹ́ t'ó ń p'ọmọ jẹ, Ènìà ìí r'ẹ̀jẹ̀ l'ẹ́nu ẹ̀ | The witch that is killing children to eat, nobody sees blood in her mouth<br>- The person who is undermining you is in secret;<br>- Deceitful people usually appear well-meaning and gentle. |
| 193. | Àjẹpọ̀ nii t'àdán | Mix-eating everything is the character of the bat<br>- Just like a bat, the person in reference can eat anything including certain forbidden foods without negative health repercussions; or<br>- The person in question may employ all kinds of tactics to achieve his goal;<br>- An individual has a devil-may-care attitude; he's not daunted in the least by others' opinion of him, he trudges on. |
| 194. | Ajogún Ẹ̀wù ni ẹ́, oò mọn'yì Agbádá ńlá | You are an inheritor of a dress, you do not really appreciate the value of an eminent Agbádá<br>- You have inherited something but you don't really know the value of it. |
| 195. | Àjọjẹ ò dùn b'ẹnìkan ò ní | Eating together is not palatable if one [of the group] does not have<br>- This is a call-out to help those members of a group [of friends] that do not have an income per se to also become self-sufficient. |
| 196. | Àjòjì ò níí wọ̀'lú k'ólè má mọ̀n | A stranger will not enter a town that thieves will not know<br>- Nothing goes on in the country that citizens will not notice. |
| 197. | Àjọrò l'à ń pè ní Àjerò | What is thought of and agreed upon together is what is called Àjerò. This is a |

| | | |
|---|---|---|
| | | pun and rhyme on the word "Àjọrò" and the city "Àjerò"<br>- What we planned and agreed together is what we should carry out. |
| 198. | Àkàrà ṣe pẹ̀lẹ́; Inú ń b'ẹ́lẹ́kọ | Àkàrà, tread carefully; the Ẹ̀kọ seller is angry. (These two meals complement one another best; you may eat Àkàrà on its own, unlike Ẹ̀kọ that you can't enjoy without àkàrà or stew or mọ́ín-mọ́ín)<br>- This personification simply means: Be careful and watch your back. |
| 199. | Àkàrá ti tú s'épo | Àkàrà balls [beignets or fritters made of black-eyed beans] have cascaded into the palm oil [have broken the seal of their container]<br>- The secret is out in the open. |
| 200. | Àkàrà wònpà òun l'ó ká'jú Ẹ̀kọ gìrí; táà bá fi Yangan dá Yangan, òun l'ó ńmu Yangan wá | A sizable Àkàrà ball [beignet or fritter made of black-eyed beans] is what is adequate for a substantial Ẹ̀kọ [hardened corn-pap]; if we don't create corn-grains with maize, this brings maize about<br>- Things would still likely return to their morally or legally correct position;<br>- Give honor to whom honor is due. |
| 201. | Akọ Igi a máa ṣ'oje ńgbàmíìn ní Kọ̀rọ̀ | A male tree sometimes does bleed in privacy<br>- This is usually said by the subject of the adage below as a rejoinder to express the deep sorrow he is feeling. |
| 202. | Akọ Igi ò gbọdọ̀ ṣ'oje | A male tree does not bleed<br>- Said to bolster up someone when they are in distress. |
| 203. | Akọ ni mo wà bí Ìbọn | Cocked like a gun I am<br>- I am always in a firing state / launch-mode for anything;<br>- Just say the word and I spring into action at any given time. |
| 204. | Akọ́dà kan ìí fẹ́ k'ọ́n gbé Idà kọjá n'íwájú òun | No executioner likes anyone to carry a sword past right in front of him<br>- People who mete out punishment or terror do not appreciate the same being |

| | | |
|---|---|---|
| | | done to them or their loved ones. |
| 205. | Akọgba tú'gba ká | He who shovels two hundred [mounds] and scatters [all] the two hundred<br>- He who works and gathers but ends up squandering all, due to his own stupidity. |
| 206. | Akọni k'ó bàjẹ́ ni, nwọn ò kì ń bá'ni dé'bẹ̀ | The instigators of "let's ruin their celebration" usually don't accompany the person they're encouraging to the event<br>- For example, colleagues who may be pushing you to talk back to your boss for some innocuous offhand comment he/she may have made might actually be pushing you just so you may lose your job. Usually if they were to find themselves in the same scenario, they would probably not talk back at all, but shrug, grin and bear it! |
| 207. | Akọni 'ó bàjẹ́ kan kò dẹ̀ ńṣe ti ẹ̀ bẹ́ẹ̀ | The malevolent that teaches how things can turn into chaos doesn't do his things like that<br>- This is an accusation of hypocrisy. |
| 208. | Àkùkọ́ ti kọ l'ẹ́hìn Ọmọkùnrin | The rooster has crowed behind the young man<br>- The man in question is dead. |
| 209. | Àkúnlẹ̀yàn, òun l'àdáyébá; a d'áiyé tán, Ojú ń kán gbogbo wa | What our individual souls chose at the point of coming to earth is what we find; now that we are on earth, all of us are in a hurry<br>- Whatever we turn out to be on earth was pre-ordained, immaterial of whether we believe it or not. |
| 210. | Àkùrọ̀ mí ti l'ómi l'ódò k'ójò tó rọ̀ si | My wetland already had water before rain fell on it<br>- Things were already working great for me before your arrival/ before I knew you. |
| 211. | Àlá t'ájá bá lá, inú Ajá l'ó ń gbé | The dream that a dog dreams, it's inside the dog it remains<br>- You'll take this [secret] with you to your grave. |
| 212. | Aláàróbọ̀ ẹ ò m'òwò t'ó ma ṣe mọ́n, Igbáa Wórobo ló kù t'ó fẹ́ lọ gbé! | Your middleman has run out of business ideas; now he wants to dabble into petty trading! |

| | | |
|---|---|---|
| | | - The person under reference does not seem to know what they want to do. |
| 213. | Alágbàfọ̀ tí wọ́n ní k'ó lọ ra'lẹ̀ k'ó máa kọ́'lé; ó ti gbàgbé wípé gbogbo Èékánná òun ní ò padà fẹ́ ẹ yọ s'ínú Aṣọ fífọ̀ k'óun ó to parí Ilé kíkọ́ | The clothes handwasher that they asked to purchase a land to start building a house; he/she has forgotten that all his/her nails would nearly come off in the clothes handwashing before they would finish building the house<br>- This allegorical expression interprets the expectation as nothing but a mirage;<br>- This is a hopeless dream. |
| 214. | Alágẹmọ́n ti bí'mọ ẹ̀ tán, àì mọ̀n-ọ́n jó kù s'ọ́wọ́ọ Alágẹmọ́n | The chameleon has birthed her hatchlings, the inability to dance rests with the hatchlings<br>- This allegory is usually expressed by parents: I have nurtured and trained you up to my utmost ability, the rest is up to you;<br>- I have led you up to the crossroads, the rest of the journey you'll have to travel on your own. |
| 215. | Aláǹgbá a yín t'ó ń lé'rí gbọ̀n-gbọ̀n-gbọ̀n, Ògiri ní ó padà fi gbá | Your lizard that is bragging and bobbing its head incessantly, it's a wall that it will eventually hit with it<br>- So much bravado and no action. |
| 216. | Alátiṣe á m'àtiṣe Ara ẹ̀<br>Tàbí...<br>Alátiṣe níí m'àtiṣe Ara ẹ̀ | Own-problem-solver will know how to resolve his own<br>The person with the problem is the one who knows how to deal with it<br>- If you don't care about your own health [or other challenges], no one else will.<br>- The person with the problem will do all they can to resolve what is bothering them. |
| 217. | Aláyọjúràn níí f'ogií gùn bíi t'ejò | A meddler who jumps and climbs trees like a snake<br>- Only a busybody who interferes in other people's affairs uninvited would do [such a thing]. |
| 218. | Alẹ́ kìí lẹ́ k'ọ́mọ Ejò má rìn; t'ọmọ Eku l'ó ni'ra | The night is never so dark that a snakelet won't be able to walk [have easy |

| | | |
|---|---|---|
| | | unhindered passage]; that of rat puppies' is the one that is challenging<br>- You might say this if you feel fearless or confident about something that you can either do now or postpone till there's more assurance of free passage like, say, a curfew has been lifted. |
| 219. | Àlejò l'owó; t'ó bá ti yà s'ọ́dọ̀ ẹ, tọ́'jú ẹ̀ | Money is a visitor; if it visits you, take care of it<br>- This opportunity is a rare one; grab it by both hands and don't let it slip away. |
| 220. | Alẹ́lẹ́ Ọ̀lẹ́ yọ̀; Àkùkọ́ kọ Ọ̀lẹ́ p'òṣé | As dusk approaches, the sluggard rejoices; the rooster crows [in the dawn] the lazy one hisses. |
| 221. | Àlọ́ ni tìẹ, Àbọ̀ ni t'èmi | Going is yours, returning is mine<br>- You have done your worst, now expect my comeback. |
| 222. | Àlọ́ yá, Oníbodè Apòmù | Going is now, the gate-keeper of Apòmù<br>- No more delays, we've got to do this now!<br>- Time is of the essence! |
| 223. | Àlọ́ká Ọlọ́ ìí p'ọlọ | The roundness of the grinding stone does not kill the mortar<br>- Things are going to be as good as before. |
| 224. | Àlọ́ká Ọlọ́ ti p'ọlọ | The roundness of the grinding stone has killed the mortar<br>- The evil you have done in the past has now caught up with you. |
| 225. | Alubàtá kan ìí dá'rin | No Bàtá drummer ever initiates a song<br>- Don't voice your opinion in the matter; it's above your pay grade. |
| 226. | Àmọ́n ni, kò sí l'ára Ẹran | It's all inedible animal byproducts, they do not make up any part of the meat<br>- It's a distraction from the issue at hand; pay no attention to it. |
| 227. | Amọ̀rọ̀bini Ọ̀yọ́ | A person already wise to a situation but asking questions about it like he didn't know<br>- Basically saying to someone why are they asking questions they already know the answer to, like someone from Ọ̀yọ́ |

| | | |
|---|---|---|
| | | might do. Ọ̀yọ́ is an important city in Yorùbá land and used to be a great empire before the slave trade began. |
| 228. | Amúnisìn ò wá Àlọ̀, àfi k'ọ́n kòó l'ójú | An oppressor (or bully) does not want a dialogue or negotiation, except one confronts him squarely (with own weapons)<br>- Shout at the devil [in question];<br>- Look your enemy in the eye. |
| 229. | Ànìkàn rìn níí j'ọmọ Ejò n'íyà | Walking alone is what makes a snakelet suffer hardship<br>- You are in this adversity because you did not seek counsel or backup before you took the decision [that landed you here]. |
| 230. | Àpaàdé'lé kò tíì jẹ́ k'a m'ológbò l'ọ́dẹ | Not bringing home its kill from the bush has not endeared the cat to be recognized as a predator<br>- His not having made his wife pregnant doesn't make anyone believe that a guy exists (as a real man). |
| 231. | Àparò kan ò ga jù'kan lọ, àf'èyí t'ó bá g'orí Ebè | One bush-fowl is no taller than another, except the one that climbs on a mound<br>- One is not better than the other. |
| 232. | Àparò ó ti já'ko | The bush-fowl has broken out of the bush<br>- What you thought the world didn't know about is now out in the open; basically, the cat is out of the bag. |
| 233. | Àpè mọ́n'ra l'à ń pe "t'èmí d'ire" | Calling to oneself is how we say "my own has become good."<br>- There is some good news and you've got to claim it for your soul. |
| 234. | Apẹ́lẹ́hìn ìí jẹ'bàjẹ́ | He who arrives last doesn't eat the rotten food<br>- He who laughs last laughs best. |
| 235. | Àpọ́nlé n'ìyàwóo Káà | Honoring and idolization is the "wife of a car"<br>- This saying is to tell off a high-and-mighty individual, as if to say "we have put you on a pedestal for so long because of your past generosity; if you keep on your haughtiness, we can let you go"; |

|  |  | - We are just exalting you for the good you may have done in the past; we don't have to keep up with your snobbery;<br>- Having a car is as respectful as having a wife. |
|---|---|---|
| 236. | Àpọ́nlé ò sí f'ọba tí ò l'ólorì | There's no honor or respect for the king who has no queen<br>- No one respects a leader who acts like a weakling or doesn't do what's expected of his esteemed office [lacking in guts/dignity]. |
| 237. | Apurọ́ mọ́n'ni ko'ni l'ojú | A pathological liar who confronts one he's lying against shamelessly<br>- Only a bold-faced liar would dare to appear in front of the person they have been lying against. |
| 238. | Ara ìjà l'eyín wà | Biting [using teeth] is part of a fight<br>- You can't moan about someone using any means available to them to fight you;<br>- It's part of the game, so don't complain about unorthodox tactics. |
| 239. | Àrà ngò rirí, mo r'órí Ológbò l'átẹ! | Hack, I'd never seen the like; I saw a cat's head on a market table-display!<br>The points-to-ponder sentence usually precedes a gossip:<br>- An unexpected event has just occurred/has been witnessed. |
| 240. | Àràbà tún'ra mú, Odò ń gb'árére lọ | The Àràbà tree had better double its efforts at reinforcement; the River [formed from recent flash flooding or storm] is actually uprooting and washing away Arère. The latter tree is second only to an Àràbà tree [in grandeur]<br>- The revolution or similar events that you hear being bandied about right now could happen in your own neighborhood before long, so watch out, and make preparations;<br>- Let what's going on around you be a lesson, so watch your back. |
| 241. | Ará-ilé l'ó ń bá ẹ pèé l'ámõdi, | It's only your close family members that |

|  | Wèrè l'ará-ìta máa pèé | might call it Àmódi (slight infection), mental illness is what everyone else will call it<br>- If you're engaged in illicit activity and no one has reigned you in at home because you're family, if you were to demonstrate half of the deeds outside, you would probably be labeled a criminal and get in legal trouble. |
|---|---|---|
| 242. | Àrífín Ilé t'òun t'ègbin; Àdàpò Owó t'òun t'ìyà; Èmi ò jù ọ́, Ìwọ ò jù mí, tí ń m'áráilé Ẹni í f'ojú di'ni | Familial insolence with deep shame; mixture of money and suffering; I'm not greater than you, you're not greater than me, that makes a family member disregard someone<br>- This is rudeness and a stigma;<br>- This signifies pride and ego. |
| 243. | Àrígiṣẹ́gi t'ó ṣẹ́'gi, Orí Ara è ló ma fi rũ | The junk bug that breaks pieces of wood, it's its own head it'll use to carry them<br>- Whoever plots evil against [the speaker] will be hoisted by his own petard;<br>- He who digs a pit for others will fall into it himself - Ecclesiastes 10:8. |
| 244. | Arìnwá ìí w'èhìn | Someone who walks backwards does not look backwards<br>- This individual came for one single purpose. |
| 245. | Àrísá Ẹkùn, t'ojo kọ́<br>Tàbí…<br>Yíyọ́ Ẹkùn bíi t'ojo kọ́ | The 'sighting & running' of the tiger is not out of dread OR…<br>The sneaking of the tiger is not out of dread<br>- If someone doesn't appear to want to engage you in a confrontation, it's not necessarily because of fear of you; more likely it's for something else that may not be so obvious to you. |
| 246. | Aríṣe bí Ọ̀yọ́ l'à ń rí, Ọ̀yọ́ ò kì ńṣe bíi Baba Ẹnìkankan | Finding something to do like Ọ̀yọ́ is what we see, Ọ̀yọ́ doesn't do [things] like anyone's father. Ọ̀yọ́ is an important city in Yorùbá land and used to be a great empire before the slave trade.<br>- This person sets the trends while others |

|  |  | follow;<br>- The person referred to in this idiom is a pace-setter. |
|---|---|---|
| 247. | Àríyá ò l'ópin | Enjoyment and pleasure has no end. |
| 248. | Àríyàn-jiyàn l'ó ń b'ọ̀rẹ́ ẹ́ jẹ́ | Arguments are what ruin a friendship. |
| 249. | Aròmàlà ni ẹ́, t'ẹnu Apẹ l'o fẹ́ gbọ́ | You are a stirrer [cook] of Àmàlà, you're only waiting to hear what the pot will say<br>- You're a trouble-maker, you're only spoiling for a fight. |
| 250. | Arúgbó ṣ'oge rí | The old [ladies] were once upon a time flirty and seductive [in vogue] before<br>- We have done this before, so stop showing off! |
| 251. | Àṣá gb'ọ́mọ Àgbébọ̀, Àgbébọ̀ ó mú'ra Ìjà; Ìran Ẹ̀dìẹ a p'àṣá rí ni? | A hawk snatched a chick, the mother-hen prepares for a fight; has a descendant of chickens ever killed a kite?<br>- The local thug/bully snatches a boy's girlfriend, the father gets ready for a fight; has anyone in the village ever challenged the thug before?<br>- Another example: some powerful individual infringes on your rights, to whom will you complain? |
| 252. | Àṣá ń b'ẹiyẹlé ń ṣ'eré, Ẹiyẹlé ń yọ̀; Ẹiyẹlé ń f'ikú ṣ'eré, kò ì 'mọ̀n p'ó fẹ́ ṣe'kú pa òun ni | The hawk is playing with the pigeon, the pigeon is rolling in tears of joy; the pigeon is playing with death, it has no inkling yet that the kite wants to kill it<br>- Watch the company you keep; don't assume everyone laughing with you wants your success and happiness. |
| 253. | Àṣá ò gbọdọ̀ wọ'lé gb'ẹiyẹlé | A hawk cannot [dare] enter to snatch a pigeon<br>- You are protected here, so do not fret! |
| 254. | Àṣá ò mọn'hun t'ólóko ń rò; Òròmọ̀ndìyẹ t'ó bá gbàgbé ìyá ẹ̀, Àṣá ò gbe l'ojú ìyáa ẹ̀ | The hawk doesn't know what the farmer is thinking about; the chick that forgets its mother, the hawk shall take the chick away right in the presence of its mother<br>- If a child doesn't listen to its parents, it will be taught a great [hard] lesson outside. |
| 255. | Aṣèbàjé ṣebí t'òun l'à ńwí; | The evildoer thinks we are talking about |

|  |  |  |
|---|---|---|
|  | Aṣebúburú ẹ kú Araá'fu | him; to the trouble-maker: well done for vigilance<br>- He who engages in illicit activities suspects everyone is always talking about him. |
| 256. | Àṣejù n'irun Àyà, ti t'orí ti tó | Chest hair is an extravagance, the one on the head should suffice [Having a hairy chest is an overindulgence, having hair on your head should make you content]<br>- It's redundant going extra step to prove your point; what you've said or done is more than enough;<br>- We've got your point; don't overstress it. |
| 257. | Aṣení ń ṣe'ra ẹ̀ | The "doer" is "doing" himself<br>- The wicked individual is only hurting himself by his actions; if no power on earth can make him pay, at least he'll get his comeuppance when karma catches up with him someday;<br>- You reap what you sow. |
| 258. | Aṣení ṣe'ra ẹ̀ | The voodoo destiny-changer has inadvertently done himself in<br>- Someone's wicked or evil plans against another person has ironically backfired on them;<br>- He/she has been hoisted by his own petard. |
| 259. | Asépẹ́ fún Wèrè jó, òun Wèrè, Ẹgbẹ́ kan nã jọ ni wọ́n | The clapper and the dancing madman are one of a kind<br>- People may find it hard to tell the difference. |
| 260. | Àṣetì kìí b'ójọ́ k'ó má yọ, Àṣetì kìí b'óòrùn k'ó má yọ l'ókè | Undo-ability never happens to the day that it'll fail to break, undo-ability never befalls the sun that it'll not shine<br>- This is an affirmation that you'll succeed in your current endeavor; or you expect a certain breakthrough. |
| 261. | Àsìkò Ekún l'à ń jẹ Eeṣin | The season of Ekún is when we eat flies<br>- We should do things when the time is right. |
| 262. | Àsìkò Eré fún Eré, Àsìkò Iṣẹ́ fún | Playtime is for playing, work time is for |

|  | Iṣẹ́ | working<br>- Everything has its own time. |
|---|---|---|
| 263. | Àṣírí ti tú, Aféfé ti fé; A ti rí fùrọ̀ Adìẹ | The secret is out, the wind has blown; we have seen the anus of the chicken<br>- Your dark secret is no longer a secret! |
| 264. | Aṣọ ńlá kọ́ l'ènìà ńlá | Plus-size clothes are not [indicative] of a person's superior status<br>- Appearances can be deceptive. |
| 265. | Aṣọ ò b'Ọmọ́yẹ mọ́n; Ọmọ́yẹ́ẹ́ ti rìn'hòòhò w'ọjà | Clothes no longer fit Ọmọ́yẹ; Ọmọ́yẹ has walked stark naked into the market<br>- This is a kind of announcement or moment of truth to indicate that the matter [issue that was hitherto pending] has certainly now got out of hand, and can no longer be rectified;<br>- The thing can't be remedied any longer, it's too late;<br>- The damage is already done. |
| 266. | Aṣọ táa bá fi lé iṣẹ́ jìnà, aà kì ń sọ́ nù, a máa ń tọ́'jú ẹ̀ ni | The clothes [tatters] we wore when we chased away indigence, we don't lose them, we always keep them<br>- We always remember the state [frame of mind] we were in when we first conquered poverty and destitution. |
| 267. | Aṣọ t'ó kángun s'éégún n'ọ́n ń pè ní Jẹ̀pẹ́ | The costume that is nearest to the masquerade is what is called Jẹ̀pẹ́<br>- The matter concerns the wellbeing of your closest relative or friend. |
| 268. | Asùn kakà kan ìí gb'òfé | No "supine sleeper" accepts 'free' [nothing]<br>- If someone does you a favor, assume that they'll expect some sort of reward or recompense;<br>- Like a lady lover who spends a lot of time with you; it's not for nothing. Bear in mind that you may have to provide for her financially as well as satisfy her sexually;<br>- Nothing goes for nothing. |
| 269. | Àt'imí, àt'ìtọ̀ l'adìẹ ń yà papọ̀ | Simultaneously does a fowl excrete feces [poop] and urine<br>- Birds eliminate waste products through |

| | | |
|---|---|---|
| | | the cloaca [sewer];<br>- All your problems will be resolved [after this time out]. |
| 270. | Ata'ná ò ṣe é m'átàná | The "pepper on the stove" is not the same as "since yesterday." This expression is as a result of a rhyming association between the first and the last words of the adage<br>- The argument is unrelated. |
| 271. | Atan'ni ò gọ̀; Ẹni à ńtàn ni ò gbọ́n | A deceitful person is not stupid; the one being deceived is the stupid one<br>- You are the one that needs to wise up. |
| 272. | Àtàrí Àjànàkú ni, kìí ṣ'ẹrù Ọmọdé | The head of an elephant is not a load for a child<br>- The problem at hand is beyond the remit of the youth. |
| 273. | Àtègbé l'ẹ́sẹ̀ ń tẹ'nà | Treading-on with impunity is how the feet step on the path<br>- There's nothing you can do about it;<br>- This metaphor could be expressed in frustration to imply, for example: This individual is so powerful that whatever they do they'll always get away with. |
| 274. | Atégùn t'ó wọ'núu'lé gbé kẹtẹpẹ Ògì, k'élélùbọ́ ó má ṣ'àfira | The wind that entered the house to carry away the sap of the corn-porridge, the yam flour better watch out<br>- This idiom is a warning to not let your guards down, but keep your wits about you. |
| 275. | Àtẹlẹwọ́ ni mo bá'là, mi ò m'ẹni t'ó kọ́ọ́ | On the palms did I find lines, I know not who made the incision<br>- I found things the way they are; I don't know who made them so. |
| 276. | Atọ́rọ̀ṣé b'ọ̀rọ̀ jẹ́ | The rectifier [pacifier] has made matters worse<br>- In matters of state: a diplomat that was sent to straighten a strained relationship has not done as he'd been tasked, but, instead, has worsened the situation by some unofficial statements of his own;<br>- In a soccer game: the defender that's supposed to assist his goalkeeper keep |

| | | |
|---|---|---|
| | | out goals has committed an error and has instead scored an own goal. |
| 277. | Àwárí l'obìnrín ńwá ǹkan Ọbẹ̀ | Looking-for-and-finding is how a woman searches for ingredients for stew<br>- If you need something bad enough, you'll do all you can to get it. |
| 278. | Awo lí t'ojú Ọ̀gbẹ̀rì da'fá nù | The initiate does not, in the presence of the novice, throw away Ifá<br>- Hush! This is not to be shared with every Tom, Dick, and Harry. |
| 279. | Awo níí gb'awo ní Ìgbọ́wọ́; b'áwo ò gb'awo ní Ìgbọ́wọ́, Awo a tẹ́, Awo a ya | It's an oracle priest that protects the secret of another; if one priest does not support the other, the oracle divinity will be dragged to ignominy and the priesthood will rupture<br>- It would be a collective humiliation if we don't pull our resources together now and overcome the challenges we currently face. |
| 280. | Àwo ò mọ̀n pé yíó j'ata; Àwó d'órí Iná tán; Àwó ń ṣ'àrànsùn | A plate did not know it was going to eat pepper; the plate got atop the fire; the plate then started to doze off<br>- It's the citizens that have forgotten or accepted the current bad situation; they no longer have the spirit to fight back or hold their leaders accountable. |
| 281. | Àwòdì Òkè ò mọ̀n'pé Ará-ilẹ̀ ẹ́ ńwò'un | The bush eagle does not know that people on earth are looking at it<br>- People in autocratic power do not care about their citizens. |
| 282. | Àwòdì t'ó ń re Ìbarà, Èfũfùú taá ní Ìdí 'Pẹ́h'; ó ní Iṣẹ́ kúkú yá ni! | The eagle that is heading to a place, the wind stings its bottom [tail] 'Pẹ́h'; it responded that its work [flying] will be that much easier!<br>- For example: If someone is trying to quit something [job, environment, etc.] and something happens that inadvertently hastens his desire for the departure he's been planning, the person welcomes the opportunity. |
| 283. | Àwòdì-òkè t'ó ń wo Ìkarahun | The bush-eagle in the sky that's eyeing a |

|  | kọ̀rọ̀, kín l'ó lè f'ìgbín ṣe | snail askew, what's it going to do with the snail?<br>- An example: the local thug eyeing a little disabled kid cockeyed, what's he going to do to the kid? |
|---|---|---|
| 284. | Àwọn Baba Mọn'ni-Mọn'ni, nwọ́n ní Ẹni t'ó bá ma j'ẹ̀dọ̀, Ìfun níí tọrọ | The elders that know everyone say whoever wishes to eat kidney, he first requests for the trachea<br>- Beware of trickery of someone asking you a favor; what is it leading to? |
| 285. | Àwọn Obìnrin ìsìnyí l'ó b'ọjà jẹ́ | It's the women of today that 'ruined' the market<br>- Young ladies of today throw themselves at men [without acquiring higher education], making them look cheap and easy to get;<br>- Your actions have put us at a disadvantage. |
| 286. | Aya Ọ̀lẹ l'à ń gbà, kò s'ẹ́ni t'ó lè gb'ọmọ Ọ̀lẹ | It's the wife of a lazy man one [may] take, no one can take a lazy man's kids. |
| 287. | Àyé gba Tápà, ó ń kọ'lé Ìgunnu | Due to lack of restrictions for the man from Tápà (in Kogi state, Nigeria), he's erecting a building for masquerades<br>- If you allowed them, people would walk over you. |
| 288. | Àyè l'ó gba Oníbàjẹ Ìda, tí wọ́n fi ń sọ'pé ó l'ágídí | It was opportunity that granted the spontaneous scoundrel that people were saying he had stubbornness<br>- The opportunity was just there for any takers, that's all!<br>- Things are not always what they seem. |
| 289. | Àyíká Odó ìí p'odó | The roundness of a [wooden] mortar does not kill the mortar<br>- No evil thing shall happen. |
| 290. | Àyíká Odó ti p'odó | The roundness of a [wooden] mortar has killed the mortar<br>- Things are no longer the way you intended to be. |
| 291. | Àyímọ́n ìí p'ọlọ́kà | Stirring here and there does not kill an Àmàlà cook<br>- Let the activist do as he pleases or say |

| | | |
|---|---|---|
| | | what he wants to say;<br>- Let whoever wants to complain [about an issue under discussion] go ahead and complain; that's not going to affect anything;<br>- It's an occupational hazard of the profession; it's part of the job. |
| 292. | Báa ṣe b'ẹrú l'a b'ọmọ | As we birthed slaves, so were free children born<br>- As children of the rich and famous were born, so were the children of the poor and unknown;<br>- What's good for the goose is good for the gander. |
| 293. | B'aá bã nà'nàkí, Ọ̀bọ l'àá wíí fún | If we intended to beat the ape, it's the monkey that we would forewarn<br>- You make your displeasure known to the subordinates who will surely report back to their boss [the real target]. |
| 294. | B'áhéré bá ń jó'ná l'ọ́wọ́, àwọn Àgbà íí lọ Oko àlọ-sùn | If the hut [farmhouse] is burning, the elders do not go passing the night there<br>- If thorny issues arise, the elders congregate and find a solution. |
| 295. | B'ájá bá ń sínwín, áá m'ojú Olówó ẹ̀ | If a dog develops insanity, he'll still recognize his master<br>- No matter how rich or powerful you become, you'll still show respect for your parents or some authority. |
| 296. | B'ájá gbe'yọ̀ kín l'ó máa fi rò? | If a dog grabs a pack of salt, what's he going to stir it in?<br>- What's the use of giving something to someone who doesn't know the value or purpose of it? |
| 297. | B'áládǐn ò bá sí ńlé, ńṣe l'ọmọ wọn ń j'ogún Ẹbu | If the palm-kernel-oil seller is away from home, the children inherit desiccation<br>- If the leaders/parents are absent, things could go poorly for the people/children. |
| 298. | B'álájá bá ń lọ l'óde, áá máa gb'óhùn Arò | If a dog owner is walking in the outdoors, he hears the noise of Arò<br>- When one walks a dangerous street, he should keep his wits about him. |

| 299. | B'álọ̀ bá lọ, Àbọ̀ ń bọ̀ | If the Going goes, the Return is coming<br>- What goes around, comes around. |
|---|---|---|
| 300. | B'áò kú, Ìṣe ò tán | If we don't die, activities and deeds are not yet over<br>- If what we currently seek appears unobtainable, we should not despair; there are bound to be opportunities before long, so keep your spirit up. |
| 301. | B'árã bá kú tán, Orúkọ Ẹni kìí kú | If one's body ages and dies, one's name remains immortal<br>- One's deed in life will succeed him;<br>- You'll be remembered by what you did while alive. |
| 302. | B'árọ̀nì ò t'àjò dé, Oníkòyí ò níí sinmi | If the chief priest [diviner] has not returned from his trip, the ruler of Ìkòyí will not rest<br>- Without the right generals surrounding him, the leader will not have peace of mind. |
| 303. | B'àṣèjé Obì t'ó ńso n'ígbà Ẹ̀rùn | Dinner-ruiner-kolanut that grows in the height of summer<br>- A lament to complain after a felony has been committed, especially when the perpetrator is someone that cannot really be made to pay for the deed, i.e. a little child, a prince/princess etc. |
| 304. | B'ẹ bá fẹ́ tẹ́ Bọ̀ọ̀rọ̀kìní, ẹ jé á jí re'lé ẹ̀ l'ákùkọ, k'á wo Ẹní t'ó tẹ́ s'ílẹ̀, k'á wo aṣọ t'ó fi b'ora | If you wish to humiliate a popular bachelor, let's visit his house in the early hours of the dawn, let's have a visual of the mat he has spread on the floor, and observe the sheet he has covered himself with<br>- This farfetched idiom alleges the subject here is given to showboating only, and not a man of any substance. |
| 305. | B'ébí bá kúrò n'ínú Ìṣẹ́, Iṣẹ́ bù ṣe | When hunger is out of the equation, poverty is reduced. |
| 306. | B'ẹ̀ẹ̀dẹ̀ ò tù, bí Ìgbẹ́ n'ìgboro ń rí | If the home is not peaceful, the outdoors [the town] will look like jungle<br>- If we don't put our affairs in order, peace of mind may become a pipe dream; |

| | | |
|---|---|---|
| | | - If what's causing discontentment among the people is not addressed and resolved, the country may find itself in turmoil. |
| 307. | B'éégún bá dán'rú è l'áṣà, yíó d'ènìà | If a masquerade attempts such a thing, he'll become human<br>- It's unthinkable to contemplate such a deed because the consequence of such action will be dire. |
| 308. | B'ẹkún bá d'alẹ́ kan, Ayọ̀ ńbọ̀ l'ówúrọ̀ | If tears linger for one night, joy is coming in the dawn<br>- Do not be despondent about the crisis you are currently facing, peace and joy is just round the corner. |
| 309. | B'ẹlẹ́jọ́ bá m'ẹjọ́ è l'ẹ́bi kò níí pé ní Ìkúnlẹ̀ | If the accused acknowledges his culpability, he won't be long on his knees<br>- If a respondent accepts his guilt, his sentence may be much reduced for saving the taxpayers money for a lengthy court proceedings. |
| 310. | B'ènìyán bá gb'ọ́gbọ́n-ọn kíkú l'ẹ́ẹ̀rùn, àwa nã ó sì gb'ọ́gbọ́n-ọn sísin s'ípadò | If someone is wise enough to die during the dry season, we too shall in turn use our collective insight and bury him in the swamp<br>- If you are clever enough to pull off what you are threatening to do, we too must try our best to outwit you. |
| 311. | B'ènìyán bá f'ogún Ọdún pinlẹ̀sẹ̀ ẹ Wèrè, Ìjọ́ wo l'ó fẹ́ já? | If someone plans for twenty years on becoming a madman, exactly when will he break out and begin playing out the role?<br>- If you want to do something, do it and stop mucking about; spare us the suspense. |
| 312. | B'ènìyán bá máa d'áṣọ fún'ni, t'ọrùn-un ẹ l'a ma kọ́kọ́ wò | If someone wants to clothe us, we first look at the clothes he's wearing<br>- For example, someone who lives with his parents wants to show you how to be successful. If he were successful himself, he wouldn't be squatting with his parents. |
| 313. | B'ènìyán bá pẹ́ l'órí Imí, Eeṣin-k'éeṣin yíó ba ńbẹ̀ | If someone tarries too long while passing stool, all kinds of flies will start to swarm round him |

|  |  | - Stop wasting unnecessary time over trivial things that only bring contempt and move quickly on to tangible stuff. |
|---|---|---|
| 314. | B'éniyán bá wọ'lé pé k'òun m'éiyẹ Ọ̀nìnì, Àwòmọn Ìran l'ó wò l'áiyé ẹ̀ | If someone entered to grab an Ọ̀nìnì (it's a West African supernatural bird that human eyes must not glimpse), that would be the last time he would ever see anything in his lifetime<br>- This proverb is a severe warning from someone to another that what they're trying to do is forbidden and could be fatal. |
| 315. | B'épà ò bá ti dáa, Ọmọ inúu rẹ̀ ò lè dáa | If groundnuts are not good, the seeds [peanuts] inside the shells will not be good<br>- If the leader is evil, the rest of his cabinet are likely to be too. |
| 316. | B'érín bá jẹ tí ò yó, Ìgbẹ́ l'ojú ó tì | If an elephant feeds and is not full, it's stool [excrement] that'll be shamed<br>- If something positive is not done in time to resolve the burning issue at hand, some innocent folks may suffer in the fallout;<br>- Example: If a wayward child commits a felony and his family turns their back on him, when he gets convicted, it's not just him that will suffer the stigma of the conviction; the family name will also get dragged in the mud along with him;<br>- If a pharmaceutical company releases an untested drug that is later found to be fatal, it's the company that will face lawsuits that could ruin their company and their reputation;<br>- If the collective diplomatic effort of governments around the world does not deter a regime (e.g. North Korea, Russia) from invading or threatening its neighbor(s), the economic sanctions that the world may impose on that country might produce the desired effect. When the sanctions start biting, citizens who feel |

| | | the hardship is intolerable enough may resort to violence, riots, protests, etc. against their government and make that regime fall;<br>- Do the needful. |
|---|---|---|
| 317. | B'éso ó bá pọ́n rẹ̀dẹ̀rẹ̀dẹ̀, aà lè fi s'ílẹ̀ l'áì ka | When fruits are fully ripe, we cannot abandon them and not pluck them<br>- When solutions are available, we exploit them to our advantage. |
| 318. | B'éwé bá pẹ́ l'ára Ọṣẹ, á d'ọṣẹ | If a leaf stays too long wrapped around soap [African natural black soap], the leaf will also become soap<br>- The notion is if someone or something has been too long in a place, he/it becomes a part and parcel of the main indigenous product or culture, with the same characteristics to boot. |
| 319. | B'éwúrẹ bá jẹ lọ, aa f'àbọ̀ s'ílé; b'ágùtán bá jẹ lọ, áá padà s'ílé dandan | If a goat roams away to browse, it will return home; if a sheep roams away to graze, it must return home<br>- This is an inspirational statement to say to someone embarking on a perilous journey that they will return home safely. |
| 320. | B'ígí bá ṣubú lé'gi, t'òkè l'a ma kọ́kọ́ gbé kúrò | If trees fell one atop the other, one would remove the top one first<br>- When there are several concerns that need attention, they are dealt with and resolved separately according to the order of priority. |
| 321. | B'íkán bá ń mọn Orù, kí Ìshasùn-ún má ṣ'àfira! | If termites could build their towering mound over a large clay water-pot, the small earthen stew pot had better watch out!<br>- If whatever is currently happening has affected the rich and the powerful that they are feeling the pinch, the underclass and those caught in a poverty trap had better double their vigilance. |
| 322. | B'íkú Ilé ò pa'ni, t'òde ò lè pa'ni | If "home death" does not kill a man, that of the "outside" cannot kill the man<br>- We are really hurt mostly by people who |

| | | |
|---|---|---|
| | | know us and our weaknesses;<br>- There are enemies within. |
| 323. | B'íkún l'ó l'oko, bí Tàkúté ni | If it's the chipmunk that owns the farm or it's the mousetrap<br>- We'll see who is the boss;<br>- If it's yours or mine, we'll soon find out. |
| 324. | B'ílé bá san, bí ò san, Àwọ̀ l'àá wò | If a house is well-to-do or not, it's the skin that we observe<br>- The evidence of a position can be noticed by the appearance of the individual, either in speech, dressing or the way they carry themselves. |
| 325. | B'ílùu Gángan-án bá wọ'lú, t'ẹbí t'ọmọ l'ó ń jóo | If a Gángan drum enters a village, both family and relations dance to the beat<br>- This personification is to say when a renowned person arrives in town, everyone welcomes him. |
| 326. | B'íná bá kú á f'eérú b'ojú; b'ógẹdẹ bá kú á f'ọmọ ẹ rọ́'pò | If fire is extinguished it covers its face with ash; if a banana tree dies it swaps position with its young<br>- It's not a complicated issue; all that needs to be done is follow tradition and let the child take over his father's role. |
| 327. | B'ínú ṣe rí l'obìí ṣe ń yàn<br>Tàbí...<br>Bí inú bá ti rí, bẹ̀ẹ l'obì ń yàn | How your mind is is exactly what the kolanut's divination will interpret/foretell<br>- We were just discussing about you, and here you are! |
| 328. | B'írọ́ ò bá jọ mọ́n'nìà, wọn ọ̀n kì ń páá mọn | If a lie does not relate to someone, no one attributes it to them<br>- No smoke without fire. |
| 329. | B'íṣẹ́ ò bá p'ẹni, Ẹnìkan lí pẹ́'ṣẹ́ | If work does not hold us back, no one tarries with the work<br>- If there's nothing else we're waiting on for the task to be carried out, we proceed without further ado;<br>- Make hay while the sun shines. |
| 330. | B'íyà ńlá bá gbé'ni sán'lẹ̀, kékeré a sì g'orí Ẹni | If a major adversity brings someone down, a little one will ascend it<br>- Kind of after an unjust punishment, one is receiving another; only this time it's being inflicted by someone in lesser status |

| | | |
|---|---|---|
| | | than the narrator;<br>- This is a muse about one's plight that they are facing another insult that has 'added salt to the injury'. |
| 331. | B'íyán ò bá tíì dé'lẹ̀, kò ní á má jẹ'ṣu; Ebí á pàà'yàn kú ni | If pounded-yam is not yet ready, it doesn't say [mean] we can't eat yam [in the meantime]; hunger will just beat man till he dies [otherwise]<br>- Have some snacks while you wait for dinner, if only to keep mind and soul together for now;<br>- It would be prudent to grab the opportunity that presents itself [right at this moment] while you wait for what you really desire. |
| 332. | B'ó pẹ́, b'o yá, Akólòló á pe Baba | Sooner or later, a stammerer will pronounce 'Baba'<br>- After a spate of trials and errors you'll succeed if you don't give up;<br>- If you persevere long enough you'll have what you so desperately seek. |
| 333. | B'ó ti wùn kí Èkúté gbọ́n tó, Ẹ̀sọ̀pẹ̀lẹ́ ni Olõgìnní ó fi mu | No matter how clever the mouse is, quietly is the way the cat will snare it<br>- No matter how cunning an enemy is, a great warrior will find a way to get him. |
| 334. | B'óbìnrín bá pẹ́ ń'lẹ̀, Ọkọ Àjẹ́ ní ń dà<br>Tàbí...<br>B'óbìnrín bá pẹ́ ńlé Ọkọ, Àjẹ́ ní ń dà | If a woman lives too long, she ends up becoming the husband of witches [Head Witch]<br>If a woman stays too long married to one man, she will end up becoming a Wiccan<br>- If a visitor overstays his welcome, he'll become a nuisance;<br>- The person in reference knows too much of your history, including secrets. |
| 335. | B'ódeé bá le'ni, Ilé l'àá wá | If 'outdoors' or an outing chases one away, it's our house we return to<br>- If someone drives us from their house, we still have our own home to return to. |
| 336. | B'ọ́gbọ́n bá tán ń'nú Àgbà, Àgbà a máa gbọ́n'mîìn ni | If an elder runs out of wisdom, the elder will gain or acquire new ones<br>- If the original plan fails, go to plan B; |

| | | - If at first you don't succeed, try, try, and try again. |
|---|---|---|
| 337. | B'óge ó báà tiẹ̀ ja'lè, a gbé'hun t'ó y'ẹni | If an elegant lady were to steal, [surely] she would nick something classy?<br>- One would expect you to do better than this. |
| 338. | B'ógiri ò la'nu, Aláǹgbá ò lè r'áyè wọ'bẹ̀ | If the wall did not split, a lizard would never be able to enter it<br>- If it weren't for what happened, the current state of affairs would not have existed;<br>- If you don't divulge information about yourself, your adversaries will not have anything to use against you. |
| 339. | B'ógún bá jẹ lọ ńkọ́, Ogbọ̀n ń jẹ bọ̀ ńgb'ẹ̀hìn | If twenty goes a-eating, thirty will return a-eating in the end<br>- You may think you can do what you like now and get away with it, but the consequence is coming;<br>- There'll be a time to face up to something one has been running away from for some time;<br>- There's a fallout for every decision one takes. |
| 340. | B'ójò ó bá ń pa'ni, a máa tọ̀ sí Ṣòkòtò Ẹni | If rain is falling on someone, he could pee inside his trousers<br>- If someone finds himself in trouble, he could say things he could be ashamed of later, after the problem is over;<br>- One would do anything to get out of his dire straits. |
| 341. | B'ọ́kọ̀ ọ́ bá r'òkun b'ó r'ọ̀sà, ó ní láti gún'lẹ̀ s'ébũté | If a ship travelled through the Atlantic ocean or river Niger, it would still berth at a port or marina<br>- All this talk has got to lead to something;<br>- All the efforts that have been invested in this business must surely produce something. |
| 342. | B'ómí bá p'ọmọ Ẹni, Omi nã l'a ma lò | If water kills one's child [i.e. by drowning], we would still use water. |
| 343. | B'ómī bá pọ̀ j'ọkà lọ, á máa dí | If water is too much in the pot of Ọkà |

|  |  | Kókó | [a.k.a. Àmàlà], it comes out with unsavory lumps in it<br>- Example: let the new government establish itself and find its feet first before everyone starts demanding for this and that, otherwise what the country may end up with won't be a model government;<br>- Too many cooks spoil the broth. |
| --- | --- | --- | --- |
| 344. |  | B'ọmọ Ẹní bá wà l'áiyé, b'áraá bá bàjẹ́, Orúkọ Ẹni ò níí bàjẹ́ | As long as one's offspring remains alive, if the body withers, one's name will not go to ruin<br>- The child that one leaves behind will continue one's legacy. |
| 345. |  | B'ọmọdé bá l'óògùn Ìjàkadì, Ẹgbẹ́ ẹ̀ l'ó ma fi nà | If a youth had a charm for wrestling, it's only his peers he'd use it to whip<br>- If someone has been trying to prove their prowess in anything, his would-be 'opponent' or 'adversary' might express this idiom to send a warning to the man that he has now met his superior. |
| 346. |  | B'ọmọdé ò bá m'ẹwẹ, tí 'ò dè m'òwè, aá j'ẹ́wẹ l'ọ́wọ́ Ọ̀tún, aá m'ówè l'ọ́wọ́ Òsì; àá wá fi hàn-án pé Ẹwẹ rèé, Òwè rèé | If a child does not recognize and cannot differentiate between leaves of Ẹwẹ and Òwè, we pluck an Ẹwẹ leaf and put it in the right hand, put that of Òwè in the left; then we show him here's Ẹwẹ and here's Òwè<br>- A child must be taught what he does not know;<br>- Remind he who doesn't know where he's found himself where he really is;<br>- Show who is obviously uninitiated how things are done. |
| 347. |  | B'ótútù ń pà'kan Ọ̀rẹ́, gbogbo wa l'ó jọ ń pa | If cold is killing one friend, it's all of us it's killing together<br>- If one friend is suffering so much from cold [flu], it would affect all their collective group of friends. For instance, if they having a get-together, the fact that one of them will not be able to participate will affect the rest;<br>- A problem shared is a problem halved |

| | | |
|---|---|---|
| | | (Gal 6:2). |
| 348. | B'ọ́wọ́ Ekú ṣe mọn l'ó ṣe fi ń bọ́'jú | As tiny as the hands of a mouse are is how it uses them to rub its face<br>- We should stick to the resources we have and manage them as much as we can;<br>- Buy a car you can afford and maintain;<br>- Send your children to a school you can afford to pay for;<br>- You only buy things that you have sufficient money to pay for;<br>- Cut your coat according to your cloth. |
| 349. | Bá ò r'ẹni bá'là, Ọlà kìí yá bọ̀rọ̀ | If we came from a background of abject poverty, becoming wealthy all alone would not come easy<br>- Without the crucial help you got at the right time, it would have been an uphill task for you to get to where you are today. |
| 350. | Bá'nú sọ, má b'énìà sọ | Talk to your soul [inner self], don't talk to humankind [don't disclose your plans to anyone]. |
| 351. | Báa bá f'ọmọ w'ọ́mọ, aá lù'kan pa | If we compared one child to another child, we would beat one to death<br>- Fingers are not equal; stop comparing! |
| 352. | Báa bá fa Gbùùrù, Gbùùrù á fa'gbó | If we drag liana, liana will in turn drag the bush<br>Three example scenarios:<br>- If the breadwinner of a household gets taken out by, say, ill health, the children may suffer greatly, especially in a household without a father with an income;<br>- If a huge storm occurs, it could destroy dwellings thereby making a large number of people homeless;<br>- If the insurance premium on an apartment goes up, the landlord may feel no compunction to also increase the rent. |
| 353. | Báa bá ńbá Olówó gbé, tí ò bá fún'ni l'ówó, ó búyi kún'ni ju k'á | If we lived with a wealthy person and he never gave us money, there would be |

| | | |
|---|---|---|
| | máa b'ólóṣì gbé k'ó tún máa f'òṣì i ẹ ran'ni lọ | more dignity than if one lived with a poor person and his poverty rubbed off on us<br>- Don't complain about how your condition as long as you are being treated without disdain. |
| 354. | Báà r'ádé, aà lè j'Ọba | If we didn't see [have] a crown, we wouldn't be able to crown a monarch<br>- Without the right items, the celebrations cannot begin. |
| 355. | Báà r'ọkọ̀, aà r'Èkó; báà r'ọkọ́, aà lè kọ́'bè | If we didn't find a vehicle [have transport], we wouldn't go to Lagos; if we didn't find [have] a hoe, we wouldn't be able to mound and shape soil. This is evidently a rhyme-inspired proverb<br>- Without the proper materials, the festivities cannot begin. |
| 356. | Báa ti ń yọ́ọ́ só, bẹ́ẹ̀ náà l'à ń yọ́ọ́ gbọ́ | As we sneakily fart, so do we slyly overhear [the hissing of the fart]<br>- If you think you are smart, there are always people who are smarter. |
| 357. | Báá ti ṣe l'áá wí, Ẹnìkan lí yà'na è l'ódì | What we intend to do is what we talk over, no one gives their in-laws the silent treatment<br>- Speak your mind - you won't die there;<br>- Make your offer known, there's no need to be afraid. |
| 358. | Báa wí, aá kũ, b'áà wí, Ọ̀run l'à ńlọ | If we speak, we'll die; if we don't speak, we'll die; it's Heaven we're headed<br>- This is said by someone wishing to speak out about the appalling state of affairs in the country when everyone appears to be scared of speaking their mind. |
| 359. | Baálé Ilé fẹ́ dá'jọ́ Ogun, ṣùgbọ́n ó ń ro t'ìyà tí 'ó j'ará Ilé | The head of the house wants to rule on the date of war but he's thinking of the suffering that will be inflicted on the household<br>- Someone with great wisdom is trying to look for alternative solutions rather than having to resort to conflict. |
| 360. | Baálé Ilé kú, Ilé da'horo | The head of the household dies, the home becomes desolate |

|   |   | - The breadwinner passes, the remaining members of the family suffer financial hardship as a result. |
|---|---|---|
| 361. | Baba l'ó mọn gúngún Ẹ̀wù, Ọmọ ò mọ́ọ́n | Only the father knows the straightness of a cloth, the little child does not<br>- Only a parent knows the upstandingness and decorum of accepted behavior in the community, a child may not. |
| 362. | B'árã'lé Ẹní bá l'ẹnu, ńṣe l'èníyàn ńl'ẹ́sẹ̀; b'árã'lé Ẹní bá l'ẹ́sẹ̀, ńṣe l'èníyàn ńl'ẹ́nu | If a relation has mouth [can talk], it behooves one to have legs [influence]; if a relation has legs, it behooves one to have mouth<br>- Find a way to outsmart your adversary. |
| 363. | Báwo l'a ṣe pín'tan Ajá t'ó kan Lèmọ́nmù? | How did we manage to split the dog's thigh that a part ended up at the Imam's house? [Muslims don't eat dogs]<br>- This idiom is directed at a meddler who is insinuating himself into a discussion or an argument [that doesn't really concern him], offering unsolicited opinions;<br>- What's the issue going on here got to do with you, sir? |
| 364. | Báwo l'aá ti ṣe mọn Àkùkọ Ẹdìẹ n'ínú Ẹyin? | How does one decipher a cock from a bunch of eggs, i.e. which of the eggs are going to turn out to be cocks?<br>- How do you tell which is which?<br>- The matter is a conundrum. |
| 365. | Bèbè l'ó y'ómi ká, t'ó jẹ́ ó d'ẹlẹ́gbin | It's the littoral land [embankment] that surrounds the river, which makes it filthy<br>- A leadership or government is only as good as the ministers that make up the cabinet. |
| 366. | B'ébù ò bá rà, aò lè f'ojú k'ègbodò. | If the yam seedling does not rot, we cannot reap new yam<br>- We cannot proceed on a course of action if the means of achieving it are not put in place. |
| 367. | Bèèrè o tó wọ̀ọ́ | Ask before you enter it<br>- Whatever you want to do, ask first for permission of whichever authority or whomever is in charge. |

| | | |
|---|---|---|
| 368. | B'éiyé bá ṣe lọ ni ẹ jẹ́ k'á sọ'kòò è | Let's aim the stone towards the trajectory of the bird<br>- Let's not focus more attention on an issue than it merits. |
| 369. | B'énìà ò bá rìn'rìn Àwàsà, nwọn ò lè f'èkùrọ́ lọ́ọ̀! | If someone did not walk the walk of Àwàsà, no one would offer him palm kernels<br>- If one didn't behave in a suspicious way, no one would suspect and accuse them of anything. |
| 370. | B'ẹrú bá ti pẹ́ ńlé, áá máa b'álájọbí! | If a slave lasts too long in the home [of his/her master], he/she would be insulting the freeborn<br>- Too much familiarity breeds contempt. |
| 371. | Bí a bá gé'tàkùn, t'ógbẹ́ bá ba Ìrókò, yíó mọ̀n pé Ìtàkùn t'ó lọ́ mọ́n'un l'ó k'ọ́gbẹ́ bá'un | If we were cutting a rope [in the bush], if the cutlass hit the Ìrókò tree, it would know that it is the rope that is clinging to it that has made the lumberjack hit it<br>- You're partly feeling the brunt of the punishment that is intended for those you surround yourself with;<br>- The injury is not personal or intentional. |
| 372. | Bí a bá gún'yán n'ínú Ewé, bí a se'bẹ̀ n'ínú Èẹpo-ẹ̀pà, Ẹní máa yó, á yó | (During a feast): if we ground pounded-yam in a leaf, cooked the stew in a groundnut shell, those who would be full and satisfied would be full and satisfied<br>- No matter what you do for some people, there'll be those who will be pleased and grateful, and those that will not be. You can't satisfy everyone, in other words. |
| 373. | Bí a bá ń jà bíi k'á kú kọ́ | If we are quarrelling, it's not till one of us drops dead<br>- No matter what, we should still be there for each other even when we disagree. |
| 374. | Bí a bá ń sun'kún, a máa ń r'íran | If we're crying, we are always able to see<br>- No matter what the situation might be, you always know what's right and what's wrong. |
| 375. | Bí a bá ní Ẹran Oníwo ní ó kan'ni pa, kìí ṣe bíi t'ìgbín | If we say an animal with horns will head-butt someone to death, it's not such as a snail |

|  |  |  |
|---|---|---|
|  |  | - A boastful saying. For example: if news has been circulating that B is planning to take over A's company, A could contemptuously retort that it won't be someone like B;<br>- The story of Goliath probably illustrates this metaphor best: if, on the night of his famous battle with David, anyone would have said to Goliath, "you know, in my dream, I saw someone beat you in a fight", Goliath might have replied, "well, not like David." |
| 376. | Bí a bá ni k'a fi Aşiwèrè s'ílẹ̀ k'ó şeé wò lóõtọ́, yí ó ba nǹkan jẹ́ | If we adjudge and leave the madman to actually try it, he might ruin things<br>- Entrusting such an important task to the individual in question would not be such a smart idea. |
| 377. | Bí a ò bá r'ẹni f'ẹ̀hìn tì, bí Ọ̀lẹ l'àá rí | If one doesn't have any support/backer, one appears to be a lazy man/skiver<br>- Two heads are better than one. |
| 378. | Bí a şe gbọ́n n'ílé Ọkọ l'a şe gbọ́n n'ílé Àlè | As astute as we become in our husbands' houses, so are we wise in our lovers'<br>- As we're getting ready, so are our enemies getting ready also, to meet us force with force, fire with fire; so get your wits about you, people!;<br>- You think you're the only one who is smart; well, we'll see about that. |
| 379. | Bí a ti ń ge l'ọ́wọ́ nã l'ó ń bọ̀'rùka | As we snip her fingers, she keeps putting on rings<br>- We are telling her off about one thing, she is doing another. |
| 380. | Bí aà bá rá Ọmọ Ìyá Ẹni n'íkõ, Ọmọ Baba ò ní b'ẹ̀rù Ẹni | If we don't give a knock on the head of one's maternal sibling, the paternal sibling will have no fear of us<br>- If we don't employ some scare tactics, or mete out punishment to an underling for breaking a regulation, others will have no respect for any rules henceforth. |
| 381. | Bí aà bá rí Àdán, a máa f'òòdẹ̀ ş'ẹbọ | If we can't find a bat, we use a vesper-bat to do sacrifices |

|  |  |  |
|---|---|---|
|  |  | - In the absence of proper normal channels, find and use other means to achieve your goals. |
| 382. | Bí Àáyá bá sọ'pé òun gbọ́n, Ògúngbè nã gbọ́n; bí Àáyá bá ń tiro, Ògúngbè a máa bẹ̀rẹ̀ | If the monkey asserts that he's smart, the baboon too is clever; if the monkey limps, the baboon will crouch<br>- If you (or they) think they're cunning, well, so am I;<br>- Two can play that game! |
| 383. | Bí Aáyán ẹẹ́ bá ṣi Ijó jó, ṣàdédé a máa f'ara k'ásà Adìẹ | If your cockroach danced awkwardly, it might sometimes imitate the behavior of a chicken<br>- Who do you think you are? |
| 384. | Bí Àfòmọ́ bá ń fò mọ́n'gi Àràbà, t'ó ń fò mọ́n'gi Ìrókò, ó ní láti yọ'gi Ìbépẹ sọ́tọ̀ | If the creeper clings to Àràbà [oak] tree, clings to Ìrókò tree, it always stays clear of the pawpaw tree<br>- Could be a sort of prayer that the troubles currently sweeping the country [or layoffs occurring at the organization where you work] will not affect you;<br>- Relax, nothing is going to touch your kith and kin. |
| 385. | Bí aò bá r'ẹni f'ẹ̀hìn tì, bí Ọ̀lẹ l'àá rí; Bí aò bá r'ẹni gbọ́kàn lé, aá tẹ'ra mọ́n'ṣẹ́ Ẹni | If we had no one to lean on, we would look like layabouts; if we had no one to depend on, we would put more effort in our occupations<br>- If one lived in a country where influence of big names one knew didn't guarantee a path to easy jobs, one would strive more in his education and make sure to graduate with excellent grades. |
| 386. | Bí aò kú, Ìse ò tán | If we don't die, activities/events do not end<br>- Don't despair, if at first you don't succeed, you should try and try again. |
| 387. | Bí Aṣení bá ń yọ́'lẹ̀ dá, Ohun búburú a máa yọ́ wọn ṣe | As a 'doer' [voodoo destiny-changer] is slinking about betraying friends, bad things come sneaking out to turn on them<br>- As wicked ones go about their evil business, so does karma go about roping them in. |

| | | |
|---|---|---|
| 388. | Bí Àtùpà [Fìtílà] á ṣe l'ágbára tó, kò leè rí ìdí ara ẹ̀ tán. | As powerful as a lantern might be, it cannot see its own base fully. Either use Àtùpà or Fìtílà in a single context, not both.<br>- No matter how powerful a king or warlord is, he cannot be fully certain of unequivocal loyalty among his ranks and guess who could betray him. |
| 389. | Bí àyé bá gba'wọ̀fà, áá fẹ́ n'ípọn l'áyà bí Ìrá | If the slave had the opportunity, he'd want to have a thick chest like a porcupine<br>- If you let people have free reign over [exploit] your kindness or generosity, they'll walk all over you;<br>- Give them an inch; they take a mile;<br>- Watch out: The first sign that someone might be taking advantage of your kindness is if they only get in touch when they need something. |
| 390. | Bí Bàtà á bá ti ń ró pọnlá-pọnlá, ó ṣe tán tí ó ya nìyẹn | When shoes [or slippers] start making a peculiar flap-flap noise, they are ready to split<br>- When the people want a change, riots, protests, disturbances etc. will be the order of the day. |
| 391. | Bí ẹ bá ń gbọ́ Dòdóńdááwà Dòdóńdááwà, Ènìà ní ńbẹ l'éhìn-in Dòdó; Dòdó kan ìí dáá wà! | Dòdóńdááwà [Dòdó supposedly stays all by itself].<br>If you hear Dòdóńdááwà Dòdóńdááwà, it's a human being that's behind Dòdó; no Dòdó ever stays alone<br>- Behind every successful man there is a woman; so to speak. |
| 392. | Bí Ẹbí bá da Àjànàkú, Ifọ́nrán Owú kan lásán gbée dè | If a relation betrayed an elephant, a mere thread of wool could ensnare her<br>- If a leader is betrayed to his enemies by one of his own family, the shock would be so much that a little nudge is all it would take to bring him to his knees. |
| 393. | Bí Ẹ̀bìtì ò bá p'eku, á f'ẹyìn f'ẹléyìn | If a trap will not kill a rat, it will return the palm nut [bait] to the palmnut owner<br>- If someone will not carry out what he was hired to do, it behooves him to return |

| | | |
|---|---|---|
| | | all that was given to him to execute the project in the first place. |
| 394. | Bí ẹẹ̀ m'erin, ẹẹ̀ gbó'hùn Erin; b'ẹẹ̀ m'ọ̀sà, ẹẹ̀ j'iyọ̀ l'ọ́bẹ̀? | If you didn't know the elephant, didn't you hear the sound of the elephant; if you didn't know the she-river, didn't you eat salt in stews?<br>- The name of the man in reference precedes him;<br>- Show respect for the man of the moment and hail him. |
| 395. | Bí Èní ṣe rí, Ọ̀la ò rí bẹ́ẹ̀<br>Tàbí...<br>Bí Èní ṣe rí kọ́ l'ọ̀la ó rĩ | As today is, tomorrow won't be<br>- What is the norm today may not necessarily be the case tomorrow (or in the near future). |
| 396. | Bí Eré, bí Eré, Àlàbo'rùn ún di Ẹ̀wù | Like play, like a jest, the shoulder scarf turns into a dress<br>- Gradually, what we thought was a joke is fast becoming a certainty. |
| 397. | Bí Eré, bí Ìnàjú, Igi-imú Ẹlẹ́dẹ̀ ẹ́ ń w'ọgbà | Like playing, like craning the eyes, the tip of the nose of the pig is advancing to enter into the pigpen<br>- Little by little, the person referred to in this symbolic expression is foolishly entering a trap. |
| 398. | Bí Ẹsẹ̀ Àjèjì bá ti ńran'lẹ̀, áá ma p'onílé ní bàbá ẹ̀ | If a visitor (stranger) stays too long in the compound, he would be addressing (or relating with) the landlord as his father<br>- Too much familiarity breeds contempt. |
| 399. | Bí Ewúrẹ́ Ẹni; t'áa bá ń lée títí t'ó sá wọ'lé Alágídí; t'àá bá tètè d'èhìn, Ìyà t'ó yẹ k'ó jẹ Ewúrẹ́ ọ̀hún, Olówó Ewúrẹ́ lè jẹẹ́ | Like one's goat; if we are chasing it till it enters the home of Alágídí [an irrational man]; if we don't retreat quickly, the punishment that is intended for the goat, the goat's owner may suffer it<br>- This allegory warns of doubling down on foolhardiness. |
| 400. | Bí Ìdágìrí bá wọ̀'lú, Ẹsẹ̀ gìrì á tẹ̀le | If disorder or trouble comes to town, innumerable feet will follow it<br>- If anarchy occurs, countless thugs and marauders will accompany it. |
| 401. | Bí ìgbàt'ènìyán bá kọ́'lée Koríko, t'ó wá gbé'lé Ìdáná ẹ̀ s'órí Òkè | It's like when someone builds a house of straws and installs his kitchen atop it |

|      |                                                                                                              |                                                                                                                                                                                                                                                                    |
| ---- | ------------------------------------------------------------------------------------------------------------ | ------------------------------------------------------------------------------------------------------------------------------------------------------------------------------------------------------------------------------------------------------------------ |
|      |                                                                                                              | - The step you've embarked on is not conducive to your survival or wellbeing; neither logical nor appropriate.                                                                                                                                                     |
| 402. | Bí Ìgbín fà, Ìkaraun è a tèle                                                                                | If a snail crawls, its shell follows it<br>- Where you find one, you'll likely find the other or if the leader does something, his followers will follow suit.                                                                                                     |
| 403. | Bí Ìjàpá bá r'àjò, a máa mú'lé è dání                                                                        | If the tortoise goes on a journey, it takes its house [shell] with it<br>- Wherever the king goes, his retinue accompanies him;<br>- Wherever the US president goes, the Secret Service agents are always at his side.                                             |
| 404. | Bí Ìlú bá tú tán, Ewé Ológbòtujè l'ó ń kù                                                                    | If a village evacuates, Ológbòtujè leaves are what's left<br>- There'll be no one to be found after a disaster except shrubs [after years of desertation].                                                                                                         |
| 405. | Bí Inú Ilé kan-án bá wà t'ó yẹ k'ó ma dàrú t'ó ń tòrò l'ọ́wọ́, wọ́n l'ọ́mọ Àlè ibẹ̀ niò tíì d'àgbà           | If there is a household that should be tumultuous but is currently orderly, they say the bastard within the family has not yet matured into adulthood<br>- This is a derogatory expression to an outspoken individual the speaker is hinting may be the eponymous troublemaker. |
| 406. | Bí Irẹ́ bá jẹun yó tán, a máa wá Bẹ́'kù-bẹ́'kù kiri                                                          | If the porcupine has eaten till its belly is full, it will start looking for tummy popper all over the place<br>- If someone has been given an unexpected [more like underserved] thing, gift, position or power, he may eventually seek ignominy [his natural habitat] to return to. |
| 407. | Bí Irín bá já, Irin nã la ma fi só                                                                           | If steel breaks, it's steel we'll use to mend it.<br>- For example, if you have a hangover, try and have the same drink [that gave you the hangover] when you wake up.                                                                                             |
| 408. | Bí Ìwọ ọ́ bá ṣe Rere, Ara kì yíò a                                                                           | If you do good, your body will feel                                                                                                                                                                                                                                |

|  | yá ọ | 'weightless' OR If you have done well, won't your body feel light?<br>- This metaphor dictates that if you've not been nasty to a particular person(s) in your life, you can always count on them as allies in time of need. As there has been no old axe to grind or no angst that might make you feel undeserving of their support when you need it most, you can freely enlist their help, surely. |
|---|---|---|
| 409. | Bí Kẹ́tẹ́kẹ́tẹ́ ti lè gb'ẹ̀rù tó, kò leè gbé Gẹdú, àfi t'ó bá ti ṣe tán àti wọ'lẹ̀ l'óòyẹ̀ | As capable as a donkey is in carrying loads, it cannot carry timber, except it's ready to sink into the ground alive. |
| 410. | Bí Kókó bá ń f'ẹni l'ẹ́fẹ̀, aà kì ń j'orí Ìmàdò | If Koko is joking and frolicking with someone, we do not eat the head of Imado<br>- Despite how rosy things may look, we must not forget who we are and leg our guards down. |
| 411. | Bí ò ṣe'ni, a kì ńgbọ́n | If it doesn't happen to one, one doesn't get wiser<br>- Experience is the best teacher. |
| 412. | Bí Òjó bá ńrọ̀, Ìrì ò tún gbọdọ̀ máa ṣẹ̀ | When it rains, it should not dew<br>- When the powers that be are talking, the minions should keep quiet. |
| 413. | Bí Ọká bí'mọ s'ílẹ̀, yíó gb'oró; bí Olõgìnní nã bá bí'mọ, yíó di Ẹhànnà | If the adder births a child, it'll be tough; if the cat also births a child, it will become a terror<br>- Children look like their progenitors. |
| 414. | Bí Ọmọdé bá kúndùn àti máa su Imíkímí, àwọn Àgbà nã ó sì fi Ewé Èsìsì fi lùú n'íkín | If a child is fond of making different kinds of faeces, the elders will use the leaves of Èsìsì to beat his anus<br>- If someone behaves in a way that demonstrates how clever they think they are, we show them how smarter we can be. Consequently, we stop him in his tracks and dissuade him from what he's trying to do. |
| 415. | Bí Oníṣègùn àtàtá bá r'áyè ro Ẹjọ́ Ẹnu è, yí ó jàre Ẹni t'ó f'iwọ pa | If an important medicine man has time to explain himself, he'll be absolved of the death he has caused |

|  |  | - A manipulative offender or guilty man who is a good orator with sweet tongue and is articulate can talk himself out of trouble. |
|---|---|---|
| 416. | Bí Òwe bí Òwe l'à ń lù'lù Àgídìgbo; Ọlọgbọ́n l'ó ń jo, Ọ̀mọ̀nràn níí mọ̀n'dí ẹ̀ | Proverbially do we beat the drum of Àgídìgbo; a sage is the one who dances to it, Ọ̀mọ̀nràn [the well informed one] is he who knows the reason<br>- If someone has a devilish plan against you, watch their body language and behavior toward you;<br>- Let this bible verse be your watch-word: Matthew 7:15 NIV: "Watch out for false prophets. They come to you in sheep's clothing, but inwardly they are ferocious wolves." |
| 417. | Bí Òwe bí Òwe l'à ń lù'lù Ògìdìgbó; Ọlọgbọ́n l'ó ń jo, Ògbèrì l'ó ń mọ̀n'dí ẹ̀ | Parabolically do we beat the drum of Ògìdìgbó; a sage is the one who dances to it, Ògbèrì [the well informed] is he who knows the reason<br>- Try to cultivate the culture of "by their actions will you know them" and pay attention to subtle but evil machinations from your friends and/or colleagues; even members of your family are not excluded. |
| 418. | Bí Pẹ́pẹ́iyẹ bá j'òkúta, Omi ní ó fi su | If a duck eats [swallows] a stone, it's water that'll come out of it when it passes stool<br>- No matter what you plan against me, I'll overcome it;<br>- Nothing will happen to me despite your attacks. |
| 419. | Bí Ṣàngó bá ń p'àràbà, t'ó ń fa Ìrókò ya, bíí t'igi Ńlá kọ́ | If Ṣàngó the god of thunder is striking down the Àràbà [oak] tree, tearing apart the Ìrókò tree and all, not like Igi Ńlá<br>- All your threats may work with others, but they certainly won't work with me. |
| 420. | Bí Sòbìyà ò bá d'egbò, Olúgànmbe l'àá kéé sí | If edema (guinea worm) does not become a sore, Olúgànmbe is he who we call<br>- If things don't work according to plan or expectations, we call the experts. |

| | | |
|---|---|---|
| 421. | Bí Sùúrù ú bá pọ̀ l'ápọ̀jù, Agọ̀ níí s'ọni í dà | If patience is way too much, it relegates one to the position of a fool<br>- Too much patience is nothing more than a fool's errand. |
| 422. | Bí yíò ṣ'èmi, bí yíò ṣ'èwọ, l'aà fi ń nà'yá Ẹgbẹ́ Ẹni | Lest it be me, lest it be you, is why we don't beat the mother of our peers [taking it in turns to beat each other's mom]<br>- This statement is to highlight the idiocy of making unpredictable covenants;<br>- Lucky we didn't make that bet, isn't it?<br>- You might think it would never happen, but what if it does? |
| 423. | Bíbí Ire ò ṣe é f'owó rà | A good birth cannot be bought with money<br>- If you were birthed well (in wealth or in poverty regardless), it would reflect in your character in later life. |
| 424. | B'íná Ẹni í bá ń jó, k'á tètè fi jó ǹkan gidi ni, nítorí k'ó tó lọ mọ́n'ni l'ọ́wọ́ | If one's fire is burning, [the trick is] we quickly burn something solid with it, so as not to burn one's hand. This would be lighting a match in the proverb<br>- Seize the opportunity that you have right now;<br>- Make hay while the sun shines. |
| 425. | Bín-ńtín ni Ata ń mọn t'ó fi ń ṣ'ọkọ Ojú | Miniscule is the pepper that it 'rules' the eyes<br>- Someone may be little but his power may shake his bigger adversaries. |
| 426. | B'írọ́ bá lọ l'ógún Ọdún, Ọjọ́ kan l'òtítọ́ á ba | If a lie has been gone for twenty years, one day the truth will catch up with him<br>- This personification is typically expressed by some group when they feel a matter should be dropped, with the hope that it will one day resolve itself, even if it takes years;<br>- Or, it is expressed when the truth has [finally] emerged and they've caught someone in a long-enduring big lie. |
| 427. | B'ó ṣe ńṣ'ogójì l'ó ńṣ'ọ̀ọ́dúnrún; Àrùn t'ó ńṣ'Abọ́yadé, gbogbo Ọlóya l'ó ńṣe | As it afflicts forty so does it afflict three hundred; the disease that afflicts Abóyadé affects all worshippers of Ọya deity |

|     |     |     |
| --- | --- | --- |
|     |     | - The upheaval going round the country is mutually felt by everyone. |
| 428. | B'ó ti wùn k'óòrùn k'ó mú tó, Sánmọ̀n dúdú díẹ̀ yíó wà | No matter how hot the sun shines, there'll be a few black clouds (even if tiny specks)<br>- Life is full of sadness and joy. |
| 429. | B'ójọ́ Ọ̀rọ̀ kán bá pẹ́ jọjọ, Ìtàn níí dà | If the time to hold a discourse [among families, typically] keeps getting deferred for so long [several years], it becomes a handed-down legend<br>- Time is of the essence;<br>- Don't leave until tomorrow what you can do today. |
| 430. | B'ọ́kọ̀ kan ò r'Ejìirìn, Ẹgbẹgbẹ̀rún ẹ á lọ | If one vehicle doesn't go to Ejìirìn [or any place for that matter], a thousand of it will<br>- If a person won't do something for someone, there're countless others who will. |
| 431. | B'óko ò bá jìnà, Ilá kìí kó | If the farm is not far [from home], okras never over-ripen and get hard. This is because the farmer can just nip out to the farm and pluck them anytime he wants since distance is not an issue<br>- If no bad blood exists already, then the matter can still be settled. |
| 432. | B'óo bá l'ógbón, fi s'íkùn Arà ẹ; Aiyé ò fẹ́ k'ó y'ẹni | If you have wisdom, keep it in your own 'belly;' the world does not ever want one to 'be in acquiescence' [center of attention]<br>- Knowledge is power; keep your knowledge to yourself. |
| 433. | B'óo ba o pá; b'óò ba o bùú l'ẹ́sẹ̀ l'ọ̀rọ̀ Ọmọ Aráiyé | If you catch up with him, kill him; if you don't catch up with him, shear him in the leg (by applying voodoo potion to someone's footstep spiritually that can manifest in a deep cut in the physical) is the legend of human beings<br>- Devastation and ruination is what people secretly wish their fellow human beings, so be careful and watch your back. |
| 434. | B'óo bá ṣe ń dè Okùn l'èmi nã ó máa túu | As you knot the rope so shall I unravel it<br>- I shall see to it that all your efforts come |

| | | |
|---|---|---|
| | | to nothing. |
| 435. | B'óo bá ṣe t'ẹ́ní ẹ l'o ma sùn le | How you have spread your mat is how you are going to sleep on it<br>- You've made your bed, now lie in it;<br>- How you have built your house is how you're going to live in it. |
| 436. | Dàda ò lè jà, ó l'Ábūrò t'ó gbó'jú l'ọ́wọ́ | Dada (John Doe) may not be able to fight but he has a kid brother who is brave<br>- One may not be able to defend himself but there's help at hand. |
| 437. | Dàdàǹbìrî mī ti wá lu'gi; tí Dàdàǹbìrí bá dẹ lu'gi, àá fẹ́ẹ kù ni | My Dàdàǹbìrí has smacked a tree; and, if Dàdàǹbìrí has smacked a tree, we no longer see it [any more]<br>- Now that I have done what was necessary, the problem should no longer exist. |
| 438. | Dídùn l'ó dùn táà ń b'ọ̀rẹ́ jè'kọ; t'ilé Ogé t'óge é jẹ | The pleasure and enjoyment is what makes us eat Èkọ [hardened corn-pap] with a friend; what Oge [lady of vogue] has at home is sufficient for Oge to eat<br>- It's because of our friendship that I'm asking you this favor, if you're going to be indignant about it, then I'll enlist someone else's help;<br>- You know it's not as if I don't have mine, but I need one right now;<br>- If music be the food of love, then play on. |
| 439. | Díẹ̀ díẹ̀ n'imú Ẹlẹ́dẹ̀ ń w'ọgbà | Little by little is how the nose of the pig enters the pigpen<br>- Gradually, gradually, the insurmountable difficulty is becoming tractable;<br>- Could also mean: Little by little, the subject in this symbolic expression is heading where some people [waiting] want him. Typically to capture him/her, or hold them hostage in one nefarious plot or another. |
| 440. | Ẹ jẹ́ k'a pe Wèrè l'ọ́kọ Ìyàwó k'ó lè jẹ́ k'a r'áyè ṣe ti wa | Let's call the mad one the bridegroom so he'll let us find space to do our thing<br>- Let's humor those who may be against |

| | | |
|---|---|---|
| | | us so we can have peace of mind to do what we need to do. |
| 441. | Ẹ jẹ k'a s'ọ̀rọ̀ ńbi t'ọ́rọ̀ọ́ bá wà | Let's talk where there's an issue to discuss<br>- Let's discuss pressing issues at hand and stop mucking about. |
| 442. | Ẹ jẹ k'a ṣé bí nwọ́n ti ń ṣé k'ó bàa lè rí b'ó ti ń rí | Let's do it as they do it so it can come out the way it normally should<br>- It's a rallying cry to a group to do things the way those before them had done things and get the same positive results. |
| 443. | Ẹ jẹ k'a ṣí'ṣọ l'ójú Eégún | Let's unmask the masquerade<br>- Let's pull our resources together and expose the bad deeds that those in power are secretly engaged in;<br>- Sometimes positively uttered to say (in case of a wrapped gift), let's open the present and see what's in it! |
| 444. | Ẹ jẹ k'a tọ́'jú Igbá Ilé; bí t'okó máa gbó, aà kúkú mọ̀n | Let's take care of the calabash that is growing at home; if the one in the farm is going to ripen, we don't really know<br>- Let's appreciate what we've got, value and nurture them;<br>- Better the devil you know than the saint you don't know. |
| 445. | Ẹ jẹ k'a t'ibi Ìṣáná k'íyè s'óògùn | Let's from the matchstick take notice of medicine<br>- Let's observe the matchstick and relate its effectiveness / liken its lighting ability to the potency of the occult;<br>- If we observed closely, one would notice the anomalies in things or events that have been happening lately. |
| 446. | Ẹ má f'ajá s'ẹnu Ìkõkò | Don't put the dog in the hyena's mouth<br>- Don't put [the person being referred to] in serious trouble. |
| 447. | Ẹ má f'ọwọ́ Ọlá gbá wa l'ójú | Don't slap us in the face with your hand of wealth<br>- This hyperbole is directed at a person of a higher position or wealth than the speaker(s): Don't treat us like dirt and use your position to disregard our opinions. |

| 448. | Ẹ má jẹ á f'ọ̀pá pọ̀ọ̀lọ̀pọọlọ p'ejò | Don't let's employ a very long stick to kill a snake<br>- Call a spade a spade;<br>- Don't let's beat about the bush. |
|---|---|---|
| 449. | Ẹ má jẹ k'a pẹlú Ọ̀bọ́ já wùrà | Don't let's join the monkeys brachiate energetically across [from one tree to another]<br>- Don't let's jump to conclusions. |
| 450. | Ẹ má wu l'égbò; Ewé ni k'á já | Do not disturb the bruises; look for herbs to pick<br>- Don't rehash the motive for the strife; let's look for peace. |
| 451. | Ẹ ń d'ẹ̀rù Okó ńlá b'arúgbóo wa | With your rhetoric, you are frightening our elderly ladies with huge penises [like they'd never seen one before]<br>- Stop scaring us with what someone will do to us; let them do it. |
| 452. | Ẹ pa mí s'ílé, ẹ má pa mí s'íta<br>Tàbí...<br>Pa mí s'ílé, má pa mí s'íta | Kill me indoors, don't kill me outside [keep my skeleton in the cupboard]<br>- Keep my secret among us here [within those who already know], don't expose it in public [outside of this group].<br><br>*For more on the usage of ẹ, ẹ̀, ẹ́, o, ò, ó, ọ, please consult the "Personal Pronouns" page.* |
| 453. | Ẹ ṣi á wòó<br>Ṣi á wòó | Open it and let's see<br>- Let's hear what you have in mind. |
| 454. | Ẹ so Ewé e Gbéjẹ́ẹ́ m'ọ́wọ́ | Tie the leaf of Gbéjẹ́ẹ́ [live in peace] to the hand<br>- Go settle down or go keep calm and have a peaceful existence. |
| 455. | Ẹ ti f'ewúro s'ẹ́nu, k'ẹ wá k'ojú s'áráiyé k'ẹ sọ fún wọn b'ó ṣe dùn tó | You have put bitter leaf in the mouth [and chewed it], now face the world and relate to them how sweet it was<br>- You have done the inconceivable. |
| 456. | Ẹ w'ẹnu Ilẹ̀, ẹ w'ẹnu Ọkọ́! | "Ẹ" is the formal of 'you' or someone you cannot address by name. Look at the land's mouth, look at the hoe's mouth [blade]!<br>- Ponder the great foundation that has |

| | | been laid, look at how things are working out perfectly! |
|---|---|---|
| 457. | Ebi ni ò pà'Jẹ̀ṣà t'ó l'óun ò j'ẹ̀kọ Ọ̀yọ́ | [It's because] hunger has not killed an Ìjẹ̀ṣà who says he will not eat the hardened corn-pap of an Ọ̀yọ́ cook<br>- This is a centuries-old idiom that pokes fun at Ìjẹ̀ṣà people (who are used to eating more rigid version of hardened corn-paps) than those made by an Ọ̀yọ́ cook that is typically soft. In effect, this idiom berates the subject of not being really hungry or they wouldn't be so fussy.<br>- You have different options, or you wouldn't refuse what is being offered to you;<br>- You complain only because alternatives are available. |
| 458. | Ẹ̀bi ò sí l'ọ́wọ́ Ẹni t'ó ṣè'wọ̀sí s'ómi Adágún; ṣé Orí l'ó mọn'hun t'ó d'ómi dúró s'ójú kan, tí ò jẹ́ ó r'íbi sàn lọ, t'ó jẹ́ ó d'eléērí | A guilt does not exist with he who has been rude to the stagnant water; it's fate that knows what kept a running water rooted in one spot, that wouldn't allow it to find an outlet to flow into, that made it become a squalid place [full of detritus]<br>- This expression, as an allegory, could be applied to describe the poor economic and infrastructural state of the Nigerian nation. The country whose currency, in the early 1980s, was one of the two most powerful in the world, equal to the British pounds sterling and only 46 kobo (cents) to the US dollar, is now a very poor shadow of its former self indeed, due to a succession of corrupt leadership and atrocious policies that have plagued the country for circa 43 years now [this is 2024]. |
| 459. | Ẹdìẹ kan ò níí kú k'a fọ́n Ẹyin ẹ dà s'ínú Igbó | A chicken will not die and we chuck its eggs into the bush in anger<br>- We can't say because a man who owed us money has died, we throw his children in jail or worse. |

| 460. | Èéfín n'ìwà | Character is smoke<br>- One's personal behavior is like smoke that one cannot mask. |
|---|---|---|
| 461. | Eegun ìí t'ọwọ́ Àgbà á d'ẹnu Ajá | A bone doesn't from an elder's hand get into a dog's mouth<br>- It's nothing important enough to bother the leadership (or senior hierarchy) with. |
| 462. | Eégún ńlá níí k'ẹ̀hìn Ìgbàlẹ̀ | The grand masquerade is the one that brings up the rear in a competition<br>- This metaphor perceives the person or entity in reference as the main event/attraction [of the show]. |
| 463. | Èèpá ń p'ara ẹ̀, ó l'óun ńpa'já | The flea is killing itself, yet insists it's killing the dog<br>- He's only inadvertently working against himself without realizing it;<br>- The subject of this proverb is going to be hoisted by his own petard, or has already been. |
| 464. | Èèrà ò fẹ́ Pòpórò dé'nú | Ants don't love dry castor bean 'up to mind' [deeply in their mind]<br>- The ants only appear to love the dry castor bean but only gather inside it for self-interest only - food;<br>- There's only a few people who genuinely love those who have risen out of penury and succeeded, partly because they feel they have failed and have been left behind in the rot. |
| 465. | Èèwọ̀! B'óbìnrín bá ní k'ọ́n sìn'un pẹ̀lú Ọkọ òun t'ó ṣ'aláìsí, Ẹnìkan ò níí sín m'ókũ ẹ̀ | Taboo! If a grieving wife asks to be buried along with her husband at his funeral, no one will bury her with the corpse<br>- Forbidden! No one must pay attention to what is being bandied about; best thing to do [in this type of situation] is disregard the issue at all costs;<br>- The issue is not worth mentioning or does not merit debate at all. |
| 466. | Ẹgba táa bá fi kọ̀'yà, Ẹnìkan ìí sọ ọ́ nù | The whip that we utilized to reject and survive hardship, no one throws it away<br>- A reminder so that our travails of |

| | | yesteryears do not recur. |
|---|---|---|
| 467. | Ẹgbẹ́ Eégún l'eégún ń gbá l'ójú | The comrades of a masquerade are those the masquerade slaps in the face<br>- He could only do that to you [his peers], not to us. |
| 468. | Ẹgbẹ́ n bí'gbo àbí t'àjùmọ̀ngbé? | The group births an audience or that of co-tenants<br>- The person who issues this statement is telling off someone or a group of people who have been unexpectedly rude to them. |
| 469. | Ègbin kín-ńkín l'étí Àwõ Gbègìrì, ẹ jẹ́ 'a f'ọwọ́ nùún kúrò k'a ma jẹun lọ | A little insult on the edge of the bowl of Gbègìrì [soup made of toasted beans], let's flick it off with a finger and continue eating<br>- When an embarrassment is trivial, let's take it on the chin and move on. |
| 470. | Egbìnrìn Ọ̀tẹ̀, b'áa ti ńpà'kan n'ìkán ń rú | The herb-spinach of treachery, as we kill one, out sprouts another. |
| 471. | Ẹ̀gún ò ní gún Ọmọ l'ẹ́sẹ̀ k'á wá lọ yọ́ l'ẹ́sẹ̀ Ẹrú | A thorn will not prick and embed itself in the foot of a child and we remove it from the foot of a house slave<br>- Reward those who merit it; don't practice nepotism. |
| 472. | Ẹ̀hìnkùnlé l'ọ̀tá wà, Ilé l'aṣeni ńgbé | Backyard is where the enemies are, right in one's own house is where the betrayers live<br>- You can only be betrayed by those close to you. |
| 473. | Ẹ̀hìnkùnlé Ojo l'à ń gb'ókũ Akínkanjú ú gbà | The procession for the dead body of a brave warrior passes right through the backyard of the meek<br>- When the freedom fighters battle, the weaklings who would not join in the struggle will live to see the adulation heaped on the fighters when they've achieved what they were struggling for, and rue their cowardice. |
| 474. | Ehoro máa sá'ré nìṣó, Ajá ń bọ l'ẹ́hìn | Keep running ahead, hare, the dog is close on your heels<br>- Let the criminals continue their activity, |

| | | the Law is right behind them. |
|---|---|---|
| 475. | Ẹiyẹ Ìbẹ̀rù níí t'ójọ́ | The bird that has fear of predators is the one that lives long<br>- If you have fear [say, of some power], you'll live longer. |
| 476. | Ẹiyẹ ìí f'apá kan-án fò | A bird does not fly with one wing<br>- Don't worry; we all know about it so you can say what's on your mind;<br>- You are not alone in this struggle. |
| 477. | Ẹiyé lọ tán, Ìtẹ́ d'òfo | The bird has flown away, the nest has become deserted<br>- The king has died, the throne has become desolate;<br>- This adage can also be expressed when the most influential individual in a community [or family] has died and it would be hard to fill the vacuum left by their passing. |
| 478. | Ẹiyẹ méjì ìí j'áṣã | Two birds are not called the kite<br>- This allegory kind of lauds someone that they are one of a kind. |
| 479. | Ẹiyẹ ò dédé bà l'órùlé; Ọ̀rọ̀ l'ẹiyẹ́ ń gbọ́ | A bird does not perch on a roof by accident; it does so expressly to eavesdrop<br>- You don't find a respectable man in an inauspicious place without a good reason. Another example:<br>- You can't find another country's warship or submarine close to your country's coast and accept their explanation that the boat is just passing through; more likely than not, it is on a sentinel mission. |
| 480. | Ẹiyẹ ò sọ f'ẹiyẹ pé Òkó ń bọ̀ | A bird didn't tell the other bird that a stone was approaching<br>- What you might say to a friend who suddenly appears at your home without prior notice. Or you run into a friend who does not live in the same city/country as you: "oh, you didn't say you were going to be in town;"<br>- A guy has just left town, got married, got |

| | | |
|---|---|---|
| | | a new job etc. without informing someone closest to him; if this person runs into the guy, the person might utter this phrase as a gentle accusation. |
| 481. | Ẹiye t'ó bá f'ara wé'gún, ẹ̀hìn Àrò ní ó sùn | The bird that compares itself to a vulture will sleep behind a barbecue grill [people may eat all birds, but not a vulture]<br>- Don't compare yourself to others for you don't know what makes them tick. Do not attempt on your own what you may have heard other people do; they may have been trained while you have not. |
| 482. | Ẹiye t'ó ti fẹ́ fò tẹ́lẹ̀ t'a ńṣe 'sùúũ' sí | A bird that's been watching us and ready to fly that we say "shoo" to it suddenly<br>- For example, a teenage daughter who is ready to fly the coop and elope with her boyfriend and here you're, upbraiding and chastising her all the time. |
| 483. | Ẹiyẹlé ìí b'ónílé jẹ, k'ó b'ónílé mu, k'ó d'ọjọ́ Ikú Onílé k'ó yẹ'rí | A pigeon does not eat with the homeowner, drink with the homeowner, and when it comes to the day of death of the homeowner it excuses itself [so it won't have to die with him]<br>- This is a cry-out by someone requesting assistance and/or support from beneficiaries of his past generosity and philanthropy. |
| 484. | Ẹiyẹlé l'ó sì ńbá ẹ fàá; t'ẹ́dìẹ bá f'ẹsẹ̀ si, kò níí mọn n'íwọ̀nba | It's only a pigeon that is pulling it with you; if a chicken put its feet in it, it would not be negligible<br>- This is just child's play at the moment; wait until the powers-that-be got involved in it, then you would pity yourself. |
| 485. | Ẹja Àwọ̀ l'ó ń mú Gbajúmọ̀n j'ekòló; Ẹran ní ńmú'níí jẹ'din | It's the Àwọ̀ fish that makes a famous man eat worms; love of eating meat makes one eat maggots<br>- It's because of our love of something or someone that we go through some unpleasantness. |
| 486. | Ẹja gbígbẹ ò ṣeé ká | Dry fish is not bendable<br>- Someone's character cannot be changed |

| | | |
|---|---|---|
| | | when they have reached a certain age. |
| 487. | Ẹja n b'ákàn? | Was it a fish or a crab?<br>- Usually asked after someone has gone to do something that requires a positive or a negative outcome: if the person responds "fish" it was negative and the response was "crab" it means it was positive. The metaphor of the fish signifies something slipping through your grasp just as fish is slippery to grab in its habitat; the crab metaphor is self-explanatory. |
| 488. | Èjìká dùn-ún ní; mélõ ni t'ejò? | Shoulders are awesome to have; how many has a snake?<br>- Sure it's good to have power; how much do YOU have? |
| 489. | Ẹjọ́ kìí ṣe t'ẹni k'á má mọ̀n-ọ́n dá | A matter [dispute] cannot be one's and we do not know how to resolve it<br>- One should not be partial when an issue concerns one's interests |
| 490. | Ẹjọ́ l'àá kọ́, a kì ń kọ́ ìjà | How to discuss and debate is what we learn, we don't learn fighting<br>- Learn to control your temper. After the fight, it's he who can explain himself best that wins anyway. |
| 491. | Ejò t'ó kọjá l'órí Àpáta tí ò n'ípa | The snake that crawled over a rock and left no trail<br>- Someone who came to the world and died without an offspring. |
| 492. | Ejòó l'ọwọ́ ń'nú | A snake has a hand in it<br>- What challenges you're facing, someone close to you is contributing to them, though it may not be so apparent;<br>- It ain't accidental. |
| 493. | Ẹ̀kọ gbígbóná fẹ́ Sùúrù | A wrap of hot scorching hardened corn-pap demands patience<br>- This matter requires tremendous patience and tact or things could get out of hand. |
| 494. | Ẹkùn l'àna; kò ṣeé rí fín | The leopard is the in-law; he's not disrespectable<br>- The person in the context is not to be |

| | | |
|---|---|---|
| | | disrespected. |
| 495. | Èkùrọ́ l'alábãkú Ẹ̀wà | The palm kernel is the life and death partner of beans<br>- Phrase that lovers say to one another promising their eternal love. |
| 496. | Èkúté Ilé tí ò j'àkọ̀ọ̀ mọ́n t'ó wá lọ ń j'ọ̀bẹ; ṣ'ẹ́ẹ̀ mọ̀n p'ó fẹ́ tọ Ẹnu Onílé lọ ni? | The house rat that failed to eat Àkọ̀ọ̀mọ́n but chose to eat the knife instead, you know its next action is to follow the path into the landlord's mouth?<br>- The dignitary/politician that keeps prodding someone/group to discuss issues that are not really their remit. It's because he really wants the person/group he's addressing to express an opinion and give him guidance, only he doesn't want to admit he needs their counsel. |
| 497. | Èkúté Ilé t'ó f'àkọ̀ọ́'lẹ̀ tí ò jẹ, t'ó wá lọ ń j'ọ̀bẹ | A mouse that overlooked a sheath [made of leather] and not eat it, that has instead decided to eat a knife [that is made of steel]<br>- You are looking for trouble [that is beyond what you can handle]. |
| 498. | Ẹl'ẹnu rúnrùn l'ó l'àmùn Ìyá ẹ̀ | The person with halitosis or mouth odor is the one that owns his mother's waterpot<br>- Let them deal with the issue as they will; it's their kith and kin after all, OR it's their problem. |
| 499. | Ẹ̀là l'ọ̀rọ̀ | Unambiguity (simplicity) is expression or oration<br>- Make your conversation understood by being unequivocal in what you mean;<br>- The rule of thumb of.a speech is making oneself clear. |
| 500. | Ẹlẹ́mọ̀ṣọ́ t'ọ́n bá fi ṣọ́'ṣu ìí ṣọ́'gbàdo | Ẹlẹ́mọ̀ṣọ́ that is tasked with looking after a yam farm does not oversee that of corn<br>- Don't concern yourself with matters that don't concern you. In other words, mind your business. |
| 501. | Elépõ l'épo ò t'óun; Èèrá l'ó ń tà'un l'ójú | The owner of the palm oil is complaining that her oil is inadequate for her needs; on the other hand, the ant that's been |

|   |   |   |
|---|---|---|
|   |   | licking the palm oil is moaning that the oil is smarting its eyes |
|   |   | - Someone is sacrificing to give you something from his little lot and you're moaning that it isn't enough. OR, |
|   |   | - Someone is going out of their way to help you out and you're moaning that what he's done is not enough; not considering that he could use some additional assistance himself. |
| 502. | Ẹlẹrù l'ó ń k'ọfẹ | It behooves the owner of a load [portable cargo] to ask for assistance [to lifting his load onto his head] |
|   |   | - The owner of a problem/burden is the one that enlists the help of others to initiate a resolution. |
| 503. | Ẹlẹrù ní ń gbe n'íbit'ó bá ti wúwo | It's the proprietor of a load that lifts it where it is heaviest before others give him a hand |
|   |   | - The owner of a problem/burden is the one that solicits the help of others to initiate a resolution. |
| 504. | Èmi ni mo mọn'bi tí Bàtá ti ń ta mí l'ẹsẹ̀ | Only I know the spot where a shoe hurts my foot |
|   |   | - I know who I am [better than anyone else], which means I know where my strengths and weaknesses lie; |
|   |   | - Only I know the challenges I'm facing; |
|   |   | - Only the wearer knows where the shoe pinches him; |
|   |   | - Only the sufferer knows what's hurting him; |
|   |   | - Only he who has a problem knows exactly what the problem is. |
| 505. | Èmi ò kì ń p'ọtí Ilée Kíún | I don't fill the House of Kíún with beverages and alcoholic drinks |
|   |   | - I can't see the truth and either refuse to acknowledge it or suppress it because of selfish interest; |
|   |   | - I don't ingratiate myself with anyone through obsequious behavior. |

| | | |
|---|---|---|
| 506. | Èmí tí ò j'ata, Èmí yẹpẹrẹ ni | The soul that does not eat pepper, is but a precarious spirit<br>- Without nourishment, no one can stay alive;<br>- This metaphor could be expressed as a warning to someone who may have an eating disorder such as anorexia, bulimia, or someone skipping food unreasonably. |
| 507. | Ẹmọ́n kú, Ojú-òpó dí | The bush rat died, its hole caved in<br>- With the loss of this prominent personality, what other option is there? |
| 508. | Ẹni a bá l'ábà nii Baba | The man we meet in the hut is Baba [sort of 'man of the house']. This proverb probably has its origin in the association of the two obvious rhymes in the phrase.<br>- The speaker might be asserting their status as above that of the person being referred to in the situation [perhaps a seniority contest];<br>- He/she who behaves in such sterling manner merits admiration;<br>- Give respect to whom respect is owed. |
| 509. | Ẹni a bá ń báá wí, Ọba jẹ́ ó gbọ́! Ẹni a s'ọ̀rọ̀ fún, Ọba jẹ́ ó gba | Those whom we rebuke, Heavenly Father Let them listen. Whomsoever we dialogue with, Heavenly King let them heed<br>- And if ye walk contrary unto me, and will not hearken unto me; I will bring seven times more plagues upon you according to your sins (Lev 26:21).<br>- You're only being chastised for your own good, so you'd better listen. |
| 510. | Ẹni à bá tà k'á fi r'àtùpà, t'ó d'ẹni Àjítanná wò | Someone we should have sold and used the proceeds to buy a lantern, that has become somebody one wakes up very early in the morning with a lamp to catch a glimpse of<br>- Someone whom everyone used to despise [because of his penury or insignificance] has now become a great man that people queue up to see;<br>- Another great example can be found in |

|  |  | the Bible. In Matthew 21:42 and Psalm 118:22, Jesus said to his disciples in "The Parable of the Tenant:" "The stone the builders rejected has become the cornerstone." |
|---|---|---|
| 511. | Ẹni a bí'mọ fún kúrò l'álè Ẹni | Whom a lady has birthed a child for is beyond being termed a secret lover<br>- Someone who has been an old hand for as long as one can remember deserves the merit/accolade being given to them; in other words, "they've earned it." |
| 512. | Ẹni a fẹ́ l'a mọ̀n, aò m'ẹni t'ó f'ẹ́ni dé'nú | We know those we love, we don't know who loves one 'up to mind' [who truly loves us]<br>- We can't tell who means us well or wishes us the best. |
| 513. | Ẹni a lè mú l'à ń lẹ̀'díí mọ́n | The person we can grab is the one we glue our bottom to<br>- This is said to someone who enjoys kicking someone when they are down;<br>- The bully never takes on someone bigger than himself. |
| 514. | Ẹni a nà l'ara ń ta | He who has been beaten with a whip is the one that feels the smarting<br>- He who is affected by the situation on the ground is the one that invariably speaks out;<br>- He who is afflicted by a debilitating desease is the one that seeks out possible remedies. |
| 515. | Ẹni aà mọ̀n rí ì báà kú | The person we do not know may die (for all we care)<br>- The matter concerns us not. |
| 516. | Ẹní bá da'lẹ̀, á bá llẹ̀ lọ | He who tosses land, he will go with the land<br>- He who betrays will pay the price of treachery. |
| 517. | Ẹní bá da'mi s'íwájú á tẹ'lẹ̀ tútù | He who throws water ahead [as he's walking] will step on cool ground<br>- If you do your homework and do what's right, you will surely reap the expected |

| | | |
|---|---|---|
| | | reward of your effort;<br>- Another example: if you want to marry a princess, you'll have to do things that'll make the king (or queen) take notice of you, so when you come to the palace to ask for the princess's hand in marriage you will be more accepted as a suitor. |
| 518. | Ẹní bá dá'rí sọ Apá l'apã ńpa; Ẹní bá dá'rí sọ'rókò ni Ìrókò ń kò l'áyà; Ẹnikẹ́ni t'ó bá dá'rí sọ'gī Rúúruù, àt'oko ni 'wọn ó ti ru Òkú ẹ̀ wá'lé | He who dares the mahogany is the one the mahogany kills; whoever dares an Ìrókò tree is the person the tree will strike in the chest; whoever challenges and head-butts the Rúúruù tree, from the forest will they bring his dead body home<br>- The contest has been thrown open, the circle is drawn; whosoever tries to harm or kill you will himself be harmed or killed instantly;<br>- Whoever attempts it will pay dearly for it. |
| 519. | Ẹní bá dákẹ́, t'ara ẹ̀ á ba dákẹ́ | He who keeps silent, his concerns will be mute with him<br>- Speak up about issues that are of great concern to you, for no one else will. |
| 520. | Ẹní bá dan wò, á dan tán | Whoever tries it will try it to the end<br>- If you try what you've been forbidden to do, you must be ready for the consequences, one of which may be fatal. |
| 521. | Ẹní bá f'ojú d'ọba, Àwówó á wo | He who discounts or dares the King, Àwówó (the King's Wrath) will descend on him<br>- He who dares a king, government institution, or authority will face the wrath of the king/government. |
| 522. | Ẹní bá fẹ́ j'oyin inú Àpáta kìí w'ẹnu Àáké | He who wants to eat the honey inside a rock does not inspect the edge of the axe<br>- If you really mean to go far, then you'll not be bothered by disappointments and teething problems along the way;<br>- The road to success is strewn with thorns. |
| 523. | Ẹní bá fẹ́ rí Àtisùn-un Pẹ́pẹ́iyẹ, á | He who wants to see a duck fall asleep |

|      |                                                      |                                                                                                                                                                                                                                                                                                                                                                                                              |
|------|------------------------------------------------------|----|
|      | l'ówó Àdín                                           | must have money for oil [for his lamp]<br>- He who wants to see [what is being bandied about] happen may have a long wait. He'd better forget hoping to see it happen. |
| 524. | Ẹní bá f'ojú Àná w'òkú, Ẹbọra á bọ l'áṣọ             | Whoever looks at a dead body with yesterday's eyes, a ghost will strip them of their clothing. This hints at anyone who gazes upon a recently dead individual as if the corpse is still alive (and therefore the subject in this idiomatic personification appears not to exhibit any dread); alas, this dead person is now superior to you in the sense that they've attained an out-of-this-worldly level you are still probably dreading - the great beyond, a.k.a. death!<br>- Do not underestimate your opponent(s). |
| 525. | Ẹní bá jẹ Fùkù l'ará ń fu                            | They who have eaten beef lungs are the ones who are paranoid. No prizes for guessing "Fùkù" and "fu" originated this idiom. Fùkù = beef lung(s); fu = presume suspicion.<br>- If your hands are clean, your conscience should be clear. |
| 526. | Ẹní bá ju'ni lọ́ lè sọ'ni nù                         | A person who is way ahead of someone in position, wealth and power can lose someone [make someone go missing]<br>- Don't be disrespectful to a more powerful adversary as they can make your life a misery. |
| 527. | Ẹní bá ma jẹun gbọnhin-gbọnhin á ti'lẹ̀kùn gbọnhin-gbọnhin | He who wants to eat 'firmly-tightly' must shut the door firmly-tightly<br>- One had better make arrangements to cover his tracks to avoid fingers pointing at them. |
| 528. | Ẹní bá ma m'ọ́bọ ń'láti ṣe bí Ọ̀bọ                   | He who would like to catch a monkey must behave like a monkey<br>- Advice for someone who is seeking something of importance from another but is being maltreated by that person. Take heart, grin and bear it, and bide your |

| | | |
|---|---|---|
| | | time. When you've got in your hand what you've been taking this ill-treatment for so long for, then walk away. |
| 529. | Ẹní bá ń gbé'lée Díígí ò gbọdọ̀ sọ̀'kò | Whoever lives in a glass house must not throw stones<br>- You cannot criticize people if you are in a position to be criticized yourself;<br>- "Let any one of you who is without sin be the first to throw a stone" (John 8:7). |
| 530. | Ẹní bá rán'ni n'íṣẹ́ l'àá bẹrù, a kì ń bẹrù Ẹni t'a ma jẹ fún | He who has tasked us with a message is the one we fear, we don't fear the recipient to whom we are delivering it. |
| 531. | Ẹní bá rí Ewúrẹ́ Ìyá Àgbà n'ínú Òjò, òun nã l'ó máa mu so | She who notices the goat of Ìyá Àgbà [the most elderly lady] in the rain is the one who will put a leash on it and protect it from the rain<br>- Whoever witnesses two people fighting is the one whom it behooves to separate them;<br>- Whoever first notices a fire burning down a house is the one whom it behooves to raise the first alarm. |
| 532. | Ẹní bá ṣe ńdī Pẹpẹ, ní ńjẹ n'ídī Pẹpẹ | Where you have worked is where you'll get paid<br>- Where one has labored is where one earns their keep. |
| 533. | Ẹní bá t'ará Ilé è l'ọ́pọ̀ kò lè ríi rà l'ọ́wọ̀n | He who sells his relation on the cheap cannot find someone to buy him high-priced<br>- If you don't value your own, no one will see any value in them either;<br>- The way you portray someone close to you and present them to others is how the people you introduce them to will perceive them too. |
| 534. | Ẹní bá tú Ẹ̀kọ gbígbóná l'ó ń taá jó | He who unwraps the leaf off of a piping-hot hardened corn-pap is the one the hot steam splashes onto and burns<br>- Whoever ruffles the feathers of a powerful individual is the one that will face the wrath of the man; |

| | | |
|---|---|---|
| | | - He who flouts a law is the one that'll get his just punishment. |
| 535. | Ẹní bá y'ára l'ògún ń gbè | He who hastens is the one Ògún favors<br>- Whoever acts fastest is the one who invariably triumphs;<br>- Whoever draws first blood is the one who wins. |
| 536. | Ẹní bí'mọ l'ọmọ ẹ̀ ń kú | He who has a child is the one whose child dies [who might experience the death of a child]<br>- Good examples: he who is an employee is the one that experiences job promotion, salary cuts, lay-offs, etc. Or, whoever has a car and drives is the one that experiences car maintenance costs, fines, and other driving-related expenses. |
| 537. | Ẹní bí'mọ Ọ̀ràn níí pọ̀n-ọ́n | She who births a problem child is the one that will 'back' him. 'Backing' a toddler is an African tradition of carrying a child on the back while you walk, work or do your chores without encumbrance<br>- She who is nursing her child without full attention and proper discipline, if the child grows up to be wayward, then this phrase applies to the mother because the father is usually not at home to raise the child, so it's the mother's fault. |
| 538. | Ẹní bí'ni l'à ń jọ | They who begot us, we look like. |
| 539. | Ẹní d'eérú l'eérú ńtọ̀, Eléte l'ète ńyé | He who pours away ash, the ash-dust trails after him; he who connives understands his deception<br>- Your evil deed will follow you wherever you go like smoke. |
| 540. | Ẹni Eégún ń lé k'ó má ṣ'àfira; b'ó ṣe ń rẹ Ará Aiyé, bẹ́ẹ̀ l'ó ń rẹ Èrò Ọ̀run | Let whoever the masquerade is chasing be cautious; as fatigue sets in on people on earth, so do heavenly commuters [spirits of dead people] get exhausted<br>- Better watch you don't get upstaged yourself [with all your moaning];<br>- You could be next in line [to a bad experience]. |

| | | |
|---|---|---|
| 541. | Ẹní gb'ádìẹ Òtòsì, ó gbé t'aláròyé | Whoever steals the chicken of a pauper has [effectively] taken that of a whiner<br>- This idiom is a caution to those who might want to 'borrow' (even for a few minutes) a particular item from an owner who would hardly permit anyone to have it for a second; especially concerning an object belonging to someone who has little or nothing;<br>- The wronged individual here will never stop complaining and telling the world about what has been done to them, even if it's something trivial;<br>- Leave well alone if you don't want nagging. |
| 542. | Ẹní gb'ódó mì ò lè ní Ìsinmi | Whoever swallows a mortar will have no peace of mind<br>- Whoever does this kind of thing will live to regret it. |
| 543. | Ẹní gb'ókũ Àparò ó gb'áápọn | He who carries a dead bush-fowl [in the bush] carries misfortune<br>- Whoever buys something at face value such as a nice-looking used car at an auction may open himself to a whole set of angst;<br>- This idiom may also be said as a warning to someone before they do something they might regret for the rest of their life, such as marrying the wrong partner. |
| 544. | Ẹni Ilẹ̀ t'ọ́n-ọ̀n kì ń t'ẹ́ní fún ni | He's a person that belongs to the soil whom no one spreads the mat for<br>- Somebody that is not deserving of honor and respect from another;<br>- Ignore him, he's not worthy of your time and kindness. |
| 545. | Ẹni Inú ńbí ò jọ Ẹni Ọ̀rán ń dùn | He/she who is angry does not resemble someone who is hurting from a troubling situation<br>- Don't let me show you my angst, so you'd better let me be!<br>- Everyone with his/her own problems. |

| | | |
|---|---|---|
| 546. | Ẹní jìn sí Kòtò ó kọ́ Ará Ìyókù l'ọ́gbọ́n | He who falls into a ditch has taught others wisdom<br>- We learn from the mistakes of others before us. |
| 547. | Ẹni méjì ìí p'àdánù Irọ́; b'ẹni t'ọ́n ń pa'rọ́ fún ò bá mọ̀n, Ẹni t'ó ń pa'rọ́ ṣáà mọ̀n? | Two people cannot suffer the deceit of a lie; if the person being lied to doesn't see the lie, at least the liar does know he's telling a lie;<br>- Only you know your thoughts toward your fellow humankind. |
| 548. | Ẹní mi Kùkùté, Ara ẹ̀ l'ó mì | He who shakes a stump, shakes himself<br>- If you think your malicious deeds affect me, you're the one that's more affected. |
| 549. | Ẹní m'ọ̀nà níí tọ̀ọ́ | Only those who know the road ply it<br>- You don't want to involve yourself in something you know little or nothing about;<br>- You don't want to enter uncharted waters or uncharted territory. |
| 550. | Ẹní mọ'ni níí ṣe'ni | He who knows someone is the one that 'does' someone<br>- Those who are familiar with someone are the ones that are usually responsible for his predicament;<br>- If someone doesn't have any information about you, they can't use what they don't know about you against you;<br>- As Bob Marley said in his Who The Cap Fit album: "Only your friend know your secrets; so only he could reveal it." |
| 551. | Èní ń lọ, Inú Ọ̀lá ń dùn | Today is going, Tomorrow is rejoicing<br>- During the Changing of the Guard, members of the new administration are celebrating, laughing at the outgoing cabinet as if it were a misfortune to be leaving, forgetting they too will be history one day;<br>- This personification can illustrate the behavior of some myopic youth of today, who mock senior citizens for exhibiting old-age symptoms while ridiculing and |

|  |  | typecasting them as inept, not taking cognizance of the fact that they too will one day reach that stage in their lives;<br>- One day, it'll be your turn too!<br>See the proverb "ọmọ t'ó ní Bàbá 'un ò là." |
|---|---|---|
| 552. | Ẹní ń wá Ìfà ń w'ófo | He who seeks freebies seeks emptiness<br>- He who is looking for easy money sometimes risks lack;<br>- He who puts his life savings on a betting risks putting himself in penury;<br>- If you put all you have into a deal that initially promises to fetch you multiple returns, beware that you may end up with nothing. |
| 553. | Ẹní ń wá Ìwákúwã l'ó ń rí Ìríkúrĩ | He who searches desperately [for something that may not be there] is the one that sees a can of nasty worms<br>- For example: Don't meddle in things you don't really know or you may find something you haven't bargained for that may further turn your life upside down;<br>- Stop looking for evidence of an infidelity for what you find may upset the balance of things in your life. For instance the person you think might be a lover of your partner may in fact be an innocuous platonic relationship and only your partner probably didn't tell you to avoid giving you that false impression in the first place. |
| 554. | Ẹní pe Ṣoṣo á rí Ṣoṣo | Whoever calls for war will have a battle on their hands<br>- Be careful what you wish for. |
| 555. | Ẹni táà ń bọ́, kìí b'ájá | He/she who is fed does not feed a dog<br>- This adage is expressed to indicate someone is about to test a kind person's generosity;<br>- Do not ask for a mile if you have been given a yard. |
| 556. | Ẹni t'a ní k'ó f'ẹni l'ójú t'ó f'ata | He who has been asked to blow the speck |

|  |  |  |
|---|---|---|
|  | s'ẹnu; Ẹni t'a ní k'ó kín'ni l'ẹ́hìn, Ègún l'ó fi s'ọ́wọ́ | from one's eyes placed ground pepper in his mouth; he who has been enjoined to scrub our back, has bedecked his hands with thorns<br>- The people we have confided in and whom we were relying on to rescue us from our dire straits are the ones that have made matters even worse for us. |
| 557. | Ẹni táa ṣe l'óore tí 'ò dú'pẹ́, ó dàbí Olọ́ṣã kó'ni l'ẹ̀rù lọ ni | Someone we did a favor that didn't say "thanks" is like a thief has carted away someone's load [property] OR like a thief has robbed someone of his possession<br>- We have to show our appreciation to our altruist/benefactor;<br>- Appreciating someone is a virtue in itself, so express your gratitude to him who has gone out of his way to help. |
| 558. | Ẹni t'ẹ̀gũn bá gún lẹ́sẹ̀ l'ó ńṣe láká-ǹ-láká tọ Alábẹ lọ | He whose foot has been pierced by a thorn is the one that limps to the podiatric physician<br>- Anyone with a problem is the one that seeks solutions wherever he might find them. |
| 559. | Ẹni t'ọ́n bá ta l'ọ́fà l'ó ń j'aporó | He who has been shot with an arrow is the one that writhes in agony<br>- He who has been affected by some calamity is the one that feels the pain or loss. |
| 560. | Ẹni táà bá fẹ́ n'ilé è ń jìn'nà | It's someone we don't want that their home is too far<br>- You don't really want to have anything to do with this individual - you're only using the fact that they don't live in your locality as a ruse to not visit them. |
| 561. | Ẹni táa bá ń fẹ́ Ìyá ẹ̀ l'ọmọ ẹ̀ ń wun'ni | The person whose mother we are befriending is the one that interests one<br>- Nothing goes for nothing;<br>- This is a privileged situation, just be grateful and lap it up;<br>- I'm only doing this because of the influence of someone else. |

| 562. | Ẹni táa kọ́ n'íwà t'ó hù'wà, ó ní t'inú ẹ̀ẹ́ ṣe tẹ́lẹ̀ ni | Whoever heeds the advice of another has their own inner mind made up about the matter<br>- You must have had an inner disposition before adhering to someone else's advice;<br>- You are just seeking someone to support your mindset. |
|---|---|---|
| 563. | Ẹni táa rí l'à ń mọ́n l'ójú | It's the person we see that we glare at<br>- It's because of my close relationship with you that you are disrespectful to me;<br>- The better you know someone, the more you will find fault with them. |
| 564. | Ẹni tí 'ò bá gbọ́ t'ẹnu Ègà l'ó ń pèé ní Páàtó | He who has not heard what Ègà [songbird] had to say is the one that calls it Páátó [baloney]<br>- You need to listen to the complainant who feels they have been wronged - they might have a valid point;<br>- The leaders need to listen to the people who are protesting first before dismissing their grievances and agitations as unimportant or baseless. |
| 565. | Ẹni tí 'ò bá ti n'írú Ẹni kò lè mọn'yì Ẹni | Whoever didn't have one's kind of person could not appreciate one<br>- The person who has never known the goodness of another would probably think every other person out there is equally magnanimous and might shrug his shoulders and underrate the man's largess and muse "he's done this and that for me, so what?"<br>- You don't know what you've got until it's gone. |
| 566. | Ẹni tí 'ò kọ́'lé, Ìṣòro ni fun k'ó gb'owó Ilé | He who didn't build a house, it would be a bit tricky for him to collect rent<br>- You can't reap where you haven't sown. |
| 567. | Ẹni tí 'ò lè jẹun Alẹ́ Àná sùn, t'ó l'óũn máa f'ọ́mọ Ọba Àlá | A poor man who could not afford to eat last night's meal and says he plans to marry a dream princess<br>- In this context, this is an impossible dream that has no hope of coming to |

|  |  | fruition. |
|---|---|---|
| 568. | Ẹni tí a ṣe l'óore Ẹgbẹ̀fà tí kò dúpẹ́, ó ti bẹ́'gi dí'nà Egbèje | He whom we did a favor sixty times and didn't say 'thanks', has 'felled a tree' to block the seventieth assist<br>- He whom we have helped out sixty times (when we didn't have to) and has failed to show his gratitude for even once, has effectively precluded our seventieth assistance;<br>- Who would want to help an unappreciative person? |
| 569. | Ẹni tí 'ò b'írú Ẹni ò lè mọn'yì Ẹni | Someone who has not birthed one's kind cannot appreciate one<br>- This is an insulting metaphor to put someone in their place;<br>- Or, to remind someone of their inadequacy or lack of achievement of something important in life, e.g. saying to a childless person, "You are barren, so you wouldn't know how to deal with a child." |
| 570. | Ẹni tí ò bá f'ẹni, a ìí sá Àlọ̀ fun | He/she who doesn't like someone, we do not air their milled produce [e.g. cassava] in the sun for them<br>- Don't bring this person into your inner circle;<br>- You should really not be giving gifts to the type of person in this allegory as they evidently haven't earned it, so to speak. |
| 571. | Ẹni tí 'ò bá ní jẹ́ a yó, a máa ń dá'ná ẹ̀ m'óúnjẹ ni | He/she who will not let us be filled [shorten our food ration], we factor their portion in with the cooking [we include them in the meal plan]<br>- He/she who could have a negative influence in our life and well-being based on their whim, we do what we can to placate or amuse them;<br>- In some instances, this person may be murdered to get rid of them. |
| 572. | Ẹni tí ò bá ní jẹ́ k'a yó, àá ròó mọ́n'sà sè ni | He who will shorten our ration, we 'stir' him with the pot and cook [we include him in the meal plan] |

| | | |
|---|---|---|
| | | - He who could have a negative influence in our life and well-being based on his whim, we do what we can to placate or amuse him. |
| 573. | Ẹni tí ò bá ṣubú tẹ́lẹ̀ kò níí mọn b'óũn ṣe ma dìde | He who has never fallen before will not know how to get up<br>- They who had never experienced hard times before would not know what to do to bounce back up when faced with adversity. |
| 574. | Ẹni tí ò bá tĩ kúrò n'ínú Odò kìí k'ígbe Òtútù | Who has not exited from the stream does not shriek [of] Cold!<br>- I am/We are just starting, calm down;<br>- We are not out of the woods yet. |
| 575. | Ẹni tí ò j'óbẹ̀ jẹ, báwo l'ó ṣe mọn bí Iyọ̀ ọ́ dùn-ún tàbí 'ò dùn-ún? | She who didn't steal [someone else's] stew to eat, how would she know that the salt was enough or not?<br>- He who has not participated in the plot under investigation, how would he know exactly how things went down? |
| 576. | Ẹni tí ò l'ẹni t'ó máa wa ìí sọnù | He who does not have someone who would look for him never goes missing<br>- You don't get yourself involved in shady activities because you'll be on your own when things go south. Basically, you watch your back. |
| 577. | Ẹni tí ò l'óògùn Arìnyà kìí dáá ní | He who does not have the remedy for chest ailment never has things all to himself<br>- Share what you have with friends and family; don't keep everything to yourself. |
| 578. | Ẹni tí 'ó parí Ìjà, Ìjà ìí t'ojú ẹ̀ẹ́ bẹ̀rẹ̀ | He who will resolve a brawl, the fight never starts in his presence<br>- A good mediator never allows a fight to begin in the first place, so there's never a fight to break up. |
| 579. | Ẹni tí ò ṣe ní ìdíí Pẹpẹ, kò lè jẹ ní ìdíí Pẹpẹ | He who has not labored at the bottom [base or factory] of Pẹpẹ cannot eat at the bottom [base or factory] of Pẹpẹ<br>- He who has not put in the effort cannot expect to reap the reward. |

| | | |
|---|---|---|
| 580. | Ẹni tí ó tẹ'kùn àti Ẹni tí ó rin'kùn, Òkèèrè báyî n'ọ́n máa ti jọ lọ ná'jàa ẹ̀ | He who pinches a stomach to feel it and he who tickles the stomach, it's from such a distance that they will go and haggle its price<br>- Whether you think you're right and others think they're justified [over a disputed issue], all of you will never come to an agreement. |
| 581. | Ẹni tí ò tîî kú l'ó l'oko Òkè yī | He who is still not dead is the owner of the farm yonder<br>- If we are alive, there's much we can still accomplish in this life. |
| 582. | Ẹni tí ò tîî kú ò m'àrùn t'ó ma pà'un | He who is not dead yet does not know what decease he's going to die of<br>- Don't preen yourself too much and laugh at those who are facing justice at the moment<br>- You don't know tomorrow. |
| 583. | Ẹni tí Òjó pa, ó sàn ju Ẹni tí Ṣàngó pa lọ | He whom the rain beats is better than someone Ṣàngó beats<br>- If the rain beats someone, they only get wet; but if Ṣàngó [the god of thunder] beats you, the euphemism means you have been struck by lightning and will likely die;<br>- It's a matter of being alive or dead. |
| 584. | Ẹni tîí bá fọ'lú mọ́n kò fẹ́ k'á fọ'lé Òun | He who would cleanse the country does not want us to clean his house first<br>- The official who is supposed to stand up for the people and has vowed to rid the country of corruption does not want himself investigated first before he embarks on his crusade. |
| 585. | Ẹni t'ó bá fẹ́ fọ'lú mọ́n, k'ó mú'ra àti fọ'yá ẹ̀ mọn | He who would cleanse the country had better be prepared to include his own mother in the cleansing campaign<br>- The official should also include his own people and all those that will work with him to be probed first. |
| 586. | Ẹni t'ó bá fẹ́ pa Oró ní láti pa Ejò pẹ̀lú ẹ̀ | Whoever wants to kill venom has to kill the snake as well |

|   |   |   |
|---|---|---|
|   |   | - In order to have everlasting peace [or anything worth having], one may have to go a step further than what is so obvious he must do. |
| 587. | Ẹni t'ó bá Ìyà bọ̀ ńbìkan, ó lè padà bá Ìdùnnú bọ̀ Ńbòmîn | He who returned with suffering from one place may return with happiness from another<br>- No one knows tomorrow, so never write off anyone. |
| 588. | Ẹni t'ó bá mọn Iṣin í jẹ, ó ní láti mọn Kóró ẹ̀ ẹ́ yọ | He who knows how to eat ackees must also know how to remove the poisonous seeds<br>- If you know how to commit crimes and don't want to serve time in prison, logic dictates that you must also know how to avoid capture or don't do crimes at all. |
| 589. | Ẹni t'ó bá ní kín l'a ma ṣe l'à ń ṣe fún | He who has in the past said what are we going to do is whom we do something for<br>- He who has underestimated us we should try and disprove;<br>- He who has commonized our worth is the one we give a crucial helping hand. |
| 590. | Ẹni t'ó bá ṣe Nǹkan t'ẹnìkan ò ṣe rí, Ojú ẹ̀ á rí Ohun t'ẹnìkan ò rí rí | He who does something no one has done before, his eyes will surely see what no one has seen before<br>- No one can do this sort of thing and not pay the price. |
| 591. | Ẹni t'ó bá sùn l'ẹnìkan-án ma ń jí, kò s'ẹni t'ó le jí Apìrọrọ | It is someone who is sleeping that anyone might wake up, nobody can wake up someone in a coma or in an induced sleep<br>- The person under reference is only feigning competence or incompetence. |
| 592. | Ẹni t'ó bá ti jẹ Dòdò kò níí lè sọ Òdodo | He who has eaten fried plantain [Dòdò] won't be able to speak the truth [Òdodo]<br>- He who has been paid off or has taken a bribe will not be able to represent his people/community truthfully. |
| 593. | Ẹni t'ó bí'mọ a ò tíì rí nkan fún-un, k'ábọ̀ nt'orí Ẹní ń b'ínú | She who has just delivered a baby we haven't got anything to give her, much less someone who is angry.<br>Please see Explanation under |

| | | "real_meaning" here.<br>EXPLANATION:<br>Bí = birth (verb);<br>Ọmọ = child, baby;<br>Inú = stomach, tummy;<br>Bí ọmọ = **bí'mọ** (birth a baby);<br>Bí inú = **b'ínú** (birth a tummy) meaning 'be angry'.<br>This proverb comes about because:<br>the **first** part of the two-parter Yoruba word for "bí'mọ" ['birth' a baby] (verb) [shortened from **bí ọmọ** to **bí'mọ**] means the same thing as:<br>the **first** part of the two-parter Yoruba word for [bí'nú] 'be angry' (literal translation 'birth tummy') [shortened from **bí inú** to **bí'nú**]. |
|---|---|---|
| 594. | Ẹni t'ó d'ìkúùkù, t'ó ní k'á fún'ni, b'ényìàn-án bá ṣe ńlá fun, yíó dúpẹ́ jù bẹ́ẹ̀ lọ | He who closes his hand to make a fist and sends it [in salute] to someone [in appreciation], if someone does him a bigger favor, he would be more thankful<br>- The people expressing this statement are prepared to put heads together to give further assistance to the subject should he require it. |
| 595. | Ẹni t'ó fò s'ókè, ó bẹ́'jó l'órí | He who hops has 'beheaded' the dance<br>- Don't complain about the less-than-expected assistance someone has given you; at least they have tried.<br>- Half-bread is better than none. |
| 596. | Ẹni t'ó gb'épo l'ájà ò ja'lè bí kò ṣ'ẹni t'ó gbàá l'ọ́wọ́ ẹ̀ | He who steals palm oil from a shelf did not steal like the person who took it from him<br>- The thief is not to blame but who sent him to commit the theft;<br>- Don't shoot the messenger because the message is unpalatable. |
| 597. | Ẹni t'ó l'ẹlẹ́dẹ̀ l'ó l'ẹ̀ẹ̀dẹ̀; Ẹni t'ó n'ílé l'ó ni Gba-ngba Oko | The owner of the pigs owns the yard; the house owner also owns the stretch of savanna<br>- The person who hires another decides what services he wants delivered; |

| | | |
|---|---|---|
| | | - He/she who pays the piper calls the tune. |
| 598. | Ẹni t'ó ń tẹ aṣọ ẹ̀ mọ́n'lẹ̀, ó lè f'aṣọ Aláṣọ ya | She who constantly steps on her own clothes can shred someone else's clothes<br>- The person to whom this metaphor refers cannot be entrusted with any responsibility. |
| 599. | Ẹni t'ó ṣ'oore fún'ni t'ó tún ń lóṣõ tìí | An individual who helps another out [of difficulty] that still also 'crouches on' it<br>- A person who helps someone out of dire straits but never lets them forget the favor rendered. |
| 600. | Ẹni t'ó ṣ'oore fún'ni t'ó tún ń ṣ'ìrègún | Someone who gives another a helping hand, but constantly reminds the person he has helped of the favor at every opportunity<br>- Someone who helps another in time of need but never lets them forget the favor rendered. |
| 601. | Ẹni t'ó ṣu l'ó gbàgbé, Ẹni t'ó ko ò gbàgbé | He who passed stool is the one that forgot, he who cleaned up after him has not forgotten<br>- Who committed a grave felony may have forgotten, but his victim(s) will always remember;<br>- Who has made important personal contributions in another person's success will never forget, though the beneficiary may not remember. |
| 602. | Ẹni t'ó ti ń f'apá Ewúrẹ́ jẹ'yán tẹ́lẹ̀, t'àgîrì ò le ka l'ẹ́nu mọ́n | He who has been used to eating pounded yam with the shoulder of a goat, that of a frog will not be abundant for him<br>- This idiom expresses the fact that the subject in this context is used to a better life than what he's currently enjoying;<br>- This person has found themselves in a belittling situation. |
| 603. | Ẹni t'ó tún Orí ẹ̀ tù Ìfà, t'ó k'ìbọn àkìkúdórógbó ò rántí pé b'ẹ́tùú bá pọ̀jù, yíya níí yà'bọn | He who embarks on a shooting spree just because he got free gunpowder has forgotten that excessive gunpowder will more often than not burst the gun [when |

| | | |
|---|---|---|
| | | the trigger is pulled]<br>- Don't overdue things. |
| 604. | Ẹni t'ọ́n f'orí ẹ̀ f'ágbọn lí dúró jẹẹ́ | The person whose head is used to crack a coconut does not live to eat it<br>- This person or team is in dire straits right now!<br>- Whoever this type of thing [hinted in the context] happens to hardly survives it. |
| 605. | Ẹní wẹ'jú l'ẹ̀rù ńbà | He who has washed his eyes [in the occult] is the one who is afraid (because now he can see spirits and ghosts)<br>- He who supped with the devil and didn't use a long spoon is the one who has cause to fear [seeing things an ordinary man is not supposed to see]. |
| 606. | Ènìà (Ènìyàn) lí n'íkà méjì k'ó má f'ìkan ṣe'ra ẹ̀ | A man does not possess two evils and not harm himself with one<br>- The subject in reference may have power to cause pain and injury to people; he will sooner or later hurt someone close to him unintentionally without realizing it before long. |
| 607. | Ènìà bí Awun l'ó ń r'áwun he! | Someone like a tortoise is the one that finds a tortoise<br>- It takes a thief to catch a thief. |
| 608. | Ènìà lí mọn Alájá k'ó tún pa Ajá ẹ̀ jẹ | A person does not know the owner of a dog and still kill the dog to eat<br>- You can't know [or be close to] someone's family and yet do harm to any of them. |
| 609. | Ènìà lí n'ígi l'óko k'ó má m'èso ẹ̀ | Someone does not have a tree in his farm and not know its fruit<br>- One can't have children and not know the behavior of each one of them. |
| 610. | Ènìà l'ó k'ẹṣin l'óró; Ẹṣin ò n'íkà nínú rárá | It's humans that taught the horse to be cruel; a horse doesn't have any malice in him<br>- It's adults that trained children to be malicious and nasty; children weren't born with wickedness. |
| 611. | Ènìà l'ó wà l'ẹ́hìn Orò t'órò ó fi | It's someone behind the Orò idol-god that |

|     |                                          |                                                                                                                                                                                                                                                                |
| --- | ---------------------------------------- | -------------------------------------------------------------------------------------------------------------------------------------------------------------------------------------------------------------------------------------------------------------- |
|     | ń ké                                     | makes him appear to squeak<br>- There's someone behind the success of another.                                                                                                                                                                                 |
| 612. | Ènìà ò f'ẹni f'ọrọ̀, à f'orí Ẹni          | Humans do not wish anyone else to have great wealth, except one's spirit<br>- Try your best and keep forging ahead no matter what, as no one else but you know where you want to go and what level you want to be at a certain period in your life.            |
| 613. | Ènìà ò gbọdọ̀ fi Iṣẹ́ Ìgbọ̀nsẹ̀ rán Ọmọ Ẹni | One should not send his kid on an excretion errand [to have the child excrete for him]<br>- The message should be delivered in person by the person concerned to the intended party.                                                                           |
| 614. | Ènìà ò gbọdọ̀ tú Ìgbóná-ọ̀rọ̀ jẹ             | Nobody should peel hot-words [as one might peel an orange] and eat<br>- Don't rush things; calm down!                                                                                                                                                          |
| 615. | Ènìà ò kì ń j'ọba k'ó l'ójo              | You can't become a king and still have fear<br>- You can't have what you've got and not exploit the opportunity it accords you.                                                                                                                                |
| 616. | Ènìà ò r'íbi sùn, Ajá ń han'run          | Humans do not have room to sleep, [yet] a dog is snoring<br>- This metaphor may be expressed when, for instance, there is something that important guests need that subordinates and house helps might have misappropriated<br>- Or the metaphor may be expressed as an indignation: What kind of nonsense is this?! |
| 617. | Ènìà ò wà nípa Àkàrà nìkan               | Human beings are not for Àkàrà [fried bean-cakes] only<br>- There's more to life than eating;<br>- Man shall not live by bread alone;<br>- Talk about something else!                                                                                          |
| 618. | Ènìà t'ó rí Orí Erin l'átẹ kò mọn'yì Erin | He who sees the head of an elephant on a market table-display does not know the value of an elephant<br>- As it is rare to find an elephant in the bush to kill, so it is with Freedom, which is                                                                |

| | | |
|---|---|---|
| | | often taken for granted by those born after the struggle for the freedom. |
| 619. | Ẹnìkan ìí b'ómi í ṣ'ọ̀tá; Omi l'a bù wẹ̀, Omi l'a bù mu | No one shuns water; water is what we bathe with, water is what we drink<br>- This is to say everyone will want to befriend you rather than spurn you. |
| 620. | Ẹnìkan ìí dá'ná k'ó ní kí t'ẹgbẹ́ ẹ ó má jòó | No one kindles a fire and wishes the fire being started by his peers does not ignite as well<br>- No able man can stand by and refuse to give support while the whole community is looking for help. |
| 621. | Ẹnìkan ìí jẹ́ "àwá dé" | One person does not signify "we have arrived"<br>- Do not needlessly make reference to more than one person if you're referencing just one single person<br>Other examples:<br>- If someone keeps referring to "we" when no one else is seen with him, the listener might express this metaphor especially if it had not been clear from the beginning of the narrative that there was someone else involved in the discourse, to mean "wait a minute; you and who else?"<br>- This metaphor also dispels the sense of two or more people involved in anything, i.e. someone might use this phrase to say "don't rope me in", "count me out", "speak for yourself" to rebut someone trying to involve him/her. |
| 622. | Ẹnìkan ìí kán'jú tu Olú-Ọrán, nítorí Igba è ò tóó sè l'ọ́bẹ̀ | No one hastens to pluck Olú-Ọrán [the tiniest mushrooms], because two hundred of them are not enough to prepare a pot of stew<br>- The matter before us cannot be hurried; it needs tact to handle it and even with that, resolution can still not be assured. |
| 623. | Ẹnìkan ìí kéré n'ídī Ẹrùu ẹ | No one is [deemed] little standing beside their property<br>- You are what you are [position], |

|  |  | regardless of your age or height. |
|---|---|---|
| 624. | Ẹnìkan ìí kọ́ Pèé, Ihun tí ńbẹ̀ ń'nú Ọ̀pẹ̀ l'àá kọ̀ | No one lectures 'Call him/her,' it's what's in the mind of the novice that we reject<br>- First hear them out! |
| 625. | Ẹnìkan ìí m'ọ́jọ́ so l'ókùn | No one ties the day in ropes [No one can bind the day in chains]<br>- No matter what we do, we simply can't prevent the natural progression of things; what will be will be. |
| 626. | Ẹnìkan ìí yó k'ó má mọ̀n | No one gets full and does not know it<br>- Could be said by someone to convey the sense of "I know you know what you're doing, but what are you doing?" |
| 627. | Ẹnìkan l'à ń ka àìsunwọ̀n fún | It's only one person whom we count 'being bad' for<br>- Let the person in question do as he pleases. |
| 628. | Ẹnìkan l'ó pá'rí l'Ádó t'ọ́n ní gbogbo wọn l'ó pá'rí | Only one person is bald in Ádó yet they allege all of the citizens are bald<br>- Only one citizen of a country has committed a felony in a foreign country and the host country labels all the citizens of the offender's country criminals. |
| 629. | Ènìyàn ò lè dá'ná ń'nú Ilé k'íná è má yọ s'íta | No one can create a fire indoors and its fire [smoke] will not appear externally<br>- No one cooks indoors without the smoke escaping outside;<br>- You can't commit atrocities and expect no one to know about it. |
| 630. | Ènìyàn tí ò fẹ́ k'áráiyé r'ídī òun ìí g'ábẹ́rẹ́; Ohun t'ó bá ń ṣ'olúwa è ní ó máa ró m'áṣọ | He who doesn't want the whole world to see his [secret] eccentricity does not have incisions; the oddity or illness that is plaguing him will he wrap in his garment<br>- You cannot completely isolate yourself from everyone [if you wish to continue staying among the living]. |
| 631. | Ẹnu Àgbà l'obì í ti ń gbó | It's in the mouth of the elders that the kolanut ripens<br>- It's only adults who appreciate the topic under discussion and their counsel is currently sought. |

| | | |
|---|---|---|
| 632. | Ẹnu Ẹni la fi ń kọ miò jẹ | It's with one's mouth one declines and pronounces "I don't want to eat"<br>- Don't hide your displeasure about what pleases and displeases you, so use your own mouth to revoke it. |
| 633. | Ẹnu l'abẹ́rẹ́ fíí t'áṣọ ṣe | It's the mouth that the needle employs to mend clothes<br>- Since it was by words spoken and agreed on that got us to the current state of affairs, likewise it's by words spoken by mouth that we will resolve the dispute. |
| 634. | Ẹnu ò dùn, Ẹlẹ́nu á pọn lá | The mouth is not sweet yet the owner will still lick it<br>- You may loathe someone but his family loves him. |
| 635. | Ẹnu ò mọn "mo jẹ rí" | A mouth does not know "I have eaten before"<br>- No one tires of help and kindness. |
| 636. | Ẹnu Ọmọ ò gba "Ìyá pà'dí mọ́n" | The mouth of a son cannot utter "mother, close your private part"<br>- We can't disrespect or talk down to our elders;<br>- What you're proposing to say is way too big for your mouth. |
| 637. | Ẹnu-ẹnu l'ẹsẹ̀ ẹ́ fi ń p'èkùrọ́ Ojú Ọ̀nà | Gradually, gradually do the feet crack the palm kernels on the path<br>- It may be a hard slow start at the beginning but surely [the issue] will have a solution. |
| 638. | Ẹnu-ẹnu l'ẹsẹ̀ ẹ́ fi ń p'èkùrọ́ Ojú Ọ̀nà; ṣùgbọ́n kàkà kí Ẹsẹ̀ ẹ́ pa Èkùrọ́ Ojú Ọ̀nà, ńṣe ni Ara Èkùrọ́ Ojú Ọ̀nà ń dán gbin-inrin síí l'ójõjúmọ́ | Gradually, gradually do the feet crack the palm kernels on the path [having fallen from the tree over time]; but instead of the feet cracking the fallen palm kernels, the 'body' of the fallen palm kernels started looking robust and shining each passing day<br>- You are not doing your due diligence;<br>- If you delay any longer, the momentum may be lost.<br>- You need to make up your mind real quick! |

| 639. | Epo kẹ̀tẹ̀pẹ́ yàtọ̀ s'épo ń rùn | Thick palm oil is different from 'the oil is stinking'<br>- Different strokes for different folks;<br>- One man's fish is another man's poison. |
|---|---|---|
| 640. | Epo ni mo rù, Oníyangí má ba t'èmi jẹ́! | It's palm oil I'm carrying [on the head], sand-hauler don't ruin my own! (Don't let your sand get into my oil)<br>- Let me just be! Don't involve me in your illicit schemes and complicate my life! |
| 641. | Epo ni mo rù; Oníyangí yàgò l'ọ́nà mi! | It's palm oil I'm carrying, sand-hauler, get out of my way! Don't let your sand get into the oil<br>- I'm an easy-going person; please do not involve me in this matter! |
| 642. | Ẹrán kú s'ílũ̀ àìl'ọ́bẹ! | The animal has died in a community where there are no knives!<br>- Look at the opportunities that are abundant here with no one to take advantage of them! |
| 643. | Ẹran Ọba l'ó fi Iṣu Ọba jẹ | It's the king's goat that ate the king's yam<br>- It's the prince that has done the egregious thing everyone is gossiping about. |
| 644. | Ẹran táa fà fà fà tí ò já, òun nã ń pè ní Nọ́nmọ̀n | The meat that we stretch in an attempt to bite into it [with teeth] but would not snap is called tendon<br>- The speaker is promising fire and brimstone if someone does the unthinkable thing described in the narrative [that brought about the idiomatic expression]. |
| 645. | Ẹranko Ilé ni wọ́n, t'ó ń f'ojú ú d'ọdẹ | They're a domestic animal that stares at a deer hunter with contemptuous, underestimating eyes (no one hunts domestic animals so they are not accustomed to seeing hunters chasing them)<br>- They do not know the extent of the power that confronts them. |
| 646. | Ẹranko ò lè mú Ẹranko kan so; Ẹranko ò lè tú Ẹranko kan s'ílẹ̀; | An animal cannot tie an animal; an animal cannot untie the leash of an animal |

|  |  |  |
|---|---|---|
|  | ó ṣ'èèwọ̀ | - What is being proposed has never been done before or is just ethically and morally impossible; it's taboo. |
| 647. | Ẹranko t'ó bá ṣ'iyèméjì òun l'ọlọ́dẹ́ ńpa | It's the animal that doubts that a hunter kills<br>- Approach any situation with confidence and do not doubt yourself. |
| 648. | Èrè dà ń'bi Lágboókà? Tàbí...<br>Kò s'érè ń'ídî Lágboókà | Where's the gain at Lágboókà's place? OR...<br>There's no profit in the business of Lágboókà [money-counting]<br>- Why involve yourself in unrewarding undertakings;<br>- Nothing will come out of it [whatever is hinted in the context];<br>- Why do you waste your time over things that do not concern you? |
| 649. | Eré gbogbó d'ọ̀la | All plays resume tomorrow<br>- This idiom suggests the current activity or discussion is being postponed until the next day. |
| 650. | Eré Orí Igi, Àṣekù Ọmọ Ẹdun | The tree-top sports are defunct pastimes of generations of monkeys<br>- The fascinating feat/deed you find astonishing is something the "old dog" is used to;<br>- We've done it all before!<br>- It's nothing new, buddy! |
| 651. | Ẹrú kan níí mú'ni bú'gba Ẹrú | It's one slave that makes one insult two hundred slaves<br>- It's only because of the wrong done by one staff in an organization that the whole firm has become a pariah in the industry and everyone now avoids doing business with them. |
| 652. | Ẹrù ú pọ̀ l'ọ́rùn Ọ̀pẹ/Ògèdè | Loads are aplenty on the neck of the palm tree / banana tree<br>- The person in reference has a lot on their plate. |
| 653. | Ẹsẹ̀ gììrì n'ílé Amíjọ̀fẹ́ (Ańjọ̀fẹ́) | Innumerable feet in the home of Amíjọ̀fẹ́ [someone who provides a sort of meal |

| | | center for the poor and the hungry]<br>- All roads lead to where there are free gifts to be had. |
|---|---|---|
| 654. | Ẹsẹ̀ kan Aiyé, Ẹsẹ̀ kan Ọ̀run l'ó wà | One leg in Earth, one leg in Heaven is where he is<br>- The subject of this storyline is neither alive nor dead; he's hovering between life and death;<br>- The person being talked about is in grave danger of losing their life. |
| 655. | Ẹṣin Inú Ìwé ni | He's a horse in a book<br>- This "book horse" simile is to allege the person being talked about is impotent. |
| 656. | Ẹṣin Iwájú ni t'ẹ̀hìn ńwò sá'ré | The lead horse is the one the horse behind is watching to gallop faster<br>- What the leaders do is what the leaders of tomorrow are watching to replicate;<br>- What the heroes and role models of today do is what the youth are watching to emulate. |
| 657. | Ẹṣin l'ó n'ijó Àrà l'ẹ́sẹ̀; òun ní ń gb'ẹ́ni tí ń sh'oge kiri | It's the horse that has dance-moves at its feet; it's the one that carries the fashionable man all over the place<br>- It's not your show! |
| 658. | Ẹ̀sín ń r'ógun Ojú Atu'ruku Ẹṣin mú'ni | Disgrace / humiliation is facilitated by embattlement of the horse whose hooves keep kicking up dust and pebbles in one's eyes to ensnare him [when he's blinded by the dust]<br>- This empathetic hyperbole is expressed when a respected individual has fallen from grace due to some calamitous event;<br>- "Oh, what a pity!" |
| 659. | Ẹṣinṣin t'ó bá b'ọ́dẹ rìn yíó m'ẹ̀jẹ̀ yó | The tsetse fly that moves with a bush hunter will drink blood till its belly is full<br>- He who walks in the company of the rich will himself be rich if he plays his cards right;<br>- A food lover who works in a hotel kitchen will have plenty to eat. |
| 660. | Ẹ̀sọ̀, ẹ̀sọ̀ l'ejò ń g'àgbọn | Gently, gently is how a snake climbs a |

|     |     | coconut tree<br>- Do not rush into things;<br>- Approach issues with caution and stealth; take your time. |
| --- | --- | --- |
| 661. | Èsúrú ti pàdí dà, ó ti ń l'ájá | Èsúrú cluster yam has changed its formation, it has now started to grow dogs<br>- You are the one begging for mercy now. |
| 662. | Ẹtà níí kọ́kọ́ ọ́ tà k'ọ́mọ Ẹrankó tó tà | The dingo sells first before any other animal pup sells<br>- The person saying this incantational proverb is wishing someone or themselves to be the first to succeed. |
| 663. | Ètè ò sí mọ́n, Eyín d'Ìṣáná; Etí ò sí mọ́n, Orí d'èkólà-Igi | Without the lips, the teeth become matchsticks; without the ears, the head becomes a piece of wood<br>- Without clear direction and good leadership, it would be hard for a community or people to prosper;<br>- Without the tried-and-tested positive concepts being put into effect, an economy or a business can become shambles. |
| 664. | Etí kan ò yẹ'rí; Bàtà kan ò yẹ'sẹ̀ | One ear does not befit the head; one shoe does not befit the feet<br>- For example: a land with riches and so much wealth but without adequate security for its citizens is useless and an embarrassment;<br>- Introduce and implement appropriate policies! |
| 665. | Etí t'ó gbọ́ Àlọ l'ó ń gbọ́ Àbọ̀ | The ears that heard the Going are the ones that hear the Return<br>- We have to give a report to the council or people that were originally present during the plan to carry out the assignment. |
| 666. | Ewé kan ò lè já bọ́ l'ára igi kí Ọlọ́un Má mọ̀n ńpa ẹ̀ | No leaf falls from a tree that God Almighty Does not know about it<br>- Nothing happens in this neck of the woods without the powers-that-be not |

| | | |
|---|---|---|
| | | being aware of it. |
| 667. | Ewé níí b'orí Işu | It's leaves that cover the unharvested yam - A sort of prayer that you'll have the upper hand over your enemies, just as the leaves are always above the muddy mound of a growing yam. |
| 668. | Èwo l'àb'ẹ̀nìkan jà, f'ọwọ́ gún gbogbo Ilé n'ímú? | What's with quarrelling with one single person and [yet] sticking your finger on the noses of everyone in the household? - Why carry your aggression and frustration beyond the scope of the person you are upset with? |
| 669. | Èwo n'ìṣẹ́-pàlá bí Ajá ń lá'mi? | What's this nonsense like when a dog is lapping water? - If you've got something good and noble to do, do it, quit stalling; - If you want to shoot, shoot; don't talk! |
| 670. | Èwo ni t'Àlàbá n'ínú Ìbejì? Tàbí… Kín l'ó k'Àlàbá ń'nú Apá Ẹdan? | What's Alaba's interest in the being of twins? OR… What concerns Alaba with the arm of Ẹdan [Yorùbá twins' fetish doll]? Please see Explanation under "real_meaning" right here. **EXPLANATION**: The traditional Yoruba names (unisex) given to twins and those born after them are: **First twin**: Taiye or Taiwo; **Second twin**: Kehinde; **First child after twins**: Idowu, a.k.a. Èṣù l'éhìn ìbejì [the 'devil' behind a set of twins]. **2nd child after twins**: Alaba. In this proverbial context, Alaba is far removed from the twins - The matter at hand does not concern someone mentioned in the context being discussed. |
| 671. | Ewu ńbẹ l'óko Lóńgẹ́; Lóńgẹ́ pāpā Ewu ni | Danger exists in Lóńgẹ́'s farm; Lóńgẹ́ himself is a Threat - Watch out, you're being surrounded on |

| | | |
|---|---|---|
| | | all sides by danger; likely by lions in sheep's' clothing i.e. your own family and friends cannot be ruled out. |
| 672. | Ewúrẹ́ Ilé kò ní òun ò b'ágùtàn ṣe, àfi tí Àgùtán bá ní Ìyá òun ò bí Dúdú! | The domestic goat has not refused to deal with the lamb, except if the lamb affirms that its mother never birthed a black lamb<br>- The players in the story have not refused to do things together as long as the latter does not insult the former. |
| 673. | Ewúrẹ́ Ilé t'ó ń f'ojú d'ọdẹ | The domestic goat that underrates the bush hunter<br>- Too much familiarity breeds contempt. |
| 674. | Ewúrẹ́ ń w'alápatà bíi k'ó kú, Àgùtàn ń w'alápatà bíi k'ó kú; b'Ólóun Ò bá pa mí, mi ò sháà ní p'araà mi | The goat is eyeing the butcher as if he should croak, the sheep is eyeing the butcher as if he should die; if God doesn't kill me, I will not kill myself<br>- You cannot wish me away!<br>- I will only go when it's my time, not before! |
| 675. | Ewúrẹ́ ò l'óun ò ṣ'ọmọ Ìyá Àgùtàn; Àgùtàn l'ó b'ojú w'ẹ̀hìn t'ó ní Ìyá òun ò bí dúdú | The goat did not say it wouldn't be an offspring of a ewe; it was the lamb that looked backwards and declared that its mother did not birth a black [lamb]<br>- You are the one who has let everyone down - you are the betrayer! |
| 676. | Ewúrẹ́ t'ó jẹ lọ tí 'ò padà wá'lé, Igi tí wọ́n bá rí ni nwọ́n fi ń na irú Ewúrẹ́ bẹ́ẹ̀ l'ójà | The goat that has roamed away and doesn't return home, any kind of stick is what anyone will use to beat the goat in the market (as it appears the goat belongs to no one)<br>- Example: An adolescent who leaves home without reason and does not return to his parents' home [when he does come back to town] but is found wandering the streets will get tongue-lashing from all sorts of people;<br>- Hardly anyone respects this person anymore. |
| 677. | Ewúrẹ́ t'ó wọ'lé Alágídí ni, Olówó ẹ̀ á ní Sùúrù | The goat that sneaks into the house of Alágídí (an intractably-bullish man), the owner may need to exercise some |

| | | |
|---|---|---|
| | | patience<br>- The issue on the ground may require a bit of tact for if care is not taken, the guy to placate may scupper things and worsen the situation. |
| 678. | Ewúrẹ́ t'ó wọ'lé Ìyá Aláwo, Ọ̀rọ́ d'ọ̀rọ̀ Ẹ̀bẹ̀, Ọ̀rọ́ d'ọ̀rọ̀ ọ Sùúrù | A goat that enters the shop of the bone china dish seller, the matter becomes a delicate suppliant, the matter becomes a trial for patience and tact. This is because if the animal gets frightened, it might just destroy all those nice fragile but expensive wares<br>- The matter cannot be rushed; it requires extraordinary imperturbability, calmness and negotiation. |
| 679. | Èyí tí 'ò yée yín pọ̀ ju Èyí t'ó yée yín lọ, tàbí...<br>Èyí tí 'ò yé ẹ é pọ̀ ju Èyí t'ó yé ẹ lọ | What you don't understand is a lot more than what you do understand<br>- You've still got a lot to learn.<br>Please see the "Personal Pronouns" page.. |
| 680. | Ẹyin kété l'ọ̀fọ̀ ń ṣẹ̀ | The solitary egg is the one that suffers bereavement<br>- In the narrative, there's really nothing to worry about as the speaker has covered all angles and won't be alone in the struggle. |
| 681. | Ẹyin l'ó ń d'àkùkọ | It's eggs that turn into roosters<br>- The kids of today are tomorrow's leaders. |
| 682. | Ẹ̀yin l'ẹ p'olè wá jà; Ẹ̀yin nã l'ẹ p'olóko wá mu | You were the ones that invited the thief to come and steal [in the farm]; you were also the ones that called the farmer to come and catch him red-handed<br>- You were staunch supporters of the cause we are agitating for, you were the very traitors who called the authorities to come and arrest the leaders;<br>- You're being too-faced. |
| 683. | Ẹyín mú j'abẹ lọ | Teeth are sharper than a blade<br>- If you toy with me, you'll regret it. |
| 684. | Ẹ̀yìn t'ó bá máa d'epo, áá f'ara w'iná. | The palm fruits that are going to become palm oil will go through fire |

| | | - To prosper and achieve the success you crave, you may have to go through a lot of hardship. |
|---|---|---|
| 685. | F'òré e hàn mi kí nso fún e Irú Ènìà tí o jé | Show me your friends so I can tell you what kind of person you are. |
| 686. | Fálànà gbó tìe, t'ara Eni l'àá gbó | Fálànà [John Doe in this analogy] hearken unto yours, one pays attention to one's own problems<br>- Mind your own business;<br>- Listen to the plight of your own people, not issues concerning others. |
| 687. | Fìlà funfun ò şeé dé jù l'éèrùn | A white cap is not appropriate to be worn during the dry season [it collects so much brown dust blown by winds]<br>- Being aware of the current situation, you should have chosen a different tack. |
| 688. | Gb'ómo wá kí mi, Owó níí ná'ni | Requesting new parents to 'visit me with your newborn' costs [the host requesting the visit] money<br>- You can't request something to be done without it costing you;<br>- You can't make demands without making some kind of payment for the privilege. |
| 689. | Gbà ràn mí d'elérù; t'ilé Ogé t'óge é şe | Holding a cargo for someone temporarily, you're now claiming ownership of the consignment; the home chores of a maiden is enough to keep her busy<br>- This is a rebuke to someone that, "what's the issue got to do with you?"<br>- Simply put, everyone should mind their business! |
| 690. | Gbà rànmí d'elérù, Ajínidó d'oko Eni | Holding [an item] for me has made the keeper the 'load-owner' [has usurped ownership], the secret lover has somehow become the husband<br>- What business is it of yours involving yourself with things that don't concern you?<br>- Mind your business! |
| 691. | Gba Wèrè, mi ò gba Wèrè; Enu Eni l'a fi ń ko "mi ò je" | Accept madness, I'll not accept madness; it's one's mouth that one uses to say "I |

| | | |
|---|---|---|
| | | don't want to eat"<br>- Only you know what you want, what you can and can't accept. |
| 692. | Gbajúmọ̀n ìí wá nkan tì | A celebrity never searches for something and not find it<br>- You'll eventually find what you are seeking. |
| 693. | Gbañgbá d'ẹkùn, Kederé bẹ́ẹ́ wò | Trust has become the tiger, Honesty inspected it<br>- It's been revealed that the person or entity you trusted wholeheartedly has been a great deceiver after all, but honesty and justice unmasked their deceit;<br>- In other words, the truth is out. |
| 694. | Gbẹ̀dẹ̀ níí rọ'kókò l'ágbàlá | Effortlessly swing the cocoyam [leaves] in the backyard<br>- An encouraging phrase to a woman who is about to give birth that she'll deliver her baby painlessly. |
| 695. | Gbẹgẹdẹ́ ti gb'iná tán k'á tó máa w'ómi kiri | Everything was already engulfed in flames before we started looking for water<br>- This idiom is to rue the fact that a negative deed has been done - the unthinkable has already happened. |
| 696. | Gbe'rin ngò gbe'rin ín ṣe dé'bii Sòkòtòo Baba ẹ l'o wọ̀ yĩ? | Sing, I won't sing along; how did it escalate to "it's your dad's pants you are wearing?"<br>- What are we saying, and what are you saying?<br>- Don't digress and stick to the point! |
| 697. | Gbogbo Aṣo kọ́ là nsá l'óòrùn | It's not all laundry that we air in the sun<br>- It's not everything that can be discussed openly for everyone to hear. |
| 698. | Gbogbo Ẹja l'ó ń gb'ódò; Ẹni tí 'ó fií Òkè l'ó wà | All fishes live in the river; the fisherman that'll catch them is above [stands on the river bank]<br>- You and your comrades are agitating [for a cause]; the few people who are going to reap the reward of your hard work are not getting their hands dirty. Be cautious! |

| | | |
|---|---|---|
| 699. | Gbogbo Ẹni l'ó mọn Gbajúmọn; Ẹni mélõ ni Gbajúmọ̀n ọ́n mọ̀n? | Everyone recognizes the celebrity, how many people does the celebrity know?<br>- You may know of someone through various means, but he may in turn never have heard of you. |
| 700. | Gbogbo Ohun t'énìà-án bá ṣe l'énī, Ìtàn ni l'ọ́la | All the things that someone does today, it is history tomorrow<br>- You write your own story. |
| 701. | Gèlè ò dùn bíi k'á mọ̀n-ọ́n wé, k'á mọ̀n-ọ́n wé ò dàbíi k'ó y'ẹni | Head scarf is not as pleasurable as knowing how to tie one, knowing how to tie one pales beside it fitting the wearer<br>- Having something is not like knowing how to do something, knowing how to do something pales beside making it universally usable and accepted. |
| 702. | Ìbànújé ò sí f'ẹni t'éyín è ẹ́ bá ta s'íta. T'ó bá ń sun'kún, nwọ́n á rò pé ó ń r'ẹ́rïn ni; t'ó bá ń r'ẹ́rïn, nwọ́n á rò pé ó ń sun'kún ni | There's no appearance of sadness for he whose teeth are bucked. When he's crying, people will think he's laughing; when he's laughing, everyone will think he's crying<br>- Appearances are usually deceptive. |
| 703. | Ìbẹ̀rẹ̀ kìí ṣ'on'íṣẹ́; Ẹní bá ṣé d'ópin òun l'a ó gbà là | Pioneers are not the real workers; those who carry it to fruition are those that will be saved<br>- The initiators just give an idea; those who through their perseverance endure the challenges till final resolution are those that reap the rewards;<br>- "But he that shall endure unto the end, the same shall be saved." (Matthew 24:13). |
| 704. | Ìbẹ̀rù Ejò ni ò kì ń jẹ k'ọ́n tẹ Ọmọ Ejò mọ́n'lẹ̀ | It's essentially the fear of snakes that people don't step on snakelets<br>- The fear of repercussion or retaliation is what forestalls people from taking advantage of the defenseless. For example, no country messes with American citizens abroad. |
| 705. | Ibi Aiyé bá bá'ni la gbé ń jẹ ẹ́ | Where life finds one, is where one enjoys it<br>- Enjoyment and happiness is relative. |

| 706. | Ibi Ènìyán bá ti gun'gi nã l'ó ti ń sọ̀ | Where one climbs up a tree is where one passes when descending<br>- Where you put your money is where you'll find it;<br>- Where you've built your house is where you'll live. |
|---|---|---|
| 707. | Ibi gbogbo lati ń kó Adìẹ Alẹ́ | It's relatively everywhere that we shoo chickens to roost in coops at night<br>- The way some things are done in one part of the world may not be wholly exclusive to that region alone;<br>- There's nothing new under the sun. |
| 708. | Ibi gẹ̀rẹ̀jẹ̀ l'à ń b'ágbà | It is in an exalted place that we find the elderly [the wise]<br>- The emotion or behavior you are exhibiting is beneath someone of your status. |
| 709. | Ibi Lékēlékē ń gbe f'ọṣọ, Ẹiyẹ Àparò ò lè mọn'bẹ̀ | Where egrets wash their clothes, the bush-fowl bird cannot get there<br>- Where these great egrets get their white plumes is a secret that bush-fowls can't figure out;<br>- Where the secret of success of the subject in a perspective is, no one can decipher it. |
| 710. | Ibi táa bá f'ẹlẹ́mọ̀ṣọ́ ṣọ́, Ibẹ̀ l'ó ńṣọ́ | The place we entrust to Ẹlẹ́mọ̀ṣọ́ to guard is where he watches over<br>- What you've been asked to do is what you should concentrate on. In other words, mind your business. |
| 711. | Ibi táa bá r'oko sí l'àá f'àbọ̀ sí | Where we left off tilling the land is where we return to resume the task<br>- We have to restart the project where we left off before we were interrupted. |
| 712. | Ibi t'a bá wí sí kọ́ l'àá kú sí | The venue where we speak is not where we die<br>- What you think you will do after a certain event is not usually what you do;<br>- There're always other circumstances you have not factored in that just might upset things. |

| | | |
|---|---|---|
| 713. | Ibi táà ńlọ ò jìnà; Ibi t'a ńyà yî ṣe Kókó | Our destination is not far; the stopovers we're making are essential<br>- Our end-point [goal] is within our grasp but the few things that seem to be causing a delay are very important to our sustainability when we do get there. |
| 714. | Ibi táà ńrè ò pẹ́ mọ́n; Ibi t'a ti ń bọ̀ l'ó jìnà | Where we are heading is in sight; whence we came is what is far<br>- Our Promised Land approaches; the difficult times are now behind us. |
| 715. | Ibi tẹ́ẹ f'ojú sí, Ọ̀nà ò gba'bẹ̀<br>Ibi táa f'ojú sí, Ọ̀nà ò gba'bẹ̀<br>Ibi t'ọn f'ojú sí Ọ̀nà ò gba'bẹ̀ | Where you have set your eyes, the path does not lead there<br>Where we have set our eyes, the path does not lead there<br>Where they have set their eyes, there is no path<br>- It didn't happen where you thought it was going to happen; it took a different route;<br>- What we had expected is not what eventually came to pass;<br>- It was a completely different outcome than what everyone had predicted;<br>- The shotcut they're expecting is but a dead end. |
| 716. | Ibi t'ènìyán bá ṣe sí, Ibẹ̀ níí jẹ sí | Where one has labored is where he'll eat<br>- You reap what you sow. |
| 717. | Ibi t'òò sọ dé, ó yé mi ju bẹ́ẹ lọ | Where you haven't expressed it to, I understand it far beyond the point<br>- I quite understand the implication of your narrative. |
| 718. | Ibi t'órí bá dá'ni sí l'àá gbé | Where the head has created someone is where we live<br>- Where your spirit has chosen to take you is where you stay. |
| 719. | Ibi tí Igi Ọ̀gẹ̀dẹ̀ bá wó sí, Ibẹ̀ níí rà sí | The very spot the banana tree falls is where it decomposes<br>- Where one commits a crime is where one is apprehended. |
| 720. | Ibi tíò s'ílẹ̀ l'a ti ń j'iyàn ìjà | Where there's no ground is where we argue about [our prowess in] fights |

|   |   | - The situation you used to brag of being capable of handling when it was not yet an issue is now rearing its head again - let's revisit and see what you're really made of now.<br>- Let's see if you can really do what you used to boast you could do if you had half a chance;<br>- This is a sort of challenge. |
|---|---|---|
| 721. | Ibi t'ó bá dùn l'èṣù ú máa ń fẹ́ẹ́ dán-án wò | Where there's joy is where the devil likes to test<br>- Keep your wits about you - don't let anything distract you to jeopardize things!<br>- You know what you've got going, so do not pay attention to any taunts! |
| 722. | Ibi t'ó bá dùn l'eṣú máa ń wọ | Where there's joy is where the devil enters<br>- The devil delights in nothing but disharmony and strife. |
| 723. | Ibi t'ó bá f'iyọ̀ọ́ ẹ̀ sí l'ó ti ń ṣ'omi | The spot where he left his salt is where it saturates with moisture<br>- He doesn't overstep his boundaries. |
| 724. | Ibi t'ó bá le l'à ń b'ọ́mọkùnrin | Wherever is tough is where you find a young man<br>- During tough times is when you know who is a fighter. |
| 725. | Ibi t'ó bá wu Ẹ̀fùùfù-lẹ̀lẹ̀ l'ó ń da'rí Ewéko-ìgbẹ́ sí | Anywhere the light wind likes is where it directs [blows] the leaves of the forest<br>- Do as you please with me/us;<br>- Your wish is my/our command. |
| 726. | Ibi t'ónílé bá f'ojú Ọ̀nà sí l'àlejò ń tọ̀ | The pathway created by the home owner is where the visitors walk on<br>- The rules laid down by the homeowner is what the guest(s) follow and obey;<br>- The man has put his money where his mouth is, so let him have it his way. |
| 727. | Ìbínú lí mọ̀n p'ólówó òun ò l'ẹ́sẹ̀ ńlẹ̀ | Anger does not know that its 'owner' [he who is angry] doesn't have a foot on the ground [does not have power or know any influential person]<br>- Rage or irritation does not know that |

| | | |
|---|---|---|
| | | whoever has it does not have someone on whom to rely in case he lets the rage get the better of him and he acts out his anger;<br>- The perpetrator of a violence that originated from anger won't have anyone to count on after the dust has settled [i.e. after he's acted out what the anger had pushed him to do]. |
| 728. | Idà Awun l'a fi ń p'awun | The tortoise's sword is what we use to kill the tortoise<br>- With your own trickery will you be deceived;<br>- You'll be hoisted by your own petard. |
| 729. | Idà ni, tí 'ò lè b'àkọ̀ jẹ́ láíláí | The person in reference is a sword that can never spoil its scabbard<br>- A patriot that can never betray his beloved fatherland, by deed or by mouth. |
| 730. | Idà ò l'éèkù táa fi ń r'ọrí | A sword has no hilt that can take the place of a pillow at night<br>- There's no retreat from the decision that has been taken. |
| 731. | Ìdágìrì kìí dá'mọ l'éhìn Ẹkùn | Mayhem does not discourage a pack of cubs trailing behind a tiger<br>- No matter what you throw at us, we'll still be here undaunted [because of whom we rely on]. |
| 732. | Ìdákẹ́ jẹ́ẹ́ n'ìdáhùn Aṣiwèrè; bí bẹ́ẹ̀ kọ́, Wèrè á di méjì l'ójà Ọba | Utter silence is enough for an insane person; otherwise, those with the malady could double [as it might be difficult to distinguish the normal person from the schizophrenic individual as they argue] in the king's market<br>- Silence is enough for a fool. |
| 733. | Ìdí Iṣẹ́ Ẹni l'a ti ń m'ẹni l'ọ́lẹ | At one's profession is where it becomes very plain to everyone if one is really lazy or hardworking<br>- If you're really lazy, you will not be able to hide the fact when people start giving you jobs/projects;<br>- One might say this to demonstrate that |

| | | they are up to the task being discussed. |
|---|---|---|
| 734. | Ìdúró ò sí, Ìbẹ̀rẹ̀ ò sí f'ẹ́ni t'ó bá gb'ódó mì | The thought of standing or bending does not exist for someone who has swallowed a wooden mortar/pestle<br>- There's no peace for he who has done what the person in the narrative has done. |
| 735. | Ìdúró ò sí, Ìbẹ̀rẹ̀ ò sí f'ẹ́ni t'ó gbé'ná rù | Waiting or crouching is not a luxury for someone with a bowl of fire on his head<br>- Someone with a big problem does not have the time to relax. |
| 736. | Ifá n'iyì Ọdẹ, Ẹ̀jẹ̀ n'iyì Oògùn | Ifá is the pride of a hunter, blood is the dignity of juju [voodoo]<br>- Do what you need to do. |
| 737. | Ìfun'ra l'òògùn Àgbà | Vigilance is the superior medicine/juju<br>- Watchfulness is the greater weapon of protection. |
| 738. | Ìgbà Ara l'àá bú'ra | It's the time of 'body' that we swear<br>- Make hay while the sun shines;<br>- When it's time to do something, do it; don't tarry. |
| 739. | Igba Eṣinṣin kìí dè'nà án d'ọwọ̀ | Two hundred flies cannot waylay a broom<br>- Whatever opponents may throw at the person being referred to, he'll still forge ahead, because it is his destiny. |
| 740. | Igba Ewé Ìbá ò tó pọ́n'kọ | Two hundred Ìbá leaves are not enough to wrap hardened corn-pap<br>- There's not enough of us to face the problem on the ground. |
| 741. | Ìgbà Ìpọ́njú l'à ń m'ọ̀rẹ́ | During the time of hardship is when you really know who your friends are. |
| 742. | Igbá l'à ń pa, a ìí p'àwo | It's calabash that we kill, not a china-plate<br>- This is a belligerent utterance that rather than me, it will be someone else;<br>- I'm too tough for that kind of thing to faze me. |
| 743. | Ìgbà ò lọ bí Òréré | Time doesn't go like an Open Expanse of Space<br>- Time is not as wide as an open expanse of space without limit;<br>- In other words, time waits for no one. |
| 744. | Igba Ọdún, Ọdún kan ni | Two hundred years, it's one year |

| | | |
|---|---|---|
| | | - The names of things do not mean much, they are what they are;<br>- This Yorùbá proverb is also similar to a popular adage from William Shakespeare's play Romeo and Juliet: "A rose by any other name would smell as sweet." |
| 745. | Ìgbà t'ọ́n bá ní k'ó má jà l'ó ńy'ọ̀bẹ | When they say he should cease fighting is when he draws a knife<br>- After an issue has been resolved, out he comes with another accusation;<br>- When someone has offered you olive branch, don't overdo things and start another fight. Let bygones be bygones. |
| 746. | Igbá t'ó tó Igbá l'ó ńṣe Baálẹ̀ Agbọ́nmi | A scooping-calabash that is up to the Calabash is the overseer of water scoopers / dredgers<br>- He who is worth his bottle is the one that rises to the call of duty. |
| 747. | Ìgbà yī l'àárọ̀! | This period [now] is the morning<br>- This is a lament to signify "It should have happened sooner."<br>- So, you're just arriving?<br>- Mh-mmm - it's about time..! |
| 748. | Igbáa Pẹ̀lẹ́ kan kìí fọ́; Àwo Pẹ̀lẹ́ kan ìí fàya bọ̀ọ̀rọ̀ | A 'Pẹ̀lẹ́' [calm, easy] calabash never shatters; a 'Pẹ̀lẹ́' bone china plate never cracks easily either<br>- Approach and do things with tranquility. |
| 749. | Ìgbàt'íjó bá ńyẹ Ọmọlúwàbí l'ó ń kúrò l'ójú Agbo | It's when the sensible man's dance is going great he leaves the dance hall<br>- Quit while [one] is ahead;<br>- Don't try to improve on something that is already accomplished;<br>- Implies that further action runs the risk of spoiling things, i.e. fine-tuning is unnecessary. |
| 750. | Ìgbẹ́ ò jọ Ẹni t'ó ṣú | Excreta doesn't look like the person who defecated it<br>- You can't really tell who is who;<br>- Your guess is as good as mine. |
| 751. | Ìgbẹ̀hìn l'aláyò ńta | It's towards the end of a match that champions play their game |

| | | |
|---|---|---|
| | | - The greatest players/gamblers always never tip their hand / ace until when the game is almost over. |
| 752. | Ìgbẹ̀hin l'ó ń y'ólókũ Àdá | It's during the epilogue that the man with the blunt cutlass appreciates<br>- The child that refuses to get an education even when it's offered freely to him but would rather play around, will one day realize that it was for his own good that education was being pushed at him;<br>- He who fails to prepare has inadvertently prepared to fail. |
| 753. | Ìgbéraga níí ṣ'íwájú Ìparun | Pride comes before a fall. |
| 754. | Igbónígbó l'à ń gb'óhùn-un Sokodìro | The deepest forest is where we hear the voice of a kingfish<br>- We do not wish to have this type of trouble anymore! |
| 755. | Igí dá, Ẹiyẹ́ fò | The tree falls, birds fly away<br>- When you're in dire straits, friends and lovers desert you. |
| 756. | Igi Ganganran má gũn mi l'ójú, Òkèèrè l'a ti ńwòó | Not wishing for the extended tree stem that's sticking out to stab one in the eye, one would usually notice it from afar as he approaches<br>- If someone or something were to become a problem in the near future, you would probably have seen the warning signs. |
| 757. | Igi kan ìí dá'gbó ṣe | A tree does not a forest make<br>- The situation on the ground requires more'n one solution;<br>- Two heads are better than one. |
| 758. | Igi Ọ̀báọ̀nà níí gba'kú Ìyeyè é kú | It's the tree at Ọ̀báọ̀nà that dies in place of Ìyeyè [olive tree]<br>- It's someone else that's going to go down in place of the powerful man who is facing disastrous trouble. |
| 759. | Igi Ọ̀mọ̀n l'ó ń sìn'kú Ìrókò | It is the Ọ̀mọ̀n tree that buries the carcass of the Ìrókò tree<br>- The speaker is casting himself as the |

| | | |
|---|---|---|
| | | "knowledge" tree of life that'll see the end of his enemies. |
| 760. | Igi táa bá f'ojú ré'nà, òun l'ó ń wọ'ni l'ójú | The tree branch that we underestimate when clearing a path in the bush is the one that pokes one in the eyes<br>- This proverb is similar to what Jesus said: "The stone that the builders rejected has become the cornerstone;" although Jesus was referring to Himself. (Matt 21:42). |
| 761. | Igi t'ó bá pẹ́ l'óko níí h'olú; bí Àgbàdó bá pẹ́ k'ó tó y'ọmọ l'ẹ́gàn, áá di Koriko | The tree that endures longest in the farm is the one that grows mushrooms; if the maize delays in sprouting its babies in the bush, it might become grass<br>- This is an allegorical warning to workers in a factory or staff in an organization hinting that whoever outlives their usefulness will become part of the furniture or become forgotten. |
| 762. | Ihun tí ń w'ará Aiyé nã ń w'ará Ọ̀run | The objects that people on earth covet are equally craved by those in heaven<br>- This is a scornful expression to mortify certain individual(s) trying to acquire some things that are reasonably beyond their means or position. |
| 763. | Ihun t'ó dáa nã ń w'ọ̀lẹ! | What is good is also appealing to a sluggard<br>- Recognize your standard and stay within it! |
| 764. | Ìjà Ìlara ò tán bọ̀rọ̀; à ń jù wọ́n ò ṣeé wí l'ẹ́jọ́ | Malicious fight of envy does not end peacefully; "we are progressing" cannot be litigated against<br>- The envy of a progressive and prosperous society/people does not evaporate overnight. |
| 765. | Ìjà l'ó dé t'órín d'òwe | It was the tiff that broke out that made songs sound like proverbs<br>- It was a row that made friends distrust each other and no longer see eye to eye; that has turned friends into foes. |
| 766. | Ìjáfará l'éwu | Carelessness has danger<br>- Not being careful and cautious is |

| | | |
|---|---|---|
| | | dangerous;<br>- Lack of attention has hazards coded into it. |
| 767. | Ìjàkadì l'orò Ọ̀ffà | Wrestling is the idol-god of Offa [in Kwara State, Nigeria]<br>- To get a foot in the door, I'm afraid some dirty fighting is what you may have to consider;<br>- To get what you want from this people [or group or someone], this is the only language they understand, I'm afraid. |
| 768. | Ìjàkùmọ̀n kìí rìn'de Ọ̀sãn, Ẹni a bí ire niò gbọdọ̀ rìn'ru | A wild beast doesn't walk in the afternoon, a well-born is the one that must not walk around in the night<br>- You are the one who needs to recognize the proper decorum that is expected of you. |
| 769. | Ìjàkùmọ̀n lè mi, mi ò ń ṣ'ẹran Ìlú kan | I am a wild beast, I am not a one-town animal<br>- No one can lay claim to me. |
| 770. | Ìjánu t'ọ́n kó sí Ẹṣin l'ẹ́nu, Kádàrá ni | The bridle attached to a horse's muzzle is its destiny<br>- The limitations placed on certain people at birth, either by virtue of their birth race or origin, stay with them through their lifetime;<br>- You might complain, but you're stuck in your situation, I'm afraid. |
| 771. | Ìjẹ tí wọ́n jẹ Tẹ̀tẹ̀, Ẹnìkan ò gbọdọ̀ jẹ Dágunró bẹ́ẹ̀; t'ó bá ṣèṣì jẹ Dágunró, ẹ sọ fun wípé Ọ̀run l'ààlà | The way they eat Tẹ̀tẹ̀ (a type of West African spinach), no one dares eat Dágunró (a Nigerian spinach that if eaten in excess can be lethal) in similar quantity; if anyone mistakenly eats Dágunró, tell them that Heaven is the demarcation<br>- This is an allegorical warning to desist from treating others badly with impunity; one day, you might take it too far and commit a similar egregious act to the wrong person who wouldn't accept apologies. |
| 772. | Ìjẹ́rìí Aiyé ni t'ọjọ́ Àgbéǹde | Witnessing of life is that of the day of pre- |

| | | |
|---|---|---|
| | | existent hypostasis [individual existence]<br>- This metaphor indicates there is corroborating evidence right here [in the discourse]. |
| 773. | Ìjì t'ó dààmú Ológì í ti sọ Elélùbọ́ di òfò! | The tempest that affected the one selling corn-pap, has rendered the yam flour seller empty!<br>- What has affected the bigwigs, the common folks had better watch out!<br>- You'd better pay attention so you too don't meet the same fate! |
| 774. | Ijó Ogún bá le l'à ń n'íran Alágídí Ọmọ | When the battle is hard is when we remember the headstrong son<br>- A suffering people need intrepid and altruistic citizens who would stick their necks out in times of conflict. |
| 775. | Ijó t'áa bá r'íbi ni Ibi ń wọ'lẹ | The day we see evil is when evil sinks into the ground<br>- The day we identify the cause of a problem is the day we put a stop to it. |
| 776. | Ijó tí Wèré bá mọ̀n pé Ohun t'ó ńs'òun ò dáa, ijó nã l'ó ń gbádùn | The day a madman becomes aware that what's been afflicting him is not a good thing, that's the very day he's healed<br>- When an evil man does a soul-searching and accepts that what he's been doing is sinful, is the day he becomes redeemed. |
| 777. | Ìka t'ó bá ṣẹ l'ọbá ń gé | It's the finger that has offended that the king snips off<br>- He who commits a felony is the one that gets punished. |
| 778. | Ìka t'ó bá tọ́ s'ímú l'a fi ń ro'mú | The finger that is appropriate to the nose is the one we use to pick the nose with<br>- You don't ask someone to do something that is patronizing to their status OR disrespect someone with such standing in the community with such request. |
| 779. | Ìkán jù'kan, òun l'àjẹ́ fi ń sa f'ólè; tí Àjẹ́ bá gb'éiyẹ Inú è s'ílẹ̀, Olé á gbe! | One is superior to the other, hence a witch runs away from a thief; if the witch drops her lightning bird on the floor, the thief will steal it!<br>- Don't underestimate your opponent(s)! |

| 780. | Ìkàn-ǹkan l'àá yọ'sẹ̀ l'ẹ́kù | One after the other do we remove our feet from palm kernel vats<br>- Resolve one issue before starting on another. |
|---|---|---|
| 781. | Ìkọ́ kìí kọ́ Baala, Ìkọ́ kìí k'éjò l'ọ́nà | No trap ensnares the 'careful one,' no trap ensnares the snake on its path<br>- No obstacle shall come in your path. |
| 782. | Ìkọjá Àyè òun l'orun orí Kẹ̀kẹ́ | Testing the limits of fundamental human nature is dozing on a bicycle [while riding it]<br>- You are tempting fate! |
| 783. | Ìkòkò ò ní gb'omi, k'ó gb'ẹyìn | The earthen pot will not hold water and hold palm fruits<br>- Too many cooks spoil the broth;<br>- It's either you or me;<br>- Two masters cannot captain a ship. |
| 784. | Ikú fẹ́ẹ́ p'alápatà, ó ń kígbe; Ọmọ Ẹranko t'ó ti dál'óró ńkọ́? | The butcher is being stalked by a death threat and he goes screaming. What about all the animals he had mercilessly butchered in his time?<br>- So you don't like the vile things you have inflicted onto others with impunity to be visited on you too? |
| 785. | Ìkòkò t'ó máa j'ata, Ìdí ẹ á gbóná | The pot that wants to feed on pepper, its bottom will suffer searing heat<br>- If you intend to pursue this line or course of action, be ready for the hardship and hazard that is attached to it. |
| 786. | Ikú j'orun lọ | Demise is senior to sleep<br>- This matter is worse than you can possibly imagine!<br>- Death is more final [worse] than sleep. |
| 787. | Ikú l'ó m'éja ká kò | It's death that made the fish bend<br>- It's circumstances that created this undesirable situation. |
| 788. | Ikú ò kì ń p'ẹtà l'ójú'ran | Death does not kill a dingo in the arena<br>- Nothing will happen to the speaker or whom the adage is in reference of. |
| 789. | Ikú Ogun níí p'akínkanjú, Ikú Odò níí p'òmùwẹ̀, Òwò tí Àdá bá mọ̀n l'ó ń ká Àdá l'éyín | Death on the battlefield is what kills the brave, death from drowning is what kills the swimmer, the trade that a cutlass is |

| | | |
|---|---|---|
| | | good at is what makes a cutlass lose its teeth [dulls its sharpness]<br>- It's their stock in trade; they live and die by it;<br>- It's occupational hazard. |
| 790. | Ikú Ọmọ l'ó ńpa Aiyétalẹ̀ | The death from the troubles that chicks bring home is what kills the mother-bird<br>- Discipline your child, and he will give you rest and bring you happiness (Prov 29:17). |
| 791. | Ikú tí 'ò bá pa'ni, t'ó bá shí'ni ní Fìlà, ó yẹ k'a ma dúpẹ́ ni | The death that ought to kill someone, if it only knocked off their cap, we should be giving thanks<br>- It could have been worse. |
| 792. | Ikú t'ó p'ojúgbà Ẹni, Òwe l'ó ńpa fún'ni | The death that kills one's bodyguard is talking proverbially to the person<br>- Said by someone witnessing an ex-benefactor (or an ex-lover) of another being mistreated by the person and muses that they too might get the same ill-treatment someday, so they'd better watch out;<br>- An observation that the ill-treatment one is witnessing can be meted out to them also in the near future. |
| 793. | Ikú wọ'lé, Aworó bá ńsá; Alákããràgá Ọlọ́un l'ó ń ṣ'àánú Òlẹ́ | Death enters, Emptiness takes to its heels; only a fake god will show mercy to the idle man<br>- The man in question who is planning on giving a renowned loafer some money has nothing better to do with his wealth. |
| 794. | Ikú yá j'ẹ̀sín lọ | Death is more honorable than shame. |
| 795. | Ikún ń j'ògèdè, Ikún ń rè'dí, Ikún ò mònpé Ohun t'ó dún l'ó ń pa'ni | The chipmunk is eating a banana, the chipmunk is swinging its butt, the chipmunk does not know that sweet things are what kill<br>- They didn't realize that deadly things are often [deceptively] enticing. |
| 796. | Ilá t'ó bá kó a máa pa Ọ̀bẹ l'ẹnu | Okra that is overripe and tough can dull a knife<br>- In this idiom, one needs to tread carefully around this entity or personality. |

| | | |
|---|---|---|
| 797. | Ilé Ẹni l'a ti ńjẹ Èkúté Onídodo | It's under one's roof that one eats a rat that has a navel<br>- One does what one pleases in one's own yard. |
| 798. | Ilé Ẹni l'àá kọ́kọ́ ṣe k'á tó ṣe Ìgboro | It's one's house that we "do" first before we "do" town<br>- Put your house in order first before you go to town to have fun;<br>- Charity begins at home. |
| 799. | Ilé Koko nii t'agbe | Ilé Koko [home-direct] is the rooster's<br>- I'm home-bound and, to avoid this danger, will tarry no longer;<br>- This could be a wish that whoever the maxim is intended for will succeed in getting home from wherever a pandemonium is happening. |
| 800. | Ilé l'a ti ń kó Ẹ̀ṣọ́ r'òde | It's from home we dress up in full regalia before stepping out in public to show off our costume<br>- In a nutshell, charity begins at home. |
| 801. | Ilé l'àá wò k'á tó s'ọmọ l'órúkọ | It's the home we look at first before naming a child<br>- It's the state of the family situation we take cognizance of first before we make a tough decision/call. |
| 802. | Ilé l'adìẹ ò ti n'íyì | It is home that a fowl has no value<br>- It's among your kith and kin that you appear not to have merit;<br>- This is similar to a verse in the Bible: (Mark 6:4) - But Jesus said unto them, "A prophet is not without honor, but in his own country, and among his own kin, and in his own house." |
| 803. | Ilé l'òòtà ń j'ókõ dè'dí | It's home the seat waits for the bottom<br>- Home furniture always waits for people [bottom] to sit in it;<br>- The law will wait for the fugitive to return home to face the music. |
| 804. | Ilé Ọba ńlé, Ilé Ọba l'óko ni; Etí máa k'etí | The king's house in town is also the king's house in the woods; ears will touch ears<br>- The word will come out, circulate itself, |

| | | |
|---|---|---|
| | | and it will not be difficult to get the community/people organized and mobilized for the cause in question;<br>- Walls have ears; the matter will be heard by everyone. |
| 805. | Ilé Ọba t'ó jó, Ẹwà l'ó bù kun | The burning of the palace has only added more beauty to it<br>- The evil deed done to us has only strengthened us. |
| 806. | Ilé Ọlá, ilée Wàhálà ni | House of wealth is a house of commotion<br>- There are so many problems in being wealthy. |
| 807. | Ilé Ọlọ́mọ mi ni nma kú sí, Òṣì l'ó fi ń ta'ni; Ìyà l'ó dẹ̀ ń kó bá'àyàn | The house of my baby father is where I'll die, mental indigence is what it afflicts one with; anguish is also part and parcel of it<br>- This expression is intended for a stubborn wife who offers excuses for her husband's philandering [because she fears being divorced by the husband]. |
| 808. | Ilé táa bá f'itọ́ mọn, Ìrì ní ó wo | The house we constructed with saliva will be imploded by dew<br>- What we have obtained by deceit or illicit means can be taken away [after proper investigation by the authorities]. |
| 809. | Ìlọ-ǹlọ l'ó dé Ìbarà Ilé; Ìbarà ìí ṣe'lé Ọlọ | Ìlọ-ǹlọ leads to Ìbarà Ilé, Ìbarà is not the home of Ọlọ. Could be a legend: A man met Ọlọ whom he decided to marry and bring to Ìbarà on the proviso that if he should find another lady he fancies to marry, he can bring her likewise to Ìbarà. Since Ọlọ herself was brought to Ìbarà as a wife, technically therefore, she's an outsider in Ìbarà<br>- Example: an African president who uses his position to concentrate the construction of major projects only in his home town/area, to benefit exclusively his ethnic group. It's the misuse of his office that makes this possible, not through his own wealth; |

|     |                                                              |                                                                                                                                                                                                                                                    |
| --- | ------------------------------------------------------------ | -------------------------------------------------------------------------------------------------------------------------------------------------------------------------------------------------------------------------------------------------- |
|     |                                                              | - Or a minister who looted his country's treasury to stash away billions of dollars in the West. It was his misuse of his position [Ìlọ-ǹlọ] that led him to this wealth [Ìbarà Ilé], not his own sweat.                                           |
| 810. | Ìlú ò lè wà l'áì l'ólórí; tí ò bá s'ólórí, Àyè Ètùtù ò sí   | A town cannot exist without a leader/head; if there were no leader, chance of sacrifice would not exist<br>- There's got to be a county/borough [elder in town] through whom things such as business registration, issuance of licenses, permits, etc. get done. |
| 811. | Ìlú Súúrú t'ó ń ṣ'ọkọ Ìlú Bàǹtà-banta                        | A tiny village that bosses a city around<br>- A small regional authority that gives a bigger authority orders in an authoritarian way that is often resisted or resented;<br>- It's a case of little kids trying to boss the big kids around;<br>- Old England probably fits this allegory. It was small, yet, with its colonies across three continents, it controlled half the world. |
| 812. | Imú n'íkà; kò jẹ́ k'a gbóõrùn Aṣebi                          | The nose is mean; it doesn't permit us to smell the evildoer<br>- For example, a home owner with CCTV surrounding his property that just got burgled but who, due to a natural disaster, momentarily lost electric power during the time of the robbery might mutter this hyperbole to rue the fact that he doesn't have the thieves on record because of the unexpected blackout. |
| 813. | Iná Ilé l'ọmọ Ẹrankó máa yá gbẹ̀hìn                          | It's the house fire that the cub of an animal will warm itself with in the end [when the animal is ensnared, killed and brought home to be roasted]<br>- The offender may run, but in the end he'll pay for his crimes when he's brought to justice. |
| 814. | Iná níí wa'tọ́ Ẹlégbin                                       | It is fire that dribbles the saliva of a dirty person                                                                                                                                                                                              |

| | | |
|---|---|---|
| | | - It is hardship that will make you sit up and fasten your belt. |
| 815. | Iná ò m'ẹni t'ó dá'un | A fire does not recognize who started it<br>- A marauding dictator that sweeps across with violent suppression of opponents may not consider those who put him in power and spare him/them. A case in point: Adolf Hitler and Josef Stalin. |
| 816. | Iná ò m'ójú Ẹni t'ó dá'un | A fire does not know the face of the person that started it<br>- A fire does not respect the fire starter. |
| 817. | Iná Orí ò níí jó'lé; Orí ò dẹ níí kún k'a p'ejò ńbẹ, Iná nã l'a ma bá ńbẹ | Head lice will not burn a house; head will not be full [of hair] that we'll find a snake there, it's lice one might find there<br>EXPLANATION:<br>Lice = **iná**<br>Fire = **iná**<br>- Whatever is coming cannot be so bad; stop fretting. |
| 818. | Iná ti d'ilẹ l'ẹ́hìn Asun'ṣu jẹ | The fire has turned to soil behind the person who roasted yam to eat<br>- Since the terrible individual has departed, things have returned to normal. |
| 819. | Inú bíbí kò kan t'àì mọn'wàá hù | Being angry has nothing to do with being unable to behave<br>- If you exhibit bad character, don't blame it on the fact that you are upset; it's because you have an innate bad behavior, period. |
| 820. | Inú dídùn l'ó ń m'óríí yá | "Sweetening" of the belly is what makes the head swell<br>- Happiness brings enthusiasm;<br>- If you made someone contented, they would cheerfully go extra lengths to grant your request and make you happy too. |
| 821. | Inú Ẹni lí dùn, k'á pá mọ́n'ra | One cannot be happy and repress it at the same time<br>- Hey, you've got to celebrate this good fortune! |
| 822. | Inú mi ni mo mọ̀n, mi ò mọn'nú Ẹlòmîn | My mind is all I know, I don't know the mind of someone else. |

| | | |
|---|---|---|
| 823. | Inú ni kiní kan Ẹiyẹ ń gbé; Ohun t'Ọlọ́un máa ṣe, kò fi han Ẹnìkan | It's inside that "something" of a bird lives; what God will do, He doesn't disclose to anyone<br>- What the subject of this proverb will do, he won't tell anyone, but one can be sure that he'll do something [usually negative]. |
| 824. | Ipa Abẹ́rẹ́ l'okùn ún tọ̀ | The path [eye] of the needle is where the thread follows<br>- The children must learn how to do things from adults because tomorrow does belong to them;<br>- It's what you teach children today they'll take with them into adulthood. |
| 825. | Ìpa táa pa Ògbèrì, aà gbọdọ̀ p'ọmọ Awo béẹ̀! | The treatment we meted out to the novice cannot be visited on the initiate<br>- What you did [and got away with] cannot be repeated here. |
| 826. | Ìpá yàtọ̀ s'ákèǹgbè | Hernia is different from a bladder<br>- The choices aren't exactly comparable. |
| 827. | Ipẹ́ Òòrẹ̀ l'ọ̀rọ̀ yī; kò ṣeé jẹ f'ájá, kò ṣeé gbémì f'ájá; kaka níí t'ajá l'ẹ́nu | The sharp quill of a porcupine is synonymous with this matter; it's not edible for a dog, it's not digestible for a dog; it's pungent in a dog's mouth<br>- This is something to avoid at all costs! |
| 828. | Ìpẹ̀ wo l'a fẹ́ ṣe f'ẹ́ni tí Kìnìún pà'ran ẹ̀? | What kind of commiseration can we express to someone whose relation has just been mauled by a lion?<br>- The situation is unacceptable; vengeance looms. |
| 829. | Ìpele-ìpele l'aṣọ Àlùbọ́sà, Ètò Ètò ni Yangan ń to'mọ tiẹ̀ | Layers and layers are the clothing of an onion, evenly-rowed is how corn/maize aligns its children [kernels]<br>- Plan and organize things properly to get the right results. |
| 830. | Ìpín Àìṣẹ̀ l'ó ń p'alárọ̀ká | The portion of innocence is what kills the slanderer<br>- Stop gossiping about people; mind your business! |
| 831. | Ìran Alákàrà ò fẹ́ k'ẹnìkejì ó dín | The lineage of àkàrà makers (àkàrà: beignets or fritters made of black-eyed beans) does not want someone else to fry |

| | | |
|---|---|---|
| | | - To whom the idiom is addressed: You don't want someone else to be more successful than you [including your family members]. |
| 832. | Ìran mẹ́ta ò kì ń t'òṣì | Three generations can't be destitute back-to-back<br>- Three generations cannot make the same mistakes as earlier generations, surely. |
| 833. | Ìràwé ìí dá'jọ́ Ilẹ̀ k'ó sùn'nà | A dead leaf never promises Land that it's coming and it sleeps on the way or path<br>- Either the speaker himself or the speaker is referring to someone who he believes never promises and fails to keep it. |
| 834. | Ìràwọ̀ Ọ̀sán ni, ó t'óhun Àperòo gbogbo Mọnríwo | It's a star that comes out in the afternoon, it's worth a head-to-head debate of all elders [think tank]<br>- It's a strange phenomenon that demands a thorough investigation. |
| 835. | Ìréjẹ ò sí n'ínú Àwòrán; bóo bá ṣe dúró l'o ṣe ma bá'ra ẹ | There's no cheating in a photograph; how you poised yourself is exactly how you'll appear<br>- Your current life is, to a large extent, the result of your past actions and choices. |
| 836. | Ìrínisí n'ìsọ ni l'ójọ́ | How someone portrays himself or how we see someone is how we treat them<br>- Appearance makes the man. |
| 837. | Ìrírí ṣ'àgbà Ọgbọ́n | Experience is the father of wisdom. |
| 838. | Irọ́ wà n'ínú Òótọ́; Òótọ́ wà n'ínú Irọ́ | There's a lie in Truth; there's Truth in a Lie<br>- There's good in Bad; there's bad in Good;<br>- What's good for the goose is good for the gander. |
| 839. | Ìròhìn ò t'áfojúbà; Ẹní bá dé'bẹ̀ l'ó lè sọ | Reports are less than seeing-with-eyes; whoever went there he only could narrate it<br>- News is not as good as being there and seeing the event unfold;<br>- Whoever visited the scene is the one that can relate the story. |
| 840. | Ìròhìn Òkè, tí ò bá lé'kan, a sì máa dín | Bush radio, if it doesn't add extra, it'll probably omit some news |

| | | |
|---|---|---|
| | | - Bush radio is not a reliable source of information;<br>- Don't rely on this individual for your source of truth or knowledge base. |
| 841. | Ìrókò ó wó s'ílé Agbẹ́dó; Iṣẹ́ di ṣíṣe | The Ìrókò tree has fallen right inside the compound of the mortar (or pestle) maker; chiseling commences, without further ado!<br>- You've got the [unexpected] break you'd been waiting for; make the most of it! |
| 842. | Ìròmìn i **yín** t'ó ńjo l'órí Omi ni, Onílù u rẹ̀ ńbẹ ńsàlẹ̀<br>Ìròmìn i **wọn** t'ó ńjo l'órí Omi ni, Onílù u rẹ̀ ńbẹ ńsàlẹ̀<br>Ìròmìn i **ẹ̀** t'ó ńjo l'órí Omi ni, Onílù u rẹ̀ ńbẹ ńsàlẹ̀<br>Ìròmìn **ẹ** t'ó ńjo l'órí Omi ni, Onílù u rẹ̀ ńbẹ ńsàlẹ̀<br>Ìròmìn **mi** t'ó ńjo l'órí Omi ni, Onílù u rẹ̀ ńbẹ ńsàlẹ̀ | Your carnival band that dances on top of the water, the drummers are [concealed] underneath<br>This proverb has been repeated in all the possible pronoun forms of the Yorùbá language. Please note that the resultant "real meaning" rendering will be different from the one given below which is for the first proverb. Thus, see the "Personal Pronouns" page for more guidance.<br>- Evidently there is some powerful individual or group backing you up behind the scene. |
| 843. | Ìrònú Oníṣègùn bíi kí gbogbo Aiyé wà l'óde Àìsàn | The thought process of a physician is like the whole world should be in one medical condition or another. This proverb is really about an egoist<br>- You're only after your own interest. |
| 844. | Irú kan-ùn kan-ùn Ọbẹ̀ẹ Gbẹ̀gìrì | The same kind [stuff] like the soup of Gbẹ̀gìrì<br>- Birds of the same feather. |
| 845. | Irú l'óun ò tẹ́ rí, à f'ìgbà t'óun dé Òkè-Ìmẹ̀sí tí wọ́n pe òun l'éegbọn | The locust bean said it had never been disgraced before in its life until it got to Òkè-Ìmẹ̀sí where they took it for a tick<br>- The person being referred to has recently experienced woeful disgrace. |
| 846. | Irú Ọlọ́run ni ò sí; Irú Ènìyán pọ̀ ju Iyanrìn l'étí Òkun | It is a kind of God that does not exist; a kind of human being like one mentioned in the narrative is more than the sands on a beach<br>- No one should think there's none like |

| | | |
|---|---|---|
| | | them on earth;<br>- Only God is one of a kind. |
| 847. | Irú wá, Ògìrì wá | Locust-beans come, fermented-corn juice come<br>- It's a situation of sorts [full of all kinds of both respectable and undesirable elements]. |
| 848. | Irun kíkún n'ìbẹ̀rẹ̀ẹ̀ Wèrè | Overgrown hair is the precursor to madness<br>- The person referred to in this allegory is exhibiting a gloomy outlook that requires attention [of his loved ones]. |
| 849. | Ìṣ'ènìà n'ìṣ'ẹranko | As it affects humans, so does it affect animals<br>- No matter who or what we are, we all feel the same sadness and joy;<br>- Could be used derogatively by someone who considers himself a high-class or wealthy individual to sneer at those 'beneath' him to say "oh, so you also like to enjoy that kind of privilege"?<br>- The common disease that is going on in the world such as the COVID-19 pandemic can be used as another example, because the suffering is relative; doesn't care who or what you are. |
| 850. | Ìsàlẹ̀ Ọrọ̀ ó l'ẹ́gbin | The bottom of wealth has filth<br>- To know how someone has accomplished some important deed, the story behind the apparent success may not be so pleasant to hear after all;<br>- Could be taken as advice to not envy anyone for what they have become, because you really do not know what they went through or what they had done or indeed how they'd suffered to get to where they are;<br>- The bottom of wealth has a can of worms. |
| 851. | Iṣẹ́ dé Ọmọ Aláṣeje, Òwò rèé Ọmọ Aláṣelà | Work arrives [hearken, you children of workers], here is business [harken, you |

| | | |
|---|---|---|
| | | children of traders]<br>- There is plenty of job and trade opportunities for everyone;<br>- There's an urgent business deal at hand that requires joint collaboration. |
| 852. | Iṣẹ́ Ìgbọ̀nsẹ̀ ni; a kìí fíí rán Ọmọ Ẹni | It's a task of toileting; we don't delegate it to one's child<br>- This is an issue that requires one's direct hands-on input. |
| 853. | Iṣẹ́ l'ó ṣeé dá ṣe, Owó ò ṣeé dá ná | A task is what one may accomplish alone, money cannot be spent alone<br>- Who has labored hard to buy his house is not going to live in it all by himself;<br>- No matter how you have suffered, when the time comes to reap the reward of your labor, there'll always be people you would share it with. |
| 854. | Iṣẹ́ táa bá f'ófin l'òfín ńṣe | The assignment we charge the Law with is what the Law does<br>- This adage smacks of an expectation of what had been set in motion to happen;<br>- It does exactly what it says on the tin. |
| 855. | Iṣẹ́ tí a bá rán Ikọ̀ ni Ikọ̀ ńjẹ́ | It's what we send an emissary that the emissary delivers<br>- Don't blame the messenger; he only delivers messages he's been tasked with. |
| 856. | Ìṣẹ́jú mélõ l'ajá fi ń gb'éegun? | How many seconds does it take a dog to snap up a bone?<br>- Don't underestimate the subject(s) this idiom is in reference to, because they could move in a flash! |
| 857. | Iṣu atẹnumọ́rọ̀ ìí jó'ná | The yam of a reiterator never burns<br>- The person in this metaphor never lets people forget about issues that concern him/her;<br>- When someone keeps on and on about something, people will likely take notice of their gripe. |
| 858. | Iṣu Ẹni níí m'ẹ́ni í t'ọwọ́ b'epo | It's one's yam that makes one dip hands in palm oil (in the olden days, yam was typically eaten with palm oil and salt, |

| | | without a fork or a knife). Palm oil is not easily washed off, even with soap, so people don't particularly relish dipping hands in it, except out of necessity (of eating yam)<br>- It's your family and loved ones that make you do things you wouldn't normally do if you had a choice. |
|---|---|---|
| 859. | Ìsúnmọ́n'ni l'à ń mọ̀n'ṣe Ẹni | Closeness and familiarity is how we know someone's character. |
| 860. | Ìtàkùn t'ó dì m'óbì niò j'óbì í s'èso rere | The liana rope that is clinging to the kolanut tree is precluding the kolanut tree from sprouting good seeds<br>- It's the current crop of adversaries the great leader finds himself surrounded by that are thwarting his efforts to enacting great policies. An example: during the Obama administration in the US, the GOP-dominated Congress frustrated the president so much that he could hardly function as a president;<br>- The philanthropic efforts and generosity of a lone wealthy individual in a poor community can hardly be felt because there's so much poverty that all his/her efforts seems like filling buckets that are leaking like sieves with water. |
| 861. | Ìtàkùn t'ó ní k'érin má wọ'dò, t'òun t'erin l'ó ń lọ | Lianas and vines that say the elephant should not enter the stream, they and the elephant will go together<br>- Anyone who would prevent us from reaching our goal, they will perish in the struggle that we go through to reach the goal. |
| 862. | Ìtàn Ìnàkí l'ojúù mi ò tó; Ojú ù mí tó díẹ̀ ní t'ọ̀bọ | It's the story of the chimp that my eyes do not reach; my eyes reach a bit when it comes to the monkey's<br>- I may not have been around when things were great, I can certainly recall the times when things were not so good [under the current leadership]. |

| | | |
|---|---|---|
| 863. | Ìtẹ́lẹ̀ Ìdí Ẹni ìí rí'ni í tì | One's brief [underwear] is never unable to see one [in their most intimate part]<br>- They are so close that there ought to be no secret between them [those in the narrative];<br>- One's wife cannot see one in the nude and one is embarrassed, and vice versa. |
| 864. | Ìtì Ògèdè ni, kò t'óun à ń lọ'dáá bẹ́ | It's the stump of a banana tree, it's not up to something we need to file a cutlass to cut<br>- It's a simple matter that does not require much effort to resolve. |
| 865. | Ìtóò ó ti sò'mîn | The baby-gourd has sprouted something else<br>- The issue at hand has evolved and given rise to other issues or has taken an unexpected twist;<br>- The issue has opened a can of worms, so to speak. |
| 866. | Ìtòó t'ó bá so, t'ó l'óun ò f'ara t'igi, Ẹ̀fùfù lẹ̀lẹ̀ ní ó wóo | The pumpkin plant that grows, refuses to lean on a tree, the light wind will blow it down<br>- If you wish to stand alone in your hour of need and refuse all help being offered to you because you feel you are self-sufficient, be prepared to fall down alone. |
| 867. | Ìtọ̀sẹ̀ l'ó l'Ọ̀yọ́ | Prearrangement and organization is what holds Ọ̀yọ́ together<br>- The speaker is using this hyperbole to suggest that he and others could come to some arrangement to show each other a few things that might be mutually beneficial to all concerned. |
| 868. | Ìwà jọ'wà níí jẹ́ Ọ̀rẹ́ j'ọ̀rẹ́ | Having similar characteristics is what makes friends "look alike"<br>- Birds of a feather flock together. |
| 869. | Ìwà l'Ọba Àwúre | Remarkable character is the modus operandi of the king who "proclaims good fortune" on people<br>- This kind of person delights in the prosperity and happiness of others. |

| 870. | Iwájú l'ojúgun ń gbé | Forwards is where the kneecap lives<br>- Stay where you are supposed to be. |
|---|---|---|
| 871. | Iwájú l'ọ̀pá Ẹ̀bìtì ń ré sí | It's forwards the trigger stick of a trap cascades<br>- This is an affirmation that one will always progress in every way and never regress. |
| 872. | Ìwákúwã l'à ńwá Ohun t'ó sọnù | Frantic-searching is the rule of thumb when looking for a lost valuable item. |
| 873. | Ìwákúwã níí jẹ́ Ìríkúrĩ | Uncontrollable-searching equals seeing a can of worms<br>- Don't meddle in things you don't really know or you might find something you haven't bargained for that may further turn your life upside down;<br>- Stop looking for evidence of an infidelity for what you find might upset the balance of things in your life. For instance, the person you think might be a lover of your partner may in fact be an innocuous platonic relationship and only your partner probably didn't tell you to avoid giving you that false impression in the first place. |
| 874. | Iwò kan ò lè gb'eku, k'ó tún gb'ejò | A hole cannot hold a rat and also hold a snake<br>- The two cannot live together;<br>- What you or they are proposing is not doable. |
| 875. | Ìwọ l'o gb'óúnjẹ Alẹ́ ẹ f'ólógbò (jẹ) | You were the one who gave your supper to the cat (to eat)<br>- You were the one that encouraged your friend to snatch your partner [by your behavior and attitude]. |
| 876. | Ìwọ n'igi l'éhìn Ọgbà mi;<br>Ìwọ n'igi l'éhìn Ọgbà ẹ̀;<br>Ẹ̀yin n'igi l'éhìn Ọgbà mi;<br>Ẹ̀yin n'igi l'éhìn Ọgbàa ẹ̀<br>Ẹ̀yin n'igi l'éhìn Ọgbàa wọn<br>(It's beyond the scope of this book to list all the possible combinations of this single | You are the tree behind my garden;<br>You are the tree behind his/her garden;<br>You are the tree behind my garden;<br>You are the tree behind his/her garden;<br>You are the tree behind his/her/their garden.<br><br>Please see the "Personal Pronouns" page.. |

| | | |
|---|---|---|
| | *proverb that can be derived by varying the first and last pronouns).* | - The individual(s) named is the stalwart pillar behind the person(s) named. |
| 877. | Ìwọ ṣã ti f'òkìtí 'ílẹ̀ fún Lágídí | You just leave the molehill for Lágídí<br>- Why argue with an unreasonable person? Let him deal with the issue! |
| 878. | Ìwọ̀fún n'ìtẹ́lọ́rùn; Ìdodo n'ìdájì Ara | "Do as you please" is satisfaction; the navel is the 'half' of the body<br>- This adage does exactly what it says on the tin - it simply means "do as you please; it's a free world!" |
| 879. | Ìwọ̀nba ni Ta-ńpẹ́pẹ́ ń gbè'jà Ẹyìn mọn | It's up to a point that the ant sides with the palmnuts<br>- The situation is becoming rather complex, we may have to withdraw our support. |
| 880. | Ìyà méjì ò sháà ń j'ọbẹ̀; bí ò bá s'épo l'ojú ẹ, Iyọ̀ ó sháà dùn-ún | Double punishments cannot assail a pot of stew; if there is no oil on its surface, salt will at least be sufficient<br>- You can't lose both ways;<br>- One has got to give! |
| 881. | Ìyà ò tíì tán l'órí Alábùjẹkù | Suffering has not ended on the head of the left-over-food "biter"<br>- Don't think the discomfort or distress is over while the problem still remains. |
| 882. | Iyán burú Afá já, Erukú bo'lẹ̀ l'éhìn Àpáàdì, sè'yí l'áfùn Amùkòkò | The pounded yam is so bad that the foot bridge collapses, dust blanketed the ground after the broken fire-pot, like it escaped from a pipe smoker's lungs<br>- Trouble is brewing. |
| 883. | Iyán di Àtúngún, Ọbẹ̀ ẹ di Àtúnsè | Pounded yam defaults to having to be re-pounded, stew needs recooking<br>- If at first you don't succeed, try, try and try again;<br>- Go back to the drawing board. |
| 884. | Ìyàtọ́ wà n'ínú-un Kíìjìpá àt'awọ Ẹran | There is a difference between a thick cloth and leather<br>- The issues in the context are as dissimilar as chalk and cheese. |
| 885. | Ìyàwó t'a bá fẹ́ l'órí Ijó, Ìran l'ó máa wò dé Dùgbè | The wife we met during a dance competition, it's a show event (exposé) |

| | | |
|---|---|---|
| | | she'll watch till she gets to Dùgbẹ̀ (a popular section in Ibadan, Nigeria)<br>- What we acquired [cheaply or easily], we tend to lose by the same way we acquired it. |
| 886. | Ìyàwó t'áa bá fẹ́ l'ójú Agbo, Ìran l'ó máa wò lọ | The wife we proposed to at a party, it's show events (parades) she'll watch, and depart<br>- What we achieved [by deceit], we tend to lose by the same manner we earned it. |
| 887. | Jáde kúrò ńlé mi, kìí ṣe "jáde kúrò l'áiyé mi" | Leave my house is not "leave my life", i.e. "the world" in which the person [who has asked us to leave their house] lives<br>- Someone asking us to leave their house does not equate "leave this world" [meaning 'die']. So all it's not gloom gloom. Just dust yourself off and move on;<br>- We live to fight another day. |
| 888. | Jẹ́ k'ẹ́lẹ́dìn pẹdin ẹ̀<br>Ẹ jẹ́ k'ẹ́lẹ́dìn pẹdin | Let whosoever is entitled do as they please with what they have earned<br>- Let the owner do as they please. |
| 889. | Jẹ́ k'ọ̀rọ̀ yī lọ Odò k'ó lọ mu'mi | Let the matter go to the brook and drink some water<br>- Let the matter rest;<br>- Leave well alone. |
| 890. | Jẹ́ kí n kú k'o tó sin mí | Let me die before you bury me<br>- Let me finish what I have to say. |
| 891. | Jẹ-kí-njẹ níí m'áyọ̀ ó dùn | You eat and I eat [win] is what makes a game sweet [exciting]<br>- Do your business and let me do mine is the music of business. |
| 892. | K'a dúpẹ́ l'ọ́wọ́ Èjìká tí ò j'ẹrù ó bọ́ | Let's thank the shoulder that keeps loads in place from falling<br>- Let's appreciate the support of someone named in this saying [the shoulder] whose support didn't let us fail;<br>- We should thank the person who rallied round us and helped us save face in time. |
| 893. | K'a f'èníyàn mímọ̀n ṣ'ọrọ̀ | To enrich oneself through connection with someone in an influential position<br>- To exploit cronyism to its fullest |

| | | |
|---|---|---|
| | | maximum and gain what you can, consideration for others be damned. |
| 894. | K'á f'òkò kan p'ẹiyẹ méjì | Let's kill two birds with one stone. |
| 895. | K'a fi Iṣu s'íná k'a ma f'inú w'ọ́bẹ | Let's put the yam on the fire while we deliberate on finding a knife<br>- Let's put our defenses in place before we consider how we are going to launch our attack. |
| 896. | K'a lè ní Olùdámọ̀nràn l'a ṣe ń n'íyàwó | So we can have companionship is why we have wives<br>- Don't hide things from your soul mate. |
| 897. | K'a má b'ópõ re'lé Olórõ | Don't let's follow the pole to go to the house of Olórõ<br>- Do not beat about the bush;<br>- To cut a long story short. |
| 898. | K'a má bàa j'ìyà l'a ṣe ń yá Májìyà l'ọ́fà | That we might not suffer was why we lent Májìyà [the entity of 'don't suffer'] the arrow<br>- This could be said during a disaster relief or time of trouble: so we wouldn't have to go through much suffering was why we equipped ourselves well. |
| 899. | K'a má déènà p'ẹnu | Not to wear out the mouth<br>- To cut a long story short. |
| 900. | K'a pọn'mi s'ílẹ̀ d'òngbẹ | Let's fetch water and keep at home till [the time of] thirst<br>- This is to prepare oneself in case of the unexpected;<br>- To be forewarned is to be forearmed. |
| 901. | K'á rìn k'á pọ̀, yíyẹ l'ó ń y'ẹni | The more we walk in unison, the more dignified and respectable we are<br>- United we stand, divided we fall;<br>- There's safety in numbers;<br>- You are safer if you are with other people or doing something with other people. |
| 902. | K'á s'ọ̀rọ̀ k'á ba bẹ́ẹ̀ òun ni Iyí Olódodo | We say something and we find it exactly as was said is the dignity and bond of Olódodo [truth speaker] |
| 903. | K'a t'ibi Pẹlẹbẹ m'ọ̀ọ̀lẹ̀ jẹ | Let's begin eating Ọ̀ọ̀lẹ̀ (bean-cake wrapped and cooked in leaves) from |

| | | |
|---|---|---|
| | | where the lowest gradient is<br>- We should confront an issue from where it's more obvious and simpler. |
| 904. | K'a tọ̀ s'ójú kan, k'ó bàa lè hó | Let's urinate in one place, so it will boil [bubble]<br>- Let's garner our combined energies in one place to confront the issue before us. |
| 905. | K'a wá Wọ̀rọ̀kọ̀ k'a fi ṣ'àdá | Let's look for Wọ̀rọ̀kọ̀ and turn it into a cutlass<br>- The situation may not be conducive, but right now, we need to use our heads and find a common solution. |
| 906. | K'éku Ilé gbọ́ k'ó sọ fún t'oko | Let the house rats hear and inform their peers in the bush<br>- This metaphor is usually proclaimed by someone in power to inform the general public about how the new policy and direction of the leadership is going to be;<br>- Let everyone take note and spread the news; everyone is expected to obey and follow the directive [could be a curfew]. |
| 907. | K'ẹlẹ́dẹ̀ẹ́ tó d'Ọ̀yọ́, Ariwo á ti pọ̀; Òkìkí ẹ̀ á kàn | Before a pig gets to Ọ̀yọ́ [any city really], there will be lots of pomp and pageantry; its fame will have spread<br>- Before the issue currently afoot is resolved, if care is not taken, it could very easily escalate and become a huge embarrassment. |
| 908. | K'ójú má r'íbi, gbogbo Ara l'òògùn-un ẹ̀ | For eyes not to see evil, all the body is the medicine<br>- Better get out [of here] while you can! |
| 909. | K'óníkálukú dá Ọmú Ìyá ẹ̀ gbé | Let everybody lift his mother's breast alone. This is usually uttered when survival is the issue of the day<br>- Do your thing and I do my thing;<br>- Each man to his own;<br>- Do whatever floats your boat. |
| 910. | K'á di'jú k'á ṣe bí Ẹní kú, k'á w'ẹni tí 'ó d'ãrò Ẹni | Let's close our eyes and play dead; let's see who will eulogize us<br>- It is a sad truth... but does anyone really care when you are gone, apart from family |

| | | |
|---|---|---|
| | | and true friends? |
| 911. | Ká fún'ni l'ádìẹ sìn k'a máa wá ka iye Ẹyin t'ó yé | Giving [a gift] of a fowl to someone to raise and be counting the number of eggs the fowl produces<br>- You already donated it out so it's no longer yours; let it go!<br>- When you have given someone something, take your mind off of it! |
| 912. | K'a má pọ̀n Jẹ̀bẹ̀ l'ákīsà | Let's not wrap [disguise] raggedy tatters [fit for garbage] in shreds of old clothing [fit for recycling]<br>- Don't let's pretend about what the man truly is - a monster/psychopath!<br>- Call a spade a spade! |
| 913. | K'á pà'sẹ́ pọ̀ k'á lè j'iyán Ẹ̀gẹ́ l'ábà | Let us join our starch and flour together so we may eat the 'pounded yam' of cassava in the farmhouse<br>- All hands should be on deck to stop the rot so we can all rejoice and celebrate together. |
| 914. | K'á rìn, k'á pọ̀, yíyẹ níí yẹ'ni | Collectively walking and multiplying, accords honor and fulfillment to everyone<br>- The coming together of friends and neighbors brings a sense of belonging and community spirit. |
| 915. | K'á t'ibi Ìṣáná k'íyè s'óògùn | Let's from the point of book-matches take notice of juju<br>- Keep your wits about you and keep your eyes peeled;<br>- Put two and two together and make a correct guess. |
| 916. | Kàkà k'ẹ b'ólè wí, ẹ ní Oníhùnkán ṣe gb'érùu è s'íbí t'ó gbe sí? | Instead of gathering together to rebuke the thief, you countered "why did the property owner leave his stuff where he left it?"<br>- Is that what it has come down to now?<br>- Have things gotten this bad that the guilty is now the innocent? |
| 917. | Kàkà k'éku má jẹ Ṣẹṣé, á fi ṣ'àwàdànù | If a mouse cannot eat the Ṣẹṣé crop, it would render it into a waste<br>- If someone is unable to get their way, |

141

| | | |
|---|---|---|
| | | they would scupper any chance(s) that might be open to anyone else. |
| 918. | Kàkà k'ó sàn l'ára Ìyá Àjẹ́, ó fi gbogbo Ọmọ bí Obìnrin | Instead of things going great for the witch-mother, all the children she birthed are girls<br>- Instead of things getting better for someone by reaching out to those in position to assist him right now, it appears he has burned all his bridges. Meaning he had probably been wicked and mean when he was on top himself to those he now needs and therefore cannot turn to them for help. |
| 919. | Kàkà k'ákèréè mi má dun'bẹ̀, t'apá t'itan rẹ̀ ni ngó lọ si! | Rather than for my delicacy of frog meat to not taste delicious, I shall blend all its limbs and body with the soup!<br>- I will do all that is necessary to make this work! |
| 920. | Kànnà-kánná na Ọmọ Ẹ̀gà, Ìjà ńbọ̀ | The budgerigar whipped the songbird's young, fight is looming<br>- A rival has drawn a circle in the sand by insulting his adversary, the fight is about to begin. |
| 921. | Kékeré ni mo fi bá Lágbájá tan, kò ṣeé f'ọ̀bẹ bù | "It's just by a little that I'm related to Lágbájá [John Doe]" cannot be divided with a knife [cannot be measured]<br>- Blood is thicker than water. |
| 922. | Kèlèbè ba'lẹ̀ ṣ'ara gírí; Ẹni t'ó wú'kọ́ l'ó mọ̀n p'áyà ń ta òun | Phlegm touches the ground and firms up; he who is coughing is the one who knows that his chest hurts<br>- He who is facing hardship is the one who knows where his main challenges lie. |
| 923. | Kèlèbè ìí ba'lẹ̀ k'ó má kõ nkan | Phlegm does not land and not have something sticking to it<br>- The individual doesn't appear without some awful things happening;<br>- Like the plague, or like some people see the eclipse as a harbinger of doom. |
| 924. | Késekése l'à ń rí l'ọ́wọ́, aà mọn Kàsàkàsà t'ó ńbọ̀ | Quietude and passivity is what we are currently witnessing, we do not know the disturbance [agitation] that is coming |

| | | |
|---|---|---|
| | | - What we are currently experiencing may be just the tip of the iceberg; the worst may yet transpire. |
| 925. | Kìí bá'ni k'á yẹ'rí | It [a task] never defaults to us and we shift our heads away in the nick of time to avoid the matter landing on our heads<br>- The call of duty has fallen on your shoulders; refusal is not an option. |
| 926. | Kìí b'ínú, kìí b'ínú, Ọmọ Àlè l'ó ń fàá | He never gets angry, he never gets irritated, it's a bastard that forces his hand<br>- If this person is upset, it is because someone has provoked him/her. |
| 927. | Kìí dé bá'ni k'ó y'ẹrí | It doesn't fall on someone [to do] and he shirks<br>- When it's your cross to bear, no use avoiding it. Just grin and bear it like a man! |
| 928. | Kìí gbọ́, kìí gbà, Ẹran àbámọ̀n ni wọ́n máa ń padà á jẹ n'ígbẹ̀hìn | He neither hears nor accepts, the meat of regret is what they typically eat at last<br>- Never listens, never conceding, this type of individual invariably regrets not accepting apologies when extended to them;<br>- They'll live to regret not accepting placations when offered. |
| 929. | Kìí ṣ'àdédé é b'ínú, Ọmọ Àlè Ènìà níí fàá | He never gets angry anyhow, it's a bastard that causes it<br>- This person is characteristically phlegmatic; if they appear not to be, it would be because someone has really aggravated them. |
| 930. | Kìí ṣe kékeré ni Babá fi ń ju Ọmọ lọ | It's not by a little that a father is greater than his son<br>- I'll show you that I am more powerful (or richer) than you. |
| 931. | Kíkéré l'abẹ́ ń kéré, kìí ṣe mímì f'ádìẹ | Small the needle may be, it's not something for the hen to swallow<br>- Someone or something may appear minuscule, you might regret it if you took them on;<br>- Appearances can be deceptive. |

| | | |
|---|---|---|
| 932. | Kín l'a fi máa ṣe'mú Ajá t'ó ma fi gbẹ? | What can we do to a dog's nostrils to make them dry?<br>- What is the solution to this problem? |
| 933. | Kín l'o gbé t'óò ń gbin? | What have you lifted that you're panting?<br>- What have you got that you're showing off so much? |
| 934. | Kín l'ò ń wá n'ínú Igbó Ejò? | What were you looking for in a snake forest?<br>- This is a hilarious question put to someone who may have gone to where no one really expected them to ever go again, especially a place where they'd recently had a bad experience. |
| 935. | Kín l'o rí l'ọ́bẹ̀ t'óo fi wa'rú s'ọ́wọ́? | What did you find in the stew that you scooped locust beans in your hand?<br>- Sort of asking someone: what made you do what you did? |
| 936. | Kín l'a gbé, kín lẹ jù? | What did we catch; what did you throw?<br>- What are we saying; what are you saying?<br>- Your input is not in resonance with what is being discussed here, buddy!<br>- Are we on the same page here? |
| 937. | Kín l'ajá ńwá ń'Mọ́sháláshí? | What is a dog looking for in a mosque? [This proverb is so because dogs and mosques do not mix]<br>- For example, if someone is called to intervene or say something over an issue they have no business with, they may respond with this proverb;<br>- Another example: If someone feels it doesn't befit them to be in a place, an event or any other place, they may thus express their disagreement;<br>- What is this person doing in this place ([of all places]?<br>- You are out of place. |
| 938. | Kín lẹ jẹ dé'bi "Àwé, Eyín ẹ rà?" | What did you [and your mates] eat until you started muttering "Buddy, your teeth are decayed?"<br>- What sort of topic were you discussing |

| | | |
|---|---|---|
| | | that got out of hand?<br>- What led up to you guys insulting each another? |
| 939. | Kín'ìyàtọ̀ n'ínú-un Túrùkú àti Ìmàdò | What is the difference between a warthog and a wild boar?<br>- There's hardly a distinction between the two! |
| 940. | Kiní kan l'ó ba Àjàò jẹ́; Apá ẹ̀ẹ́ gùn ju'tan è lọ | One thing ruined the appearance of a flying fox bat; its arms are longer than its thighs<br>- What you/they have done would have been perfect, except for... OR<br>- This [material thing] would have been so and so, if not for this or that (depends on the context of the discussion). |
| 941. | Kínl'ó wà n'ínú Òròmọndìyẹ t'áwòdì-òkè ò mọ̀n? | What's inside a chick that the bush eagle does not know?<br>- We can use a terrorist organization as a perfect example of this idiom: What are they planning that the FBI or NSA does not know about? |
| 942. | Kó Ara ẹ ní Ìjánu | Watch what comes out of your mouth<br>- Either to rebuke or caution someone: the less you talk the better!<br>- Don't speak out of turn and implicate yourself. |
| 943. | Kò fún mi l'ágùtàn sìn, ó ní n m'ágbò ńlá wá | He/she never gave me a sheep to tend and raise, he/she is asking me to bring a big ram<br>- This saying is directed at someone who is expecting to reap where they have not sown;<br>- You think I'm stupid? |
| 944. | Kò níí burú títí fún Ẹdìẹ k'ó má dé'bi tí Ẹyin rẹ̀ẹ́ wà | It can't be so bad for the chicken that it will fail to go to where her eggs are<br>- Things cannot be so dreadful that a king/leader will abandon his subjects;<br>- The situation cannot be so dire that parents will fail to use their protective instinct to shelter their children. |
| 945. | Kò níí burú títí k'ó má k'ẹnìkan | It couldn't be so calamitous that there |

|   | | |
|---|---|---|
|   | mọ́n'ni; Ẹni t'ó kù l'aò mọ̀n | would be no next of kin left for someone; who the kin [that is left] might be is what we don't know<br>- One could not be so dirt-poor that he'd have no surviving relation, though the identity of the family member may not be known. |
| 946. | Kò s'àǹfààní t'ọ́mọ Ẹiyé fẹ́ ṣe fún Ìyá ẹ̀ tí ò ṣe k'ó d'àgbà k'ó fò lọ | There is no benefit/advantage the chick of a bird has to offer its mother other than to mature and fly away<br>- What is my reward in this enterprise other than you using my ideas? |
| 947. | Kò s'áwo kan l'áwo Ẹ̀wà | There is no single initiate from the initiates of beans<br>- There is no riddle to the problem [as it should be obvious]. |
| 948. | Kò s'áwo kan l'áwo Ẹ̀wà ju pé k'á sèé k'á dẹ̀ jẹé lọ | There is no single initiate from the initiates of beans, other than we cook it and eat it<br>- There is no riddle to the problem other than the obvious;<br>- Don't overthink things! |
| 949. | Kò ṣ'eku, kò ṣ'ẹiyẹ | It's neither a mouse nor a bird<br>- Beware of this kind of person as their loyalty is not to one single entity. |
| 950. | Kò s'ẹni t'ó g'ẹṣin tí 'ò níí ji'rùn | No one rides a horse and not bob their neck<br>- Hardly anyone can be in a position of power or influence and not exploit it. |
| 951. | Kò s'ẹni t'ó ma t'ajà Erùpẹ̀ tí ò níí gb'owó Òkúta | There is no one who would market [the product of] sand and not collect the money of sandstone<br>- A man reaps what he sows (Galatians 6:7);<br>- What goes around comes around. |
| 952. | Kò s'ẹni t'ó mọn'lé Àjẹ́ ẹ̀ 'í gbá | No one knows how to sweep her coven-stead<br>- It's difficult to please the individual in question. |
| 953. | Kò s'ẹni t'ó ń f'ọ̀bẹ t'ó 'nù j'ẹṣu | No one eats with a lost knife<br>- No one will claim to have seen an item |

| | | |
|---|---|---|
| | | that has gone missing. |
| 954. | Kò s'ẹni t'ó r'ọbẹ tíò níí j'ẹko | No one sees stew and will not eat hardened corn-pap<br>- No one sees a freebie and passes it over. |
| 955. | Kò s'énìà t'óko Baba rẹ̀ ò sì níí d'ìgbòrò | There's no one whose father's farm will not become a residential area [some day]<br>- We all have a common destiny; it'll be everyone's turn soon;<br>- All of us are still gonna die. |
| 956. | Kò s'éwu l'óko, àfi gìirì Àparò | There's no danger in the farm, except the rustle of a bush-fowl<br>- Everything is calm despite the commotion you see. |
| 957. | Kò s'éwu l'ọ́rọ̀ Ejò; t'ọmọ Eku l'ó n'ípọn | There is no danger whatsoever in the matter concerning the snake; it's the baby rat's [issue] that is beset with hardship<br>- This is a simple matter [as far as I am concerned]. |
| 958. | Kò s'íbi táa ń b'ágbà táà b'ápolo Orí ẹ ńbẹ | There is no place where we find an elder and don't find his wisdom with him<br>- There is always a solution to every problem. |
| 959. | Kò s'íbi táà ti ń dá'ná Alẹ́; Ọbẹ nìkan l'ó ń dùn ju'ra wọn lọ | There's no place where night meal [supper] is not prepared; only one stew is more delicious than the other<br>- There's nothing new under the sun;<br>- The way some things are done in one part of the world may not be wholly exclusive to that region alone. |
| 960. | Kò s'íbi t'ó gb'orò bí ò ṣe'gbó ńlá | Nowhere can contain the idol-god except a vast forest<br>- What is transpiring right now requires a different kind of thinking. |
| 961. | Kò s'óhun t'ádìẹ lè f'ẹiyẹ Àṣá ṣe | There is nothing that the chicken/hen can do to the hawk<br>- Your threats are of no consequence to the person(s) you're threatening. |
| 962. | Kò s'óhun t'ó n'íbẹ̀rẹ̀ tí 'ò l'ópin | There's nothing that has a beginning that doesn't have an end. |
| 963. | Kò s'óhun tuntun l'ábẹ́ Ọrun mọ́n | There's nothing new under the heavens again. |

| | | |
|---|---|---|
| 964. | Kò s'ólógbón t'ó lè ta Omi sí kókó Aṣọ | No clever genius can tie water in a cloth-knot<br>- The matter will remain a riddle forever. |
| 965. | Kò s'óúnjẹ f'ẹni tí ò ṣ'iṣẹ́ | No food for he who doesn't work<br>- If you can't put in the effort, you don't deserve the reward. |
| 966. | Kò s'óúnjẹ f'ọ́lẹ | No food for the lazy<br>- If you are not disabled or incapacitated in any way and you're choosy about what you do, then you don't deserve to eat. |
| 967. | Kò sí Arẹ́májà, Ajàmágbẹ̀bẹ̀ nìkan ni ò sí | There are no pacifist friends, a fighter who is so stubborn that he never accepts an apology is the only one that doesn't exist<br>- Let bygones be bygones and move on. |
| 968. | Kò sí Awo kan n'ínú Awo Ẹ̀pà | There's no divinity in the priesthood of groundnuts<br>- There's no purpose of our being in the same priesthood if we can't help each other out;<br>- We exist together to help each other, not to eat peanuts. |
| 969. | Kò sí bí Ọ̀bọ mí ṣe ṣ'orí tí Ìnàkí i tiwọn ò ṣe | There is no way my monkey holds his head that their chimpanzee cannot<br>- I'm not better than anyone else; what I may have done, anyone can do also. |
| 970. | Kò sí nkan t'ó ńbọ̀ l'ókè t'ílẹ̀ ò gbà | There's nothing coming from the sky that the land [earth] cannot accept<br>- Whatsoever the enemy intends to throw at us, we are ready to face it;<br>- Anything you wish to do, I'm ready to take you on. |
| 971. | "Kò wùn mí" ò l'ẹ́lẹ́bẹ̀ | "It doesn't please me" does not have an Ẹlẹ́bẹ̀ [pacifier]<br>- The person has made up his mind about someone or something and that's what they'll have or do, come what may. |
| 972. | Kò yẹ kí Agbọ́n Ilé máa ta Onílé | It's not fitting that the house-hornet stings the homeowner<br>- Don't bite the hand that feeds you (Pro 29:19);<br>- You should at least have a bit of respect |

|  |  | for those who got you where you are. |
|---|---|---|
| 973. | Kọ́kọ́rọ́ kan-án b'eyín Ajá jẹ́ | One key ruined the dog's teeth<br>- Something is not quite right [about the subject of the narrative];<br>- Though by all appearances he/she looks alright and presentable, something is a bit off about this person. |
| 974. | Kòkòrò tí ńj'ẹ̀fọ́, Ìdì Ẹ̀fọ́ l'ó ńgbé | The insect that is eating the spinach, actually resides within the spinach<br>- Like a case of guarding a bank vault with robbers and thieves and the vault is discovered to be empty. OR<br>- The people who are running the country are the same people destroying it;<br>- In other words, the enemy is within! |
| 975. | Kọ̀lọ̀kọ̀lọ̀ t'ó bá p'adìẹ Òkú, t'ó bá yá, òun nã á lọ b'áládìẹ | The fox that killed the chicken of a dead person, sooner or later, it too will join the chicken's owner<br>- Let him carry on the way he is acting; he'll meet his karma soon enough! |
| 976. | Kòmọ̀n-ọ́nwọ̀ l'ó l'ẹ̀wù; Ẹlẹ́nu rírí l'ó l'àmù Ìyá ẹ̀ | He who doesn't know how to don clothes is the owner of his clothes; he with the mouth odor is the owner of his mother's clay-pot of water<br>- The property is yours; do as you please. |
| 977. | K'óníkálukú dá Ọmú Iyá ẹ̀ gbé | Let everyone lift their mother's breasts up [with no assistance]<br>- To each his own;<br>- Stay in your own backyard. |
| 978. | K'óníkálukú t'ọwọ́ Ọmọ ẹ̀ b'ọsọ | Let everyone keep their toddlers' hands inside their garment<br>- This is a warning to friends and family [and sometimes the community] as to what might happen, going forward;<br>- Let everyone beware! |
| 979. | Korokoro l'à ń rán'fá Adití | Repetitively is how we divine the future for the deaf<br>- This phrase pertains to people who need to be warned of the hazards in the companies that they keep. |
| 980. | Láálã t'ó r'òkè, Ilẹ̀ l'ó ńbọ̀ | The kite that goes up, it is land that it's |

|  |  | coming to<br>- What goes up must surely come down;<br>- Avoid it as you will, the problem you're running away from will wait for you until you confront it;<br>- You may run, but you can't hide. |
|---|---|---|
| 981. | Labalábá t'ó lọ s'óko t'ó tún padà dé, Àrà mí'ìn l'ó gbé dé | The butterfly that went to the farm and somehow returned, [sure] it's returning with a different attitude<br>- Be mindful about people you thought you knew and don't leave yourself open to unpleasant surprises. |
| 982. | Láì déènà p'ẹnu... | Not to push blocks to cover the mouth<br>- To cut a long story short... |
| 983. | Láìkú Ẹ̀gìrì aò gbọdọ̀ f'awọ ẹ̀ ṣe Gbẹ̀du | Without the demise of the eland deer, we cannot use its skin to make a Gbẹ̀du drum<br>- You don't elect a new ruler while the current one is still alive or has not abdicated;<br>- No lawyer starts reading a Will while the benefactor is still breathing. |
| 984. | Láílái, Ojú-Oró ò níí j'ẹ́sẹ̀ Ẹiyẹ́ tẹ'jú Omi | Never will common water hyacinth allow a bird's feet to touch the surface of the water<br>- Never will the person in the metaphor allow another to do what they want to do;<br>- Warning of a serious parent not wanting suitors for their teenage daughter(s). |
| 985. | Lílọ níí k'ẹ́hìn-in Bọ́í | It's 'departure' that follows after the troublesome youth [when he finally leaves town or grows into old age]<br>- Dust will settle after so much upheaval;<br>- It's a solution that follows any conundrum. |
| 986. | "Má f'okoò mi ṣe Ọ̀nà", Ọjọ́ kan l'ènìà ń kọ̀ọ́ | "Don't use my farm as a path" [to your own farm], it's one day a man rejects it<br>- If you don't reject this kind of insolence but accept it, your capitulation is seen as weakness and naiveté. |
| 987. | Má fi lọ̀ mí n dá si | Don't give me the hint so I can offer my opinion |

|   |   | - This is to tell off a busybody to mind their business. |
|---|---|---|
| 988. | Má fi Pupa pe Funfun; má fi Funfun pe Pupa | Don't call the red white; don't call the white red<br>- Do not give misleading information;<br>- Call a spade a spade;<br>- Tell it as it is. |
| 989. | Má f'ojú Olóore gún'gi | Don't hire the eyes of a benefactor to poke a tree<br>- Don't reward someone who has helped you with cruelty they do not deserve. |
| 990. | Má p'ẹ̀gbẹ̀ Ògiri | Don't tiptoe around the wall<br>- Stop avoiding the real issue; come to the point! |
| 991. | Má ṣ'íwájú mi l'à ńgbọ́, a kì ńgbọ́ má k'ẹ̀hìn mi | Don't step in front of me is what we're used to hearing, not don't bring up my rear<br>- It is hard to drive forward looking in the rear view mirror. |
| 992. | Má ṣọ Orí Olórí kí Àwòdì gbé ti tiẹ k'ó gbe lọ | Don't guard the head of another that the eagle carries yours away<br>- Don't be so engrossed in other people's business that yours gets neglected and messed up. |
| 993. | Màá kúnlẹ̀ bá ẹ d'ógba | I shall kneel down and be level with your height [irrespective of your stature]<br>- This idiomatic phrase is made by someone who has lost their respect for the other party and is now ready to challenge them to a contest (if necessary). |
| 994. | Màálúù tí ò ń'írù, Ọlọ́run L'ó ń l'ẹ́ṣinṣin fún-un | The cow that has no tail, it's God that shoos away the flies that torment it<br>- When we have no one to lift us up or help us, it's God that comes to the rescue. |
| 995. | Màálúù t'ó bá j'èbù l'ó ní k'ọ́n na Fúlàní | It is the cow that ate the half-tuber of yam [in the farm] that made one [the farmer] beat the Fulani cowboy who led the cattle to graze on the man's ranch. |
| 996. | Màrìwò l'o ṣì rí, oò tíì r'éégún | Palm frond is what you have seen [so far], you haven't seen the masquerade<br>- This is just the beginning, you haven't |

| | | |
|---|---|---|
| | | seen anything yet. |
| 997. | Mélõ l'a fẹ́ kà l'éyín Adípèlé | How many are we going to count out of supernumerary teeth<br>- Like hyperdontia of the teeth, there are so many angles to the story that it's impossible to know where to begin. |
| 998. | Mélõ l'èèrà ẹ t'ó l'áràn-án ń yọ'un l'ẹ́nu | How many are your ants that they complain that worms are worrying them?<br>- How big is your ant that it's moaning of intestinal worms (where is the tummy)?<br>- How big do you think you are that you're making so much spectacle of yourself?<br>- Who do you think you are? |
| 999. | Mi ò lè fún Wàrà, mo lè da'mi Wàrà nù! | I can't milk a cow [for clotted cream], but I can certainly flip over the liquid milk<br>- I may not be able to create, but I can [certainly] destroy! |
| 1000. | Mi ò lè rí Erin k'ó wá di Ẹ̀líri mọ́n mi l'ọ́wọ́ | I couldn't have seen an elephant and it turned into a pygmy-jerboa right before my eyes<br>- I know what I saw! |
| 1001. | Mi ò lè sọ'pé mo fẹ́ j'ẹran kí nma pe Màálúù ní Bọ̀ọ̀dá | I won't say because I long to eat beef, I start calling the cow 'brother'<br>- I won't accept nonsense or any other unacceptable behavior (from the person in the context of the narrative) because I need their help. |
| 1002. | Mìò gbọ́'pé Ọmọ Arúgbó lí jẹ́ k'ọ́n ṣ'àánú Arúgbó | I have never heard where for the fact that a senior citizen has a resident grandchild precludes anyone having pity on the old one and helping him/her out<br>- This is like not wanting to assist a kid of rich and influential people on account of the wealth of the parents. |
| 1003. | "Mìò lè wá kú báyï" kìí j'ogún Ilée Bàbá ẹ̀ | "I don't want to die in this way" never inherits his father's property<br>- If you can't put in the effort, you don't deserve the reward;<br>- Nothing goes for nothing;<br>- No pain, no gain. |
| 1004. | Mo f'owó àti Ọmọ díí yín l'ẹ́nu | I sock your mouth with money and |

|  | tàbí…<br>Mo f'owó àti Ọmọ dí ẹ l'ẹ́nu | children.<br>*For more on the usage of ẹ, ẹ̀, ẹ́, o, ò, ó, ọ, please consult the "Personal Pronouns" page.*<br>- Said to interject someone who is addressing you or a group, to break their flow of conversation and say something;<br>- Apologies for interrupting another's person's speech. |
|---|---|---|
| 1005. | Mo kòó báyĩ, a máa l'ápẹẹrẹ | "I ran into him thus", it usually has takeaway examples<br>- Surely you must have a story to tell about your encounter [with the individual]. |
| 1006. | Mo ń m'ẹiyẹ bọ̀ l'ápò | I'm bringing out the bird from the pocket<br>- I'm coming out with my narrative, be patient. |
| 1007. | Mo ní mò ń bọ̀, o ní ó yá mi | I said I was coming; you said I'm early<br>- If you would only exercise patience and let me finish my narrative! |
| 1008. | Mo wà l'ẹ́hìn ẹ bí Iké | I'm behind you like a hump / kyphosis [on a hunchback]<br>- I have your back; I support you in whatever you're doing. |
| 1009. | Mọ̀n'jà mọ̀n'sá l'a fi ń mọn Akínkanjú l'ógun; Akínkanjú t'ó bá mọ̀n'jà tí ò bá mọn'sá, irú nwọn a máa kú s'ógun ni | Knowledge of warfare coupled with knowledge of running when faced with defeat is what defines a brave warrior; the soldier who knows the art of fighting but lacks the knowledge of fleeing, their kind always dies in battle<br>- Knowing when to fight and knowing when to run is key;<br>- He who fights and runs away, lives to fight another day. |
| 1010. | Mọ̀n'wà f'óníwà níí jẹ́ Ọ̀rẹ́ j'ọ̀rẹ́ | Knowing and accepting a person's behavioral characteristics makes and sustains a friendship. |
| 1011. | Mọ̀njèsí ni wọ́n, nwọn ò l'órúnkún Ẹjọ́ | They're youth, they don't have the knee for a case [to plead for mercy]<br>- They're youth with innocuous intentions trying to act like adults and they do not |

| | | | know what they're doing. |
|---|---|---|---|
| 1012. | Mọ̀nkàn-mọ̀nkàn l'oyè ń kàn | | Chieftaincy is like lottery<br>- It could be your turn next, so let's give our support. |
| 1013. | Ńtori Afọ́jú l'òjó ṣe ń kù; ńtorí Adití l'òjó ṣe ń ṣú | | It's because of the blind that the rain is preceded by thunderclaps; it's because of the deaf that a dark cloud harbingers impending rain<br>- Don't say you haven't been warned. |
| 1014. | Nǹbá ti dá'wọ́ lée, Awọ ni ò ká'jú Ìlù | | I would have started it, but the hide was inadequate for the drum face<br>- The speaker is rueing the fact that he doesn't have the means necessary to begin the project he's talking about, i.e. perhaps due to shortage of money. |
| 1015. | Ńbo l'ẹ f'orúkọ s'ílẹ̀ sí tẹ̀ẹ́ ń jẹ́ Làmbòròkí? | | Where did you 'abandon' bona fide names and named yourself Làmbòròkí instead?<br>- Now you have cottoned on to what we / I have been trying to say;<br>- So you had such a brilliant idea and never disclosed it to anyone?<br>- Now you're talking; that's more like it! |
| 1016. | Ńgb'òòjó bá p'ẹlẹ́wù Ẹtù l'ariwo "Igí dá" ń gba'lé kan-an | | When rain has drenched the man with an Ẹtù costume that's when the screams of "tree has fallen" saturate the whole house<br>- Òh-óh-òõh, so you're complaining now because you're feeling the negative effect of something you originally initiated yourself. |
| 1017. | Ńgbà t'ónílé bá ńsọ pé Ìwòyí Àná a ti sùn, k'áléjò ó má ṣ'àfira | | When the homeowner starts saying about this time yesterday we were already asleep, let the visitor not tarry<br>- This euphemistic statement is a warning that it's time to leave. |
| 1018. | Ngó gũn'yán, ngó fũn ọ jẹ, Ibi èsun Iṣu l'ènìà-án ti ń mọ̀n | | I will pound [make] some pounded yam and give you [out of it], it is from roasted yam we will know<br>- I will prepare pounded yam and give you some, it is from the start one will know;<br>- If someone was promising you heaven and earth, you would know their sincerity |

| | | by their body language if they would indeed keep their promise;<br>- "Ye shall know them by their fruits…" Matt 7:16. |
|---|---|---|
| 1019. | Ní kán-ńgírí, ní pẹlẹbẹ, Ẹ̀ẹ́ké ní láti ṣè'kan ńbẹ̀ | Chubby or thin, the cheek has to be either of the two<br>- You are either part of the team or you are not;<br>- Either you succeed or fail [in the endeavor]; we'll soon find out;<br>- Either you are alive or dead; there is no mid-point. |
| 1020. | N'ígbà Ẹ̀gún bá sì ti dé'bi "hùn," ó ti ṣe tán àti yọ nìyẹn | When a thorn [inside a foot] has reached a point of 'uhm', it's reached the moment when it's ready to pop out<br>- When a situation has reached the point where one heaves a sigh of relief, a solution is at hand. |
| 1021. | Nínú Ìkòkò dúdú l'ẹ̀kọ funfún ti jáde | From within a black pot comes white corn-pap<br>- Out of the ashes and turmoil, comes a new beginning. |
| 1022. | N'ínú Òfîì, n'ínú Ọ̀láà l'ọmọ Pándòrò ó rùú làá | In the midst of tough ecosystems and thorny constraints do pinto beans sprout and thrive<br>- Iron does not become steel until it's been through the fire;<br>- Tough times never last but tough people do. |
| 1023. | Nǹkan Ẹni ìí di méjì k'ínú bí'ni | One's joy or good fortune does not become double and the person gets upset<br>- This is as if to say: "Oh, I thought you would be delighted;"<br>- Somebody might say this to someone who has just struck it lucky but may not wish the good news disclosed because of someone else in the room who might not be happy for him, hence might put on the look of displeasure on his face. |
| 1024. | Nǹkan ìí ṣ'ọmọ-ọn kò sí ńlé | Nothing happens to a child that is not at home |

| | | |
|---|---|---|
| | | - Don't put it on he/she who was not present [during the event]. |
| 1025. | Nǹkan l'ẹdìẹ ń jẹ k'ágbàdo ó t'ó d'áiyé | It was something that the chicken used to feed on before the corn ever came to earth<br>- Before modern inventions, human beings used to exist or before all these modern technologies (the internet, smartphones, social media, GPS, etc.) came into existence, people managed to survive anyway. |
| 1026. | Nǹkan t'ó bá wà n'ínú Ọlọ́tí l'ọtí ńpá pa | What had been inside a drunkard is what he gets drunk on<br>- What you say in a moment of anger is something you'd bottled up inside but never got a chance to say. |
| 1027. | Nwọ́n ń lé mi í bọ̀ ò yẹ Ọmọ Ọdẹ | The shrills of "They are chasing me" doesn't befit a child of a hunter. In Old Yorùbá civilization and legend, a hunter was someone who had juju and supernatural powers. Their children would often more than not have been baptized [initiated] in protective power from birth that no one would dare hassle them<br>- This is unexpected of someone of your upbringing;<br>- This is unexpected of someone of your position/office and the protection that comes with it. |
| 1028. | Nwọ́n ní "Amúkũn, Ẹrù ẹ́ wọ́." Amúkũn ní, "Hàã, Òkè lẹ̀ ńwò; ẹ è wò'sàlẹ̀ [Ibi t'ó ti wọ́ wá] ni?" | They said, "disabled man, your load is askew." The man retorted, "Argh, you're looking at the top [where the load is perched on his head]; you didn't look below [where the crookedness originated]?"<br>- You're looking at problems but not taking cognizance of the root cause of them. |
| 1029. | Nwọ́n ní "Ẹléfộ ò, Ẹ̀fọ́ọ̀ rẹ yī mà tutù ò!" Ó ní "Ẹ̀fọ́ọ̀ mi lí şe Ẹ̀fọ́ Orí Ààtàn o!" | Would-be customers commend the spinach vendor and said, "eh, spinach seller, your spinach is oh so green." She |

| | | |
|---|---|---|
| | | responded defensively, "my spinach was not plucked from a landfill." <br> - Well, no one suggested it came from a refuse dump, so why mention that unnecessary fact except it did originate from a garbage dump? |
| 1030. | Nwọ́n ní "má f'oko mi d'ọ̀nà", Ijọ́ kan l'ènìà ń ṣ'òfin ẹ̀ | They say "don't use my farmland as a path [shortcut]", it's one day one makes the rule [draws the line] <br> - People will take advantage of you only if you let them. |
| 1031. | Nwọ́n ní Ẹbọ a gbé t'ìrókò Olúwéré, Ara l'ó fi ń sun | They say the sacrificial food we place at the base of Ìrókò, it's its body it uses it to burn <br> - Your diabolical effort to make someone's life a misery is ineffective. |
| 1032. | Nwọ́n ní Ẹ̀ní nma pá, Ọ̀la nma pá; Ẹnu-ẹnu l'ẹsẹ̀ ẹ́ fi ń p'èkùrọ́ Ojú Ọ̀nà | They said it's today I'm going to kill him, it's tomorrow I'm going to kill him; gradually, gradually do the feet crack the palm kernels on the path <br> - This an unlikely event as tomorrow is not guaranteed. |
| 1033. | Nwọ́n ní k'á s'òótọ́ k'á kú s'íbẹ̀ ó sàn ju k'á pa'rọ́ k'á wà l'áiyé lọ | They say to tell the truth and die there [on the spot] is a lot better than lying and staying alive <br> - It's better to tell the truth and live with the consequences than to lie and put someone in trouble [or in jail or worse] with your lies. |
| 1034. | Nwọ́n ní t'énìyán bá ń j'ẹ̀fọ́ Ọ̀dùn, t'ó ń j'ẹ̀fọ́ Òdù, ṣebí nítorí Ọmọ ni? | They say if someone eats Ọ̀dùn spinach as well as Òdù spinach, is it not because of his children? <br> - Would-be parents go through many travails because of their desire to have children. |
| 1035. | Nwọ́n ní t'ó bá kọ'jú sí ẹ kóo tá; t'ó bá k'ẹ̀hìn sí ẹ kóo tá; t'ó bá ku Ìwọ nìkan kóo tún Èrò Araà ẹ pa | They say if it's facing you shoot it; if it turns its back on you shoot it; when you're left on your own, rethink your own plans <br> - When you're alone by yourself, do soul-searching of your part (or culpability in the affair), reflect and come to a decision of |

| | | what you're going to do henceforth because no one's going to take sides with you any longer. |
|---|---|---|
| 1036. | Nwọn ò fẹ́ wa ń'lũ̀, à ńbá wọn dá'rin; ta'ní ó bã wa gbèé? | They don't want us in the city, we initiate a song; who will join us to sing it?<br>- Since we are not wanted here, isn't it better for us to stay under the radar? That way, we are not going to draw attention to our presence. |
| 1037. | Nwọn ò kì ń gb'èsan Òròmọndìyẹ l'Ádó, k'ó ṣáà ti máa jẹ l'ẹ́hìn Ìyá ẹ̀ | No one avenges Òròmọndìyẹ [the pullet/chick] in Adó, so long as it keeps foraging behind its mother<br>- No one minds the son as long as it doesn't misuse his privilege of being the prince or the son of the political leader. |
| 1038. | Nwọ́n ti b'ẹ̀rù Orí títí, Orí ti fẹ́ sá wọ'nú! | They had feared the head so much that the head has almost imploded inside the body<br>- You have been harassed and treated so badly that you can hardly find your voice and speak out again. |
| 1039. | i. Nwọ́n ti fi Iná s'órí Òrùlé sùn<br>ii. O f'iná s'órí Òrùlé sùn<br>iii. Ó f'iná s'órí Òrùlé sùn | 1. They have left fire on the roof and went to bed.<br>2. You left fire on the roof and went to sleep<br>3. He/she left fire on the roof and went to sleep<br>- They/You have, She/He has this huge problem and yet remain docile and not do something about it.<br>For **more**, please consult the "Yorùbá Alphabets & Pronunciation Guide" page. |
| 1040. | O b'ẹ́fọ̀n l'ábàtà, o y'ọ̀bẹ́ tìí; ṣ'ómi l'o ròpé ó mu kú ni? | You found a rhinoceros in a marsh, you took a knife to it; did you think it died there as a result of drinking too much water?<br>- Somebody must have been taking care of what you are now claiming [a rough diamond] because it is now showing its potential of beauty and value. This implies that this person never valued the object in |

| | | |
|---|---|---|
| | | the past [when it was rough].<br>- Or somebody must have been responsible for the [current good state] of the object you are now coveting. |
| 1041. | Ó bà ni, kò bàjẹ́ | It's only wasting away, it's not rotten<br>- It may be bad, but the situation is not unsalvageable;<br>- It's bad but it's not unrectifiable. |
| 1042. | Ó d'ẹ̀hìn Ìgbín k'á tó f'ìkarahun ẹ̀ họ'kòkò | It'll be behind a snail before we use its shell to scrape a burnt cooking pot<br>- The speaker means no one can do anything to displace/unseat the person in the discussion while he or she is still in office [or in power]. Could also be referring to himself/herself. |
| 1043. | Ó d'iwájú ó ńd'ẹjọ́, ó d'ẹ̀hìn ó ńd'asọ̀ | [In case] in the near future it results in a litigation; [referring to it] as an antecedent, it turns into malice<br>- You notify someone [to act as a kind of witness] about what you're about to do just in case things turn awry;<br>- Watch what comes out of your mouth in case what you say today gets held against you in the near future. |
| 1044. | Ó di Àjọlọ, ó di Àjọbọ̀ | It has become "we go together," "we return together"<br>- Usually said at parting time between two people especially when one party is in the loop of where the other is going. Kind of to say "I'll give you details of my findings upon my return." It is also customary for the first person to utter the first phrase "Ó di Àjọlọ," while the other responds "Ó di Àjọbọ̀." |
| 1045. | O gbọ́ kúkù Òjò, o wá da'mi Agbada nù! | You heard the rumbling of the rain, you went and threw the water in the cauldron away!<br>- You have counted your chickens before they hatch!<br>- You have been scornful of the assistance offered to you in the nick of time, and |

| | | |
|---|---|---|
| | | now those you had counted on all along have failed to turn up! |
| 1046. | Ó kù díẹ̀ kí n wí, Ojo níí sọ'ni í dà | "I was just about to say..." makes a man a coward<br>- Be man enough and speak when you feel the need to make a contribution to the debate at hand; don't keep saying this statement after the fact. |
| 1047. | O m'ájá l'ọ́wọ́ o ní o fẹ́ ṣ'ọdẹ Alákẹdun | You are leading a dog to hunt a monkey.<br>- You have forgotten that a descendant of dogs will never go on top of trees to hunt, neither will a descendant of monkeys play around on the ground [where there are trees];<br>- You want to attempt something this bold that has never been done before, even by seasoned intrepid warriors; the chances of your success are non-existent. |
| 1048. | O m'órí Àgbò méjì o wá fi ń mu'mi n'ínú-un Koto kan ṣoṣo | You coerced the heads of two rams to drink in one single trough<br>- You are forcing two adversaries to be in the same proximity;<br>- You are a sadist! |
| 1049. | Ó mọ̀n, ó mọ̀n, kò ní mọn l'óun nikan | He knows, he knows, that's not going to be limited to just him alone<br>- The secret is not likely to remain secret for much longer;<br>- Some other people probably know as well. |
| 1050. | Ò ń ṣe'yán bí Ọkà | You are treating pounded yam like ọkà (doughy pasty food [made out of yam and/or cassava flour, or unripe plantain flour])<br>- You are not according the level of devotion the [current] situation merits;<br>- You are not taking this seriously. |
| 1051. | Ó ń ṣ'ọmọ Olóòkú bẹ́ẹ̀ ni, ṣùgbọ́n a ò lè sín m'ókūu rẹ | The child of the deceased may be traumatized enough to feel like it, but we cannot bury him with his dead parent<br>- It is mere wishful thinking but what you are proposing cannot be done; |

| | | | |
|---|---|---|---|
| | | | - What you are asking is taboo! |
| 1052. | i. | Ó ń yí mi s'ébè, ó ń yí mi s'íporo | He/she is rolling me from mound to mound, he/she is rolling me between the rifts [between the mounds] |
| | ii. | Ẹ̀ ń yí wa s'ébè, ẹ ń yí wa s'íporo | You are rolling us from mound to mound, you are rolling us between the rifts |
| | iii. | Wọ́n ń yí wa s'ébè, wọ́n ń yí wa s'íporo | They are rolling us from mound to mound, they are rolling us between the rifts |
| | | | *For more, please consult the "Yorùbá Alphabets & Pronunciation Guide" page.* |
| | | | - Whomever the pronoun refers to in the discourse is deceiving the speaker(s). |
| 1053. | Ó ńbọ̀, ó ńbọ̀; Àwọn l'à ń dẹẹ́ dèé | | It's coming, it's coming; it's a [traditional] fishing-basket we set [for its arrival] in anticipation to snare it |
| | | | - Forewarned is to be forearmed about something ominous whose arrival everyone dreads; |
| | | | - We should keep our eyes open. |
| 1054. | Ó ní'hùn kan tí Àjànàkú jẹ tẹ́'lẹ̀ Ikùn k'ó tó ṣe'kùn gbẹ̀ndu s'ọ́lọ́dẹ | | There is something the elephant had consumed in the base of its belly before it pushed out its stomach to the bush hunter |
| | | | - There's something really potent that the person under reference has as a weapon or a deterrent before showing such defiance as he does. |
| 1055. | Ò ńṣe mí, ò ńgbà mí; báwo l'a ṣe fẹ́ dúpẹ́ Ẹni t'ó ńṣe'ni, t'ó tún ńgba'ni? | | You are "doing" me, you are saving me; how do we show gratitude to the person that is "doing" someone, and [in the same breath] saving one? "Doing" means to control someone with supernatural means [black magic] |
| | | | - This is about someone acting like they love and care for you, yet do things that make you wonder if they are enemies or what; |
| | | | - I don't know where I am with you. |
| 1056. | O r'ẹsẹ̀ ẹ Wèrè, oò bũ; Ìjọ́ wo l'o fẹ́ rí t'ọlọgbọ́n? | | You found the feet of a madman you didn't hack at them, what day will you find those of a sage? |
| | | | - If you don't grab this opportunity, when |

| | | |
|---|---|---|
| | | next do you think another will present itself? |
| 1057. | O r'óko Olóko k'o t'ó gbìn'pà si | You saw the farmer's ranch before you planted groundnuts on it<br>- You can't just do things with impunity; you should have sought permission;<br>- You knew what was going to happen when you did that. |
| 1058. | Ó ṣ'íyán, kò dúró gb'ọbẹ̀ | He/she bought pounded yam, but didn't wait to collect the stew<br>- They started something but didn't finish it;<br>- He asked a question but he didn't wait for the answer;<br>- She started something [great] but was too impatient to see it through;<br>- This allegory might also have a sad tone to it: They bought a house or a car but they didn't get to live in it or drive the vehicle [due to untimely death]. |
| 1059. | O ṣu, oò nù'dí; Ẹni mélõ l'o fẹ́ ma fẹ̀'dí hàn? | You used the toilet, you didn't wipe your ass; how many people are you going to expose your anus to?<br>- Someone expresses their surprise or amazement at what you just narrated that they'd never known/heard of; and you respond, "well, how many people was I supposed to call up and narrate the whole sob story to?" |
| 1060. | Ó tán l'ẹnu àmọ́n kò tán n'íkùn | It's exhausted in the mouth but it still exists in the stomach [mind]<br>- Though there's some semblance of truce right now, there's more of that rancour where it came from. |
| 1061. | O ti d'ọ́kọ dé'lée Dàánímọ́n | You have prostituted yourself till [you reached] the home of Dãnímọ́n [bad man, outlaw]<br>- You've done the unthinkable!<br>- You've crossed the boundary and you must pay the price;<br>- You have overstepped your boundary |

| | | |
|---|---|---|
| | | [this time] and must face the consequences. |
| 1062. | Ó ti di àfisẹ́hìn, èyí t'éégún ún fi'ṣọ | It has become a throwback, the way a masquerade throws or flips his costume from the front to his shoulder in one fluid motion<br>- It has become a thing of the past; it's only a memory now. |
| 1063. | Ó ti di Akáwún [tàbí Káún]; ó ti ń já'bẹ | The person under reference has become a potash that makes a dish taste over-salted<br>- She's just too big for her boots/pants. This idiomatic personification alludes to becoming so "swollen" with conceit that one's pants or boots no longer fit. |
| 1064. | O ti gé'gi Ìgbá, oò tún jẹ'rú mọ́n<br>Ẹ ti gé'gi Ìgbá, ẹẹ̀ tún jẹ'rú mọ́n | You have cut down the eggplant tree, you will not eat locust beans again<br>2$^{nd}$ variation of proverb. {As above, but with the formal use of 'you' or someone you cannot address by name).<br>*For **more**, please consult the "Yorùbá Alphabets & Pronunciation Guide" page.*<br>- You have bitten more than you can chew. |
| 1065. | i. O ti r'óko Ikún ńlẹ̀ k'o tó gbin Ẹ̀pà si<br>ii. Ó ti r'óko Ikún ńlẹ̀ k'ó tó gbin Ẹ̀pà si | You had seen the farm of chipmunks on the ground before you planted groundnuts there<br>He/she saw the farm of chipmunks on the ground before he/she planted groundnuts on it<br>- You knew the farm was full of animals that would eat the crops you were planting;<br>- Stop complaining! You knew very well what was going to happen before you took the decision to do what you did. |
| 1066. | O ti tẹ Ọká n'írù mọ́n'lẹ̀ | You have stepped on the python's tale<br>- In this metaphoric term, you have stirred up a hornets' nest;<br>- You have wronged the unforgiving individual. |
| 1067. | Ó tú mi l'áṣọ n'íta gba-ngba | He/she has undressed me in the open |

| | | |
|---|---|---|
| | | [publicly]<br>- He/she has disgraced me openly. |
| 1068. | i. O tu'tọ́ s'ókè o f'ojú gbã.<br>ii. Ó tu'tọ́ s'ókè ó f'ojú gbã.<br>iii. Wọ́n tu'tọ́ s'ókè wọ́n f'ojú gbã | i. You spat above [tilt your head towards heaven and spit] and collected the spittle fallout with your face.<br>ii. He/she spat above and collected it with his/her face.<br>iii. They spat skywards and collected it with their faces<br>- The person(s) mentioned in this context are ready to draw a circle and fight. |
| 1069. | Ó wun'ni k'á j'ẹran pẹ́ l'ẹ́nu, Òhùnfà ọ̀fun ni ò jẹ́ | It pleases one to chew meat for long in the mouth, the swallowing reflex won't let one<br>- One wishes he could stay longer at an event, but duty or something calls;<br>- It is an idiom that means to say "I wish I could." |
| 1070. | Ó yẹ kí Ẹrú sá, ó yẹ kí Olówó ẹ nã wáa | It behooves a house-slave to run away; it's also proper that his master search for him<br>- If a child behaves like a child, an adult should also behave like an adult. |
| 1071. | Ọba kan kìí d'ábã; Àṣẹ l'ọbá ń pa | No king proposes; decrees are what a king enacts<br>- Said by an adviser to someone in power: the leader does not require anyone's input or suggestion [on the issue being considered here]. |
| 1072. | Ọba t'ó bá sán Bàntẹ́ wọ'lé Odù nã l'à á máa ń yẹ́ẹ́ sí | The king that was properly kitted out in loincloth to enter the shrine is the one we respect<br>- The man who has fulfilled the requirements [to belong] is the one we recognize and honor. |
| 1073. | Ọ̀bàyéjẹ́ Ènìà níí ru Gángan wọ̀'lú | Only an ungrateful and nonchalant fool would carry a Gángan drum on his head to enter a town/village. This is a show of nonchalance and ingratitude toward your hosts<br>- Be grateful for what you have and don't |

| | | |
|---|---|---|
| | | embarrass yourself before your benefactor. |
| 1074. | Ọbẹ̀ t'ó dùn, Owó ló paá | The stew that is so delicious must have cost a lot of money to prepare<br>- To own such a thing of excellence or beauty requires spending lots of money. |
| 1075. | Ọbẹ̀ t'ó máa pẹ́ lí kan | The stew that will last does not go sour<br>- A structure [building] that is going to last does not wobble;<br>- If it's going to work out, you usually will get an inkling from the onset. |
| 1076. | Ọbẹ̀ tóo sè é máa tó ru pa'ná | The soup you are cooking will soon boil over to extinguish the fire<br>- The police are almost onto you [and your criminal act];<br>- What you have been keeping a secret is almost out in the open. |
| 1077. | Obìnrin t'ó bá f'ojú d'orò, ó ń wá Ìyọnu Òrìṣà | A female who commonizes or underestimates an Orò idol-god, she's looking for trouble from Òrìṣà (messenger-god)<br>- Whoever attempts to do what you have in mind is looking for life-changing trouble. |
| 1078. | Obìnrin t'ó ńlọ t'ó ńbọ̀ tíò gbé'lé, t'ọwọ́ t'ọwọ́ ni k'ẹ kọ̀ọ́'lẹ̀ nítorí tíò bá p'ara ẹ̀, áá p'ọkọ | The woman who goes and comes but never stays at home, with both hands should you divorce her because if she doesn't end up killing herself, she'll end up killing her husband<br>- Get rid of those who don't appear to have loyalty to your cause or lack fidelity. |
| 1079. | Òbúkọ ọ́ ní t'òun di méjì l'ọ́dọ̀ Ìyá òun; ó ní òun l'ó bí òun, òun dẹ̀ tún l'ọkọ ẹ̀ | The buck says his own is a double score with his mother; he said she birthed him, and he is also her husband<br>- It's a win-win situation;<br>- One might even use this adage to say, "It's a great coincidence, that!" OR "Touché!" |
| 1080. | Ọ̀bún r'íkú Ọkọ tì'ràn mọ́n; ó ní at'ijọ́ t'ọkọ òun ti kú oun ò tíì wẹ̀ | A wife with body odor [because she hardly ever bathes] has something to blame her stench on; she said since her husband |

| | | |
|---|---|---|
| | | died she has not taken a bath [because she's in mourning]<br>- Someone who would habitually not do something for anyone but says if it weren't for so and so, he would be there to give a hand. Everyone knows he's full of bulls;<br>- Oh yeah? Tell that to the birds!<br>- Believe that, you'll believe anything. |
| 1081. | Ọ̀bùn ràdìràdì ní ó r'ẹrù Afínjú wọ'lé | The messy or sloppy individual is the one that will carry the belongings of the clean and methodical person into the house<br>- For example, those that oppose a government policy are the ones for whom the policy was written [to benefit] in the first place. |
| 1082. | Ọbuntun ò níí gbé s'Áìmú | The young maidens will not 'hang' or 'be suspended' in Àìmú (Untaken Land), i.e. they will always find suitors<br>- No matter what, the plan/idea will take off someday;<br>- Something has got to give;<br>- The situation will not remain stagnant forever. |
| 1083. | Ọ̀daràn Ẹiyẹ t'ó ń mun'sàn | A criminal bird that sucks oranges<br>- Someone who has done something one cannot punish or rebuke them for. |
| 1084. | Ọdẹ ìí p'ọdẹ ẹ́ j'aiyé | A hunter does not kill another hunter and live<br>- There has been a huge betrayal of trust and someone is baying for some kind of retribution with this statement. |
| 1085. | Òde l'ó ń d'ọ́mọ ẹ̀ l'ábọ̀ | It's outdoors lifestyle that bids its child "welcome", "nice to see you again"<br>- Don't complain if you experience stressful moments attending night clubs, parties and other partying life. It's occupational hazard. |
| 1086. | Òde ńlá ò r'íbi sá rè f'óòrùn | A big outing [parade] has no hiding place from the sun<br>- We [group or club members] excuse you |

| | | |
|---|---|---|
| | | to attend to other things;<br>- We are here till your return or till you release us [to go];<br>- We are in no rush to leave. |
| 1087. | Ọdẹ t'ó ńṣọ́ Elédùmarè, Orí Ẹ̀gùn l'ó máa kú sí | The hunter that is watching to spot God, his chosen summit (or watch tower) is the very location where he'll die<br>- He who waits to see happen something that had hitherto never been possible is only waiting in vain. Rather like hoping to see snow in West Africa. Whoever nurses such hopes will die before that happens. |
| 1088. | i. Odò ẹ́ ti gbẹ́'gi ni púmpú, kò sì ní f'ara re.<br>ii. Odòo ẹẹ́ ti gbẹ́'gi ni púmpú, kò sì ní f'ara re | i. Your brook has 'sharpened wood in short order' (like any tree growing inside a stream never grows beyond a few centimeters), and the brook will not fare well.<br>ii. His/her brook has 'sharpened wood in short order' (like any tree growing inside a stream never grows beyond a few centimeters), and the brook will not fare well<br>- The person under reference has done a willful and wicked thing and he's going to suffer the repercussion. |
| 1089. | Odò ò kì ń kún k'ó yí b'ẹja l'ójú | A river never fills up and overwhelms the fish's eyes<br>- Fish can never be inundated with water;<br>- Despite all challenges in a person's life, he would still know whence he came. |
| 1090. | Odò t'ó bá gbàgbé Orísun ẹẹ́ máa ń gbẹ ni | A river that forgets its source is bound to dry up<br>- One should not forget where he comes from;<br>- A man with no history is a lost man. |
| 1091. | Òdú ni, kìí ṣ'àìmọ̀n f'olóko | It's an Òdú spinach, it's not unknown to the owner of the farm<br>- The individual being referred to is well-known by everyone or everyone must have heard about him and what he does or what he stands for. |

| | | |
|---|---|---|
| 1092. | Ọdún mẹ́ta tí Rélùwéè ti ń sá'ré, ẹ kú Iwájú l'ó máa ń k'ílẹ̀ | Three years that a train has been going, "hello at the fore" is how it'll be saluting land<br>- The entity [or country] is so far gone and advanced you'll never be able to catch up with them;<br>- Could be said to someone that as long as their parents are alive, he/she could never be the same age as their parents;<br>- This idiom is hinting that the issue here is a mathematical impossibility. |
| 1093. | Ọdún ò níí dun k'á má rí nǹkan Àjọ̀dún | A season will not arrive without citizens finding food stuff to celebrate it<br>- A seasonal celebration will not arrive and we won't be able to find things to celebrate it, so everyone can relax. |
| 1094. | Òfin táa bá t'orí Ẹrú ṣe ó ti di dandan k'ó d'órí Ọmọ; à ṣé nǹkan Ọ̀hún ò tíì kan'ni ni | The law we passed because of the house-slave must one day affect the [freeborn] child; and now that the child [of the law maker] has fallen foul of this same law, the political leader is now running helter-skelter to get the law repealed<br>- Warning to political leaders to be considerate when trying to introduce draconian laws. |
| 1095. | Ògà t'ó nṣe jẹ́jẹ́, Ikú paá, k'a máì tíì wá sọ t'ọ̀pọ̀lọ́ t'ó ń jan'ra ẹ̀ mọ́n'lẹ̀ | The chameleon that lived its life in tranquility, death managed to claim it; not to discuss that of the toad that bounces itself on the ground willfully<br>- A gentle and careful person succumbs to death, how much more a man with a reckless and violent disposition. |
| 1096. | Ògangan Ọ̀nà l'aláké ńsọ | Right in the middle of the road does the Aláké [sand flea] digs<br>- Right on the head does the speaker or the person in reference strike the nail; he doesn't beat about the bush. |
| 1097. | Ọgbọ́n Ẹnìkan ò jọ; Ìmọ̀nràn Ẹnìkan ò jọ bọ̀rọ̀. Ìmọ̀nràn t'énìà kan ṣoṣó bá gbà, Asán ni | Wisdom of one single person doesn't cut it; counsel of just one person doesn't hack it at all; the advice that a single person adopts is zilch |

| | | |
|---|---|---|
| | | - We need to come together and use our collective wisdom. |
| 1098. | Ọgbọ́n lí tán n'íkùn Àgbà | Wisdom never exhausts in an elder's belly<br>- A great leader will always think of a way out of a challenging situation. |
| 1099. | Ọgbọ́n Inú Ọlọ́gbọ́n ni Ọlọ́gbọ́n fi ń jẹun | The wisdom that is within a wise man is what the wise uses to earn his daily bread<br>- You use what you've got to earn your keep. |
| 1100. | Ọgbọ́n j'agbára | Wisdom is greater than strength. |
| 1101. | Ọgbọ́n l'a fi ń p'ẹmọ́n, Àyà gbà-ǹgbà l'a fi ń p'ejò, Pẹ̀lẹ́kùtù l'a fi ń ro'ko Ìdí-ọ̀pẹ | With cleverness do we kill Ẹmọ́n [a kind of rat with light-yellow fur], with boldness does one kill a snake, with utter calmness do we trim the bush in the base of a palm tree [especially when young]<br>- The issue under discussion requires boldness and extreme tact. |
| 1102. | Ọgbọ́n Ọlọ́gbọ́n ò jẹ́ k'á pe Àgbà ní Wèrè | The wisdom of a sagacious man doesn't permit us to address an elder a madman<br>- Taking a page out of the book of a wise philosopher, one knows never to call an elder [in the community] a psychopath. |
| 1103. | Ọgbọọgbọ́n ni Àgbá fi ń sá fún Màálúù | The elderly [senior citizens] use wisdom to run from a cow or a herd of cows<br>- Use your wit or common sense to control a bad situation before it gets out of hand. |
| 1104. | Ògirí l'étí | Walls have ears<br>- Usually whispered between two people or in a group before sensitive conversation begins;<br>- Do not speak too loudly;<br>- You never know who has ears sharp enough to pick up strays of your utterances. |
| 1105. | Ògó tà, Ògó ò tà, Owó Aláárù á pé | Cudgels sell, cudgels do not sell [in the market], the money [fee] of the market-wares carrier will be complete<br>- Whether you make a great sale/profit or not, it's no skin off the nose of the transporter who delivered your wares to the market; you've still got to pay them |

| | | |
|---|---|---|
| | | their fare in full;<br>- Whether a team wins or loses, the players will still get paid. |
| 1106. | Ogún Ọdún tí Irọ́ ti ńlọ n'íwájú, Ọjọ́ kan l'òtítọ́ ń báa | Twenty years' head start that a lie has had, it'll take just one day for the truth to catch up with it<br>- No matter how long you've been living a lie, beware; the truth is only round the corner. |
| 1107. | Ogún Ọmọdé ò lè ṣ'eré f'ógún Ọdún | Twenty children cannot play together for twenty years<br>- Sooner or later, a time will come when childhood friends disperse and go to their different destinies;<br>- Time waits for no one. |
| 1108. | Ohun nílá ò kì ń rá'hun | A huge utensil [pot] does not render invisible what you put in it. It may not be ideal to use a giant pot to cook a handful of grains but if you look hard enough, one can still see the grains in the pot. Placing the food in the large pot has not rendered it invisible; maybe just inappropriate<br>- A salient example: say you need to store a set of kitchen applicances but can't find the right storage in time. Instead you find a warehouse [which is way too large] and so you rent it. What does it matter, as long as you are able to store your stuff?<br>- It's all you've got; it'll have to do. |
| 1109. | Ohun Ojú ńwá, l'ojú ńrí | What the eyes are searching for is what the eyes find<br>- If you look for trouble, you'll eventually find misery, so to speak. |
| 1110. | Ohun Ọwọ́ mi ò tó, nma fi Gòngò fàá | Whatever my hand cannot reach, I'll use a sickle to draw it<br>- If there's something you're trying to get your hands on but is not easily obtainable, you may use what you have to try and get it: could be a lady's affection, a plum position at work, could be influence, money or both. |

| | | |
|---|---|---|
| 1111. | Ohun t'a maa jẹ lí jẹ́ á gbọ́n | What we want to eat prevents us from being wise<br>- Self-interest impedes progress for the people or inhibits us from taking the right course of action. |
| 1112. | Ohun táà ńwá lọ sí Sókótó wà l'ápòo Ṣòkòtò | What we are travelling to Sókótó [a Northern Nigerian city] to search for is right inside the Ṣòkòtò (pants) we have on<br>- Look for solutions to your challenges within your community;<br>- You may not have to suffer so much for what troubles you if you'll only look for resources available around you. |
| 1113. | Ohun t'ágbà á fi ń j'ẹ̀kọ, Abẹ́ Ewé l'ó ń gbé | What the elders eat Ẹ̀kọ with, it's underneath fallen leaves that it lives<br>- The power that gives adults ability to do certain things is hidden out of sight of the young ones;<br>- Someone might say this to indicate that they are not willing to share a knowledge or information to the person(s) they say this proverb to. |
| 1114. | Ohun táà bá f'ara ṣ'iṣẹ́ fún lí pẹ́ l'ọ́wọ́ Ẹni | What we didn't work for [to possess] does not stay long in one's hand<br>- We do not value what we obtained so cheaply, hence if we lost it in a short time, we wouldn't worry too much about it. |
| 1115. | Ohun táa bá f'ara ṣ'iṣẹ́ fún níí pẹ́ l'ọ́wọ́ Ẹni | What we have labored for with our body is what lasts long in in one's hand [one's keep]<br>- What we have labored for and suffered a lot of hardship to acquire in our lives is what we nurture most with care and love, and try our best to preserve it. |
| 1116. | Ohun táa bá f'ẹ̀lẹ̀ mú kìí bàjẹ́, Ohun táa bá f'agbára mú níí le koko mọ́n'ni | Whatever we grab with humility never perish, what we grab with force is what turns out to be challenging with one<br>- Let patience and humility be your watchwords. |
| 1117. | Ohun táa bá fi pamọ́n l'ó n'íyì | What we keep [in a hiding place] is what has merit |

|   |   |   |
|---|---|---|
|   |   | - People generally keep what they consider valuable secret, in a safe place or restrict its knowledge only to a select few;<br>- For classified government information to remain top-secret, the secrecy behind it has to be maintained. |
| 1118. | Ohun táà bá jẹ rí ìí dá'ni l'ọ́rùn | What we have never eaten before doesn't break one's neck<br>- No one craves for a meal they've never had before;<br>- We don't miss what we never had. |
| 1119. | Ohun táa bá ní l'à ń náání | It is what we have that we cherish<br>- If you don't value what you have, no one else is going to value it. |
| 1120. | Ohun t'ẹiyẹ bá jẹ l'ẹiyẹ ma gbé fò | What a bird has eaten is what it'll carry and fly with<br>- This figure of speech is best suited for someone on a road trip: use the bathroom, fill your tank and get all the snacks you need now as there might be no such opportunity after you exit here until final destination;<br>- Better grab what you can before [the anticipated] trouble starts. |
| 1121. | Ohun t'énìà án bá fi ju Ènìyàn lọ, àá fíí hàn-án ni | Whatever one has that eclipses his rival's, we show it to him<br>- This person needs to be put in their place. |
| 1122. | Ohun t'ènìyán bá fi s'ílẹ̀, òun l'ewúrẹ́ ńgbé, tàbí...<br>Ohun t'a bá fi s'ílẹ̀, òun l'ewúrẹ́ ńgbé | It's what someone leaves behind (or forgets) that the goat grabs, OR...<br>It's what we leave behind (or forget) that the goat grabs<br>- If you don't value your asset(s), others might see their value and snap them up. |
| 1123. | Ohun t'ó bá'jú l'ó bá'mú | What touches the eyes touches the nose [as well]. It is entirely dependent on the scenario or context when one may use this metaphor<br>- What a loved one or a family member is going through will likewise affect the whole family, be it positive or otherwise; |

| | | |
|---|---|---|
| | | - Any economic woe that befalls a country, such as inflation, recession, etc. must directly affect its citizens;<br>- Another example: in a situation where, say, a former public benefactor is undergoing a perceived unfair and biased investigation; some people might rally round him/her and declare this metaphor: "If there ever was a time to show our unwavering solidarity, it is now!"<br>- This concerns us all, folks! |
| 1124. | Ohun t'o sè t'ílé fi jó'ná, gbogbo Aiyé l'ó máa gbọ́ | What you cooked that the whole house burned down, the whole world will hear it<br>- I shall disclose the secret you have been keeping close to your chest. |
| 1125. | Ohun t'ó wà l'ẹ̀hìn Ọ̀fà ó ju Èje lọ | What is behind six is more than seven<br>- Things are not what they seem;<br>- There are more to this than meets the eye. |
| 1126. | Ohun tí 'ò dáa ò l'órúkọ méjì; kò dáa nã l'ó ń jẹ́ | What is not good doesn't have two names; 'not good' is its name<br>- Call a spade a spade. |
| 1127. | Ohun tí Ajá máa jẹ, Èṣù l'ó ń ṣeé | What the dog is going to eat, the devil provides it<br>- What we need to achieve our purpose will provide itself. |
| 1128. | Ohun tí Ojú Ìlábìrù ń rí, Ojú Aṣọ ò lè to | The stuff that the eyes of a weaver experience, the eyes of the clothes cannot see it<br>- An example of this allegory is: If children knew what their parents go through to raise and educate them, the children would be blown away in awe of the sacrifices;<br>- Another example: The hardship that some migrant workers in Western countries go through (such as poor living conditions, lack of access to health care because they are undocumented, fear of being caught and deported, and loneliness) to send money to their loved |

| | | |
|---|---|---|
| | | ones in their respective native countries, the dependants have no idea. |
| 1129. | Ohun t'ó bá dé bá'ni, Orí Ẹni l'a fi ń gbe | Whatever happens to someone, we use one's head to carry it<br>- Acknowledge your inner demon;<br>- Face your demons. |
| 1130. | Ohun t'ó bá jọ'hun l'a fi ń wé'hun | It's what approximates an issue that we evaluate issues with<br>- If we are looking for evidence, we always compare similarities of earlier occurrence(s). |
| 1131. | Ohun t'ó bá ti yá lí pẹ mọ́n | What is ready does not tarry much longer<br>- What are you waiting for?<br>- Let's make hay while the sun is shining! |
| 1132. | Ohun t'ó bá w'ọmọ ọ́n jẹ, òun l'à á fi ń lọ́ọ́ | It's what a child loves to eat that we offer him/her<br>- To keep the peace and have your way, do what the troublesome individual craves. |
| 1133. | Ohun t'ó máa jí Baara á jí Baara | What will wake Baara will wake Baara<br>- If you won't take heed and protect yourself or do something that's going to be beneficial to your wellbeing, it's your problem and all eyes will see and you'll be shamed. |
| 1134. | Ohun t'ó ń bi'ni á máa bi'ni; Ohun t'ó ń bèèrè á máa bèèrè | That which asks someone will ask someone; what analyses will always analyze<br>- What will be will be; the speaker has accepted his fate. |
| 1135. | Ohun t'ó ń ti'ni l'ójú j'olè lọ ń bẹ | Something that shames more than being a thief exists. |
| 1136. | Ohun t'ó pamọ́n, Ojú Ọlọ́un l'ó to | Things that are obscure or hidden, only God's Eyes see them<br>- Said to someone or a group who may be economical with the truth or simply not forthcoming with the way things really are. |
| 1137. | Ohun t'ó yẹ'ni l'ó y'ẹni; Okùn Ọrùn ò y'ẹdìẹ | What befits one is what suits someone or what's apposite; a rope or a leash does not befit a hen/rooster |

| | | |
|---|---|---|
| | | - We should not be found engaged in unbefitting activity. |
| 1138. | Ohun t'ójú Aláìmooré ńrí, Òṣìkà á j'ìyà a ẹ̀ lát'aiyé lọ | What the eyes of an ingrate see, the wicked will suffer it in this world onward till the next<br>- God hates wicked people. "The Lord tests the righteous, but His soul hates the wicked and the one who loves violence" (Psalm 11:5). |
| 1139. | Ọjà t'ọmọ bá ti wọ̀, ó ti di Ọjà Òkùtà | A business or market that children have entered [concerning children] has become a trading activity with loss<br>- An arrangement that involves children is said to be an unprofitable undertaking because raising children costs a lot of money. |
| 1140. | Ọjọ́ gbogbo ni t'olè; Ọjọ́ kan ni t'olóun | Every day is for the thief; one day is for the owner<br>- Everyday people hear only about the "atrocities" of the peaceful activist/agitator who is fighting for his people's liberation; the hoopla will be nothing compared to what everyone will hear about the vicious atrocities committed by those in government who label him a terrorist instead. |
| 1141. | Ọjọ́ Ikú l'ọjọ́ Ìsinmi | The day of death is the day of rest<br>- This matter is "till death do us part;"<br>- No rest until the job is done. |
| 1142. | Òjò l'ó p'àlàpà t'ó fi d'ohun Àmúgùn f'ẹran | It was rainfall that beat the uncompleted foundation wall and battered it to be a thing of climbing for domestic animals<br>- It was a circumstance that made someone a laughing stock or a disrespected person in the community;<br>- It was circumstances that made a rich man (who is now somehow poor) become a buddy of a poor inconsequential man. |
| 1143. | Ọjọ́ Oore pé, Aṣiwèrè gbàgbé | The day all the caring assistance completes [i.e. eventually results in desired sanity of the sick man], the |

|      |                                                                                         |                                                                                                                                                                                                                                                                                                                                                                                                                                                                                                           |
|------|-----------------------------------------------------------------------------------------|-------------------------------------------------------------------------------------------------------------------------------------------------------------------------------------------------------------------------------------------------------------------------------------------------------------------------------------------------------------------------------------------------------------------------------------------------------------------------------------------------------|
|      |                                                                                         | schizophrenic forgets<br>- Can be equated with someone whom his community supported to achieve great success but who seems to have forgotten where he/she would have been without these folks, and now turns his/her back on them;<br>- Can also be likened to a nation that many countries fought for to achieve independence. This nation may now appear to have forgotten where they would have been without the support they got, and now treats some citizens of those very countries woefully. |
| 1144.| Òjò Òrú ìí pa'ni Ire. Bí ò bá p'olè, a p'òfófó, a pa Aṣẹ́wó, a pa Dókọdókọ             | A night rain never drenches innocent decent folks. If it doesn't soak thieves, it'll beat gossips, it'll drench prostitutes as well as adulterers<br>- Decent folks don't engage in suspect nightly activities; they would be sleeping snugly in their beds during such nighttime downpours.                                                                                                                                                                                                            |
| 1145.| Òjó rọ̀ kò ì dá, ẹ ní kò tó t'àná                                                      | The rain is falling and has yet to stop, you say it's not up to yesterday's downpour<br>- This idiom hints that the speaker has not yet finished with his narrative, but everyone is already judging his discourse; some patience is advised to hear him out first.                                                                                                                                                                                                                                   |
| 1146.| Ọjọ́ t'ọ́n bá pa Wèrè n'ọ́n ma mọ̀n p'ó l'ẹ́bí                                        | The day they kill a mad person is when they'll know he/she has got relations<br>- The day they harm one of us is the day they'll find out that we have powerful supporters.                                                                                                                                                                                                                                                                                                                           |
| 1147.| Ọjọ́ tí Ajá bá f'eyín sọ Irin, Ìjọ́ nã l'eyín Ẹnu ẹ̀ẹ́ máa wọ́ dànù                  | The day a dog bites on an iron is the day all his teeth will fall out of his mouth<br>- The day a popular man commits a heinous crime is the day he loses all his influence;<br>- The day one breaks the law and scamper is the day he becomes a wanted man.                                                                                                                                                                                                                                          |

| 1148. | Òjó tí ń pa Igún-un wa, Ọjọ́ ti pẹ́ | It's been a long while that the rain has been beating our vulture<br>- We have been suffering for a long time, with virtually no respite. |
|---|---|---|
| 1149. | Ojọ́ọ're níí jẹ́ Ọ̀kẹ́rẹ́; Ọjọ́ Ọ̀kẹ́rẹ́ p'ebi sùn ló pọ̀ | A good day is called Ọ̀kẹ́rẹ́ [squirrel], the number of days the squirrel went hungry are countless<br>- Only the speaker knows what he's been through. |
| 1150. | Ojú á tún'ra rí, Òwé Àkàlàmàgbò | Eyes will re-see themselves, the proverb of the ground horn bill<br>- We shall meet again! [with a veiled threat or intimidation] |
| 1151. | Ojú Àwo l'àwó fi ńgb'ọbẹ̀ | The face of a bowl is what it uses to collect soups<br>- Ok, we're ready - let's hear the indictment;<br>- We face our challenges head-on, not scamper and bury our heads in the sand. |
| 1152. | Ojú Ẹni l'àá s'òdodo; Aṣẹ̀hìndeni ò wọ́'pọ̀ | Right before someone might the truth be said; when you turn your back, it's uncommon to find someone that'll look after your interest<br>- In other words, we don't know each other's mind. |
| 1153. | Ojú Ẹní máa là á rí Ìyọnu | The eyes of someone who's gonna be wealthy will see plenty of ups and downs<br>- An ambitious individual's hardship of today is a sign of success and wealth to come. |
| 1154. | Ojú ìí pọ́n'ṣin aì ma là | An ackee's eyes never go through trauma without opening<br>- No matter what, there'll be a solution to the problem [at hand]. |
| 1155. | Ojú kan Ẹ̀pà, Ojú kan Erèé ni | It's a matter of "one eye does the peanut have, one eye does the black-eyed bean have"<br>- The speaker is expressing the fact that she has only one single child. |
| 1156. | Ojú kan l'àdá ń ní; Èyí t'ó bá l'ójú méjì, Idà l'à ń pèé | The cutlass has only one "eye"; the one that has two "eyes", it's a sword we call it |

|  |  | - The speaker is stating that he is not two-faced;<br>- He or she neither double-dates nor does he/she double-deal. |
|---|---|---|
| 1157. | Ojú kan tí Ọká bá jó'kõ è sí, Ibẹ ni Ohun tí ó jẹ ẹ ti ma báa | One spot that the viper quietly sits is where what he's going to eat will come to him<br>- The enemies of the speaker will inadvertently reveal themselves [confess] to him and face their just punishment. |
| 1158. | Ojú l'àá m'epo, Ẹ̀ẹ̀kẹ́ l'àá mọn'yò | With the eyes do we recognize [good] palm oil, in the cheeks do we recognize [taste] salt<br>- Okay, let's see the proof of the result!<br>- I didn't think it could happen, but seeing is believing;<br>- The proof of the pudding is in the eating. |
| 1159. | Ojú l'alákàn-án fi ń ṣọ́'rí | The eyes are what the crab employs to guard the head [early warning signal]<br>- Use whatever alarm system you have as sensor/antenna of impending danger. |
| 1160. | Ojú l'o fi ri, Ètè ẹ ò bàá | With your eyes you see it [food], your lips will not touch it<br>- You're admiring the girl, but you won't get to marry her;<br>- You see the new car, but I won't allow you to drive it;<br>- Now you see it, now you don't. |
| 1161. | Ojú l'a f'ẹni, Ọ̀rẹ́ ò dé'nú | Affection is on face value [i.e. when you are with the friend], friendship is hardly truly sincere. |
| 1162. | Ojú l'a rí l'à ń s'òdodo; Aṣèyìn de'ni ò wọ́pọ̀ | Face-to-face is when we might be honest; those who might hold the fort conscientiously [take over the reins] when we are away are uncommon<br>- We're generous with the truth when we face each other; this is rarely the case when we turn our back! |
| 1163. | Ojú l'àgbà ń yá, Àgbàlagbà ìí yá'nu | An elderly person may show grandiloquence, an elderly person will not be full of 'talk' [rhetoric] |

| | | |
|---|---|---|
| | | - It is not expected of the person [in the narrative] to talk so much, but remain patient with a show of dignity. |
| 1164. | Ojú l'ó ń r'ójú ṣ'àánú | It's eyes that see eyes to do kindness<br>- You can't see the obvious challenges someone is facing without having compassion;<br>- In this instance, empathy is what's required. |
| 1165. | Ojú mẹ́wã ò j'ojú Ẹni | Ten eyes don't look like one's eyes<br>- What is yours is yours;<br>- You can't feel someone's pleasure [or discomfort, sorrow or drunkenness, etc.] with them. |
| 1166. | Ojú ni Fèrèsé Ọkàn | Eyes are the windows to the soul<br>- If someone is in harmony or conflict with you, you can always tell by their eyes, if you look deep enough;<br>- "Your eyes are windows into your body. If you open your eyes wide in wonder and belief, your body fills up with light." Matthew 6:22-23 MSG |
| 1167. | Ojú Ọ̀run-ún t'ẹiyẹ ẹ́ fò l'àì f'ara kan'ra | The sky is wide enough that birds can fly without touching each other<br>- The world is big enough that two enemies don't have to see one another;<br>- The market is wide enough that a business niche can have many competitors. |
| 1168. | Ojú ṣe méjìi Awòran; Àtélẹsẹ̀ ẹ́ ṣe méjìi Arìnnà; b'áwẹ́ Ìdí bá ṣe méjì, áá j'òkó l'ẹ́ní | The eye becomes two for a spectator; the sole of the foot becomes two for a walker; if a buttock becomes two, one can sit on a mat<br>- There should be no dissenting voices with any of my decisions; other people have done it without so much as a ruckus;<br>- It is my choice; I have earned it, so everyone should respect it. |
| 1169. | Ojú t'ó bá máa bá'ni ka'lẹ́ lí t'ààrọ̀ ọ́ ṣe'pin | The eyes that wish to remain with someone till twilight won't produce boogers in the morning |

| | | |
|---|---|---|
| | | - If something was going to be ours forever, we would get clear and unambiguous positive hints early enough, if we observe very closely;<br>- If a cause is going to be a success, you'll notice the right indicators will be flashing early enough. |
| 1170. | Ojú t'ó bá r'íbi tí ò bá fọ́, Ire ló kù tí ó rìí | The eyes that saw evil and failed to lose their vision, goodness is what's left for them to see<br>- He who had been through the throes of life (or death) and survived to relate the tale will accept any other challenge of life as a second chance. |
| 1171. | Ojú t'ó ti mọn'ni rí kò lè l'óun ò mọn'ni mọ́n | The eyes that have known someone before cannot say they do not know the person again<br>- Once you have had dealings with someone, they can hardly deny knowing you [when next you run into one another]. |
| 1172. | Ọká lì j'ọkà; kín l'ọkàá wá dé'nú Ọká; à ṣé Ẹran tí ń j'ọkà l'oká ńjẹ | The python doesn't eat ọkà; what is ọkà doing in the belly of a python; Oh-Oh-Oh, so the animal that eats ọkà is what the python eats?<br>- What are all these calamities?<br>- What is causing all these intrigues? |
| 1173. | Ọká ti bí'mọ ọ́n lẹ̀, ó b'óró | A python has birthed her snakelet, she has birthed venom<br>- Someone has been poisoning the mind of some other person(s) in the narrative;<br>- Do not be surprised if you start experiencing instances of malice from certain quarters henceforth. |
| 1174. | Ọ̀kánjúwà àt'olè, Gẹ́ńgẹ́ l'ó ń jẹ | Greediness and stealing, there's correlation between them<br>- They are birds of the same feather. |
| 1175. | Ọ̀kánjúwà àt'olè, Ọgbọọgba n'ọ́n jẹ | Greed and stealing, there's equality between them [they are the same]<br>- That bad behavior and this one in question, they are equally bad;<br>- They are birds of the same feather. |

| | | |
|---|---|---|
| 1176. | Òkèèrè l'ọ̀rẹ́ ti dùn ún ṣe | It's from afar that friendship is 'sweet' to maintain; friendship is best enjoyed from a distance<br>- To make a friendship last, it's best not to live together with your friends;<br>- You may like someone from afar but when you get close to them, you find out what they are really like. |
| 1177. | Ọ̀kẹ́rẹ́ bí ǹkan Ọbẹ̀, ó l'óun bí ǹkan | The squirrel has birthed a thing for a pot of stew, she thinks she's birthed something. This idiom applies in West Africa where squirrels are roasted or used as meat in a pot of stew<br>- Said by someone possibly jealous of another: what do you think you've got?<br>- What you think you've got that is making your head swell, you wait until the new laws come into effect and see if it isn't rendered worthless. |
| 1178. | Ọ̀kẹ́rẹ́ g'orí Ìrókò, Ojú Ọdẹ́ dá | The squirrel climbs up the Ìrókò tree, the face of the hunter clears<br>- What you'd been banking on [placed your money or pinned your hopes on] has slipped from within your grasp or the plan has gone 'pear-shaped';<br>- Now you see it, now you don't. |
| 1179. | Ọ̀kẹ́rẹ́ jọ'kún, Olóõgìnní j'ògbò, Àdán ò yàtọ̀ sí Òòbẹ̀ l'áàjìn | The squirrel looks like a chipmunk, the cat looks like a genet, the bat is not distinguishable from an owl in the dark<br>- The offspring of someone has got to look like them. |
| 1180. | Òkété gbàgbé Ìgbòsí, ó dé'gbà Alátẹ ó ká'wọ́ lé'rí | The giant pouched rat forgot Ìgbòsí, when he got to the rat seller's table-display [dead] in the market, his arms were clasped on his head in sorrow<br>- You abandoned your culture; you have now returned to the same cradle you had ignored for so long because you're now nothing. |
| 1181. | Òkété ní Ọjọ́ gbogbo l'òún mọ̀n, òun ò mọn Ọjọ́ mîn | The giant pouched rat declares that although he knew all days, he does not |

|  |  | know another day<br>- We may not know yet what's going to happen, we surely will when the time is upon us. |
|---|---|---|
| 1182. | Ọkọ burúkú ṣe é fẹ́; Àna burúkú niò ṣe é ní | A lady could marry a nasty husband; however, horrid in-laws are the ones not good to have<br>- It's one thing to make an embarrassing gaffe; to make a plethora of blunders in a given situation is a worse proposition. |
| 1183. | Òkò ò gbọdọ̀ t'ẹnu Ìbọn jò | Pebbles should not leak from a gun muzzle<br>- You must not leak this secret; effectively you are muzzled from disclosing the information you've just learned. |
| 1184. | Oko ò ní jẹ́ ti Baba, t'ọmọ, k'ó má l'áàlà | A farm cannot belong to both father and son and not have a demarcation<br>- Don't assume what you're seeing is a joint effort;<br>- We may have the same parents, yes, but was what he did something I would do?<br>- You need to pay attention and know what I'm capable or incapable of. |
| 1185. | Ọkọ t'ó bá t'ọ́kọ l'ó ńṣe Baálé l'ọ́ọ̀dẹ̀ | A husband that is worthy of being called Husband is the one that runs his family home successfully<br>- A just and indefatigable man is the one worthy of the position of leadership. |
| 1186. | Òkóbó ìí bí'mọ s'ítòsí | The impotent man never births a child close by [that everyone can easily affirm he is indeed a father now]<br>- You need to prove to those who have this metaphoric thought that what you are claiming is definitely true. |
| 1187. | Òkú Ajá ìí gbó | A dead dog does not bark<br>- This axiom is usually in reference to someone who may have just been outdone, defeated or overcome. |
| 1188. | Òkú ìí san'wóo Pósí | A corpse does not pay for its coffin<br>- The item is gratis for the person asking for the price; |

| | | |
|---|---|---|
| | | - The seller is not charging the buyer for the product. |
| 1189. | Òkú ò gbọdọ̀ f'ara pamọ́n f'ẹni t'ó ma sín | A corpse cannot hide its body from those who will bury it<br>- You can't hide your personal details and other information from entities that require them to give you something you need, i.e. government departments, visa applications, banks, doctors, immigration et al;<br>- It would behoove you to be nicer to those who could help you. |
| 1190. | Òkun ìí hó riri k'a wàá riri | The sea does not boil wild and we scoop it in our bucket wildly<br>- We have to tread carefully so the situation being debated does not get out of hand;<br>- Patience and tact will not be out of line here. |
| 1191. | Okun Inú l'a fi ń gbé ti Ìta | The strength inside [inner strength] is what we employ to sustain that of the outside<br>- The family support that awaits us at home is what sustains us when we are away from home. |
| 1192. | Òkùn kan ìí gùn-gùn-gùn k'ó má n'íbi táa ti fàá wá | A rope cannot be so lengthy that it does not have a source whence it was pulled<br>- There is no one without history/background. |
| 1193. | Ọkùnrin l'àdá | Man is the cutlass<br>- A man is the symbolic cutlass in leading the way in a thick forest brush; hacking at weeds and tree branches to clear a path through which his family may walk. |
| 1194. | Ọkùnrín r'éjò, Obìnrín paá; ṣebí k'éjò má ti lọ ni! | A man spots a snake but it's a woman that succeeds in killing it; as long as the snake doesn't get to escape, what difference does it make?<br>- It doesn't matter who negotiates and gets us what we want, as long as we get it! |
| 1195. | Ọlá Àbàtà l'ó ń m'ódòó ṣàn | The resources [influence] of Àbàtà kolanut |

| | | |
|---|---|---|
| | | is what makes the stream flow<br>- That you are where you are is proof of the privilege of your association with a certain influential individual that you are enjoying. |
| 1196. | Olè ìí j'àgbà k'ó má ṣeé l'ojú firí | A thief does not progress to leadership and no longer does a double take [upon sighting any object of value belonging to another]<br>- Once a thief, always a thief. |
| 1197. | Olè l'àá fi nǹkan-án ṣọ́ | It's a thief we entrust our most precious objects to guard<br>- The most secure entity [as noted in the content] than this is inexistent. |
| 1198. | Olè l'ó m'ẹsẹ̀ Olè é tọ̀ | Only a thief knows how to trace the path of a thief<br>- Birds of a feather flock together. |
| 1199. | Olè t'ó gbé Kààkàkí Ọba, ńbo ní ó ti fọ́n? | The thief who steals the king's trumpet, where will he blow it?<br>- There is absolutely no point in acquiring this object, or going this route. |
| 1200. | Òlẹlẹ̀ t'ó bá wọ'nú Èkọ kò tún jáde mọ́n | Òlẹlẹ̀ (dish made of blended black-eyed peas and wrapped in leaves and boiled).<br>Èkọ (hardened corn-pap is a dish made of corn/maize, also wrapped in leaves and boiled). The two complement one another.<br>**EXPLANATION**:<br>In this proverbial context:<br>Òlẹlẹ̀ that 'enters' Èkọ will not come out again<br>- When something has been assigned to someone, that person expects to keep it for life and never cedes possession. |
| 1201. | Ọlọ́bẹ̀ l'ó l'ọkọ | A [female] culinarian is the one that 'owns' the husband<br>- A husband sticks with the wife who is an excellent cook and will not look for a replacement;<br>- The way to a man's heart is through his stomach. |

| 1202. | Olófõfó ò gb'ẹgbẹ̀wá, Ibi Ọpẹ́ l'ó mọn | A rumormonger doesn't get a tenth [of two thousand]; the limit of gratitude is "thanks"<br>- Mind your own business;<br>- A gossiper never gets a financial reward, beyond "thank you." |
|---|---|---|
| 1203. | Olójú ò ní la'jú ẹ̀ s'ílẹ̀ kí Tàlùbọ́ọ̀ kó wọ̀ọ́ | The eyes owner will not open their eyes to the ground [wide] and let flying insects enter them<br>- No one will open their eyes and let dust or speck get into them;<br>- The person with the problem will not allow anything to jeopardize their case. |
| 1204. | Olóókùnrùn t'ó ń f'isó dúpẹ́ l'ọ́wọ́ọ̀ Babaláwo | An ungrateful person that says thanks to Babaláwo [diviner] by farting in his face<br>- An ungracious individual that insults his helper. |
| 1205. | Ọlọ́mọdé ò m'ẹ̀là; ó l'óun m'ẹ̀là kátakàta | A child does not recognize barriers; he retorts that he can distinguish some scattered partitions<br>- This is an inadvertent acceptance of a challenge. |
| 1206. | Olóógìnní ti t'àjò dé, Èkúté Ilé ẹ p'ara mọ́n | The cat has returned from his trip, you house-rats better hide<br>- The landlord has returned, you tenants had better behave yourselves;<br>- The king has returned, everyone had better be at their best behavior;<br>- The powerful leader has returned, anyone thinking of a coup had better be careful. |
| 1207. | Ọlọ́pã, èwo n t'èpè | Policeman, what's with the cursing?<br>- This is said when someone says something that is not at all expected of someone in their class or position. |
| 1208. | Ọlọ́rọ̀, a b'etí dídí | The host of the "word," hard of hearing<br>- This metaphor is a direct confrontation by the loved one(s) of a defendant to chastise them, "we have been warning you to stay away from the people who are now accusing you of this offense all this |

| | | |
|---|---|---|
| | | time but you never paid attention."<br>- Also means the accused is usually the last to hear about a problem concerning them. |
| 1209. | Ọlọrun ò dá mi ń'írù sun jẹ | God did not create me with a tail to roast and eat<br>- The hyperbole refers to someone affirming that they've got what someone is asking them if they've got;<br>- Also means "thank God I'm not destitute;"<br>- "I'm not without means". |
| 1210. | Ọlọun ií ṣe Nǹkan k'ó má f'àyè Ọpẹ́ s'ílẹ̀ | God never does anything without leaving room for our gratitude<br>- No matter what our situation may be, there's always a reason to be thankful to our Creator. One might utter this idiom especially when there's been a story of a lucky escape or of appraising, say, a disabled lady who happens to be very beautiful and attractive;<br>- Anything that might make someone say in amazement, "Wow! God Is wonderful!" |
| 1211. | Olówó Ẹni kìí burú títí k'ó ní k'a má ṣ'ẹ̀yọ́ | One's 'owner' can never be so evil that he'll order us not to excrete (in the context of slave and master)<br>- A leader cannot be so mean that he would deny his subordinates time to ease themselves when they feel the need;<br>- An employer cannot be so rigid and strict that they won't let their employees use the bathroom, or just to be happy for a moment and laugh, no matter what their job is. |
| 1212. | Olówó gbà'yàwó Ọ̀lẹ | A wealthy man has snatched the lazy man's wife<br>- This is an afflicted person's lament that they have been cheated by someone in a higher position than they. |
| 1213. | Olówó l'ó ń jẹ'yán ìdí Ito | Only the rich eat pounded yam at the base of the Ito tree. (In the olden days in |

| | | |
|---|---|---|
| | | Yorùbá land, one needed to be rich to eat at this spot)<br>- You have to be rich to do that, wow! |
| 1214. | Olówó ń ṣ'ọrẹ Olówó, Òtòṣì ń ṣ'ọrẹ Òtòṣì | The wealthy are friends with rich people, the poor man is friends with poor people. |
| 1215. | Olówó ò níí f'owó ra Ẹrú, k'ó tún ma san'wó Ẹrù f'álábārù! | You can't spend money to buy a slave and thereafter start paying a load-carrier (or courier) to carry loads for you!<br>- What's the point of having what you have if you won't use it?<br>- Make use of what you've got! |
| 1216. | Omi Àná tí 'ò mu Baba ní Kókósẹ̀, ó ti fẹ́ ma wọ́ gbogbo wa lọ tuurutu | The stream of yesterday that didn't reach the ankle of Baba, it's about ready to start dragging us all away<br>- The little rascal of yesterday has now become the hoodlum that terrorizes the whole neighborhood. |
| 1217. | Omi Ẹ̀kọ, Ẹ̀kọ ni | The juice of the hardened corn-pap is also corn-pap<br>- If you are looking for a tool and can't find it in time, but find a similar alternative, so long as it does the same job, why not grab it?<br>- Like father like son; like mother like daughter. |
| 1218. | Omi gbígbóná ìí pẹ́ l'ẹ́nu; Ọwọ́ ìí pẹ́ ní Isà Àkéekèe | Hot water does not stay long in the mouth; a hand does not tarry in a scorpion's burrow<br>- Hurry and make use of this rare window of opportunity! |
| 1219. | Omi l'àá kọ́kọ́ tẹ̀ k'á tó tẹ'yanrì | It's water our feet first touch before the sand<br>- Let's settle the matter first before we ask "what can we do to fix the damage?"<br>- Let's establish what happened first before we seek amends. |
| 1220. | Omi l'ó dà'nù, Akèngbè ò fọ́! | It's the water that got spilt, the gourd-vessel didn't get shattered<br>- It could have been worse; the situation can still be salvaged;<br>- You can still forge ahead despite the |

| | | |
|---|---|---|
| | | unexpected disappointment. |
| 1221. | Omi l'ó ma r'éhìn Iná; Àgò l'ó ma d'édìẹ gbẹ̀hìn | It's water that'll see the end of fire [extinguish it]; it's a coop that'll cover chickens in the end.<br>- No matter how long we live, we will still die someday;<br>- The person expressing this metaphor is saying he/she will triumph over current enemies or over those conspiring against him/her. |
| 1222. | Omi ò ṣeé ta ní Kókó | Water can never be tied in a knot<br>- There's no comeback from where things are. |
| 1223. | Omí pọ̀ j'ọkà lọ | The water is too much for the ọkà (doughy pasty food [made out of yam and/or cassava flour, or unripe plantain flour])<br>- There is so much to do and the ability to cope is not guaranteed!<br>- We failed because we were overwhelmed! |
| 1224. | Omi táa fi rọ Ọmọ ìí pá Ọmọ l'órí | The water with which we feed a toddler (with the child positioned sideways on the lap) does not choke him/her<br>- What you're being given will not be an anathema to you. This is like a prayer. |
| 1225. | Omí t'ẹ̀hìn wọ'gbín l'ẹnu | Water has managed to enter the mouth of a snail through its back [shell]<br>- The situation is dreadful and quite possibly a loss of life has occurred. |
| 1226. | Omi táa bá dà s'órí, Ilẹ̀ l'ó ń bọ̀ | The water we pour on the head, it's the floor/ground it's coming to<br>- There are always repercussions for our actions, be it positive or negative. |
| 1227. | Omi tuntún ti rú, Ẹja tuntún ti wọ'nú ẹ̀ | A new river has sprung forth, new fishes have entered it<br>- The river has been renewed with fresh water [through asteroids] and new varieties of fish have entered it;<br>- This is a new beginning;<br>- New things with fresh hopes are already springing up. |

| 1228. | Ọmọ Àjànàkú ìí jẹ́ Ààrá; Ọmọ t'ẹ̀kùn-ún bá bí, Ẹkùn l'ó máa jọ | The calf of an elephant is never called Thunder, the cub that a leopard births, will look like a leopard<br>- You have not birthed bastards. |
|---|---|---|
| 1229. | Ọmọ Àlè níí r'ínú tí kìí bí; Ọmọ Àlè n'ọ́n ń bẹ̀ tí kìí gbà | Only a bastard would see a cause to be angry and he's not; [having said that] it's only a bastard that is begged and doesn't accept [apologies]<br>- Once an apology has been offered, just accept it. |
| 1230. | Ọmọ bẹẹrẹ Òṣì bẹẹrẹ | Loads of children, loads of punk rascals<br>- The speaker is generally asking what's the point in having so many children. |
| 1231. | Ọmọ burú, Ìkan l'àá bí | A terrible child, we only birth one<br>- This suggests the person referred to in this term as being so egregious, no one will pray to have two of them in their family. |
| 1232. | Ọmọ Ẹni ì bá jọ'ni à bá yọ̀ | If one's offspring were to resemble someone [in deed and character really], we would have cause to rejoice<br>- This is a direct accusation to a child: "You have disappointed me;"<br>- This idiom is directed towards a wayward child who is being upbraided. |
| 1233. | Ọmọ Ẹni ìí ṣè'dí bẹ̀bẹ̀rẹ̀ k'a f'ìlẹ̀kẹ̀ s'ídî Ọmọ Èlòmîìn | One's daughter cannot have a nice big bum and we pass her over and endow someone else's daughter with sequinned beads<br>- The great asset you have should be kept in the family or for the benefit of your people; you don't make a present of it to others;<br>- Keep it in the family. |
| 1234. | Ọmọ Ẹní kú yá ju Ọmọ Ẹní 'nù lọ | One's child is dead is a lot better than one's child is missing<br>- You can count your losses and move on. |
| 1235. | Ọmọ Ẹni ò dáa kò ní k'á le f'ẹ̀kùn pa jẹ | The wickedness of one's child does not drive one to chase him toward the path of a tiger to be mauled<br>- No matter what someone close to us has |

| | | |
|---|---|---|
| | | done, we cannot wish evil to befall them. |
| 1236. | Ọmọ́ gọ̀, ẹ ní ó má kũ; kíní ń p'ọmọ bí ò ṣ'agọ̀? | A child is a moron, you said he should not die; what kills a child faster than stupidity?<br>- This is what you get if you just fold your arms and do nothing to put your house in order. |
| 1237. | Ọmọ Iná l'à ń rán s'íná | It's the offspring of the fire that we send to the fire<br>- We send word to those we are quarrelling with through someone they know and trust and whom they'll listen to. This is only uttered during conflicts however. |
| 1238. | Ọmọ́ ńbẹ n'ínú Ẹrú, Ẹrú nã ńbẹ n'ínú Ọmọ | There is a child [trait] in a slave, there is also a slave [trait] in a child [of the freeborn]<br>- There is good as well as bad in everyone. |
| 1239. | Ọmọ́ ń wá'ṣẹ́, ó r'íṣẹ́ | A child is looking for work, he finds work<br>- You willingly enrolled in the course (or exam) you're studying for, so don't moan about the difficulty or hardship you may be facing;<br>- It was you who volunteered to assist [in this project]; don't complain now about being overwhelmed. |
| 1240. | Ọmọ Ojú ò r'ọ́lá rí, t'ó ń s'ọmọ ẹ̀ l'ọ́lá n'íyọnu | A person who had never experienced wealth that named his newborn child "wealth is fraught with difficulties and challenges"<br>- This metaphor is derogatorily said to someone who shows off every little and mundane material acquisition to the point that they exasperate friends and neighbors. |
| 1241. | Ọmọ Ọ̀lẹ l'àyè ò gbà; Ibi gbogbo l'ó gb'alágbára | A bastard may lack free reign [of space]; everywhere accepts the powerful individual<br>- Better know your place and mind how you trespass. |
| 1242. | Ọmọ ọlọ́mọn l'à ń rán ńṣéẹ dé t'òru-t'òru | It's someone else's child we send on an errand that requires a dead-of-night |

| | | |
|---|---|---|
| | | return
- You engage someone else's child or property to perform unsavory deeds, but never yours. |
| 1243. | Ọmọ Ọsàn l'ó ń kó Kóńdó bá'yã ẹ̀ | It's the child of the orange [tree] that causes batons and bats to strike its mother
- It's oranges on an orange tree that make people who are trying to pluck the oranges hit the tree with sticks and bats and all what not;
- It's the child that has committed a felony that makes his parents receive such scathing criticisms from everyone. |
| 1244. | Ọmọ Ọwọ́ ìí kú l'ojú Ọwọ́, Ọmọ Ẹsẹ̀ ìí t'ojú Ẹsẹ̀ ẹ́ kú | A finger never dies before the hand [that it's attached to], a toe never dies before the foot
- This personification is an inspirational maxim to [usually] the parents of a child who is suffering from a grave illness. |
| 1245. | Ọmọ r'ọmọ ń p'òṣé n'ígbà Orò; ó ní ìgbàtí Ìyáa Lámọnrín ò bá bí òun | A child dressed in tattered clothing beholds another who is well-dressed [Lámọnrín, a.k.a. Jane Doe] during a festive event. She hisses and muses: well, since the mother of Lámọnrín did not birth her…
- What someone might say when they take stock of their life and wish if only their parents had been those wealthy parents of Lámọnrín, their lot in life would be a lot better today. |
| 1246. | Ọmọ́ só sí'ni l'ẹ́nu, ó bu'yọ̀ si; Isó rèé, kò ṣeé pọ́nlá, Iyọ̀ rèé, kò ṣeé tu dànù! | A child passed gas in one's mouth and added a pinch of salt. Fart for a start is not lickable but neither is salt spit-able!
- Someone may have done a great thing for others but he has also done something unremarkable that effectively cancelled out this good deed. You can neither tolerate this offense nor ignore this individual's contribution to society, sort of. A case of mitigating circumstances. |

| | | |
|---|---|---|
| 1247. | Ọmọ t'ẹ̀kùn ún bá bí, Ẹkùn ní ó jọ | The cub that a tigress births, resembles a tiger<br>- The child must surely look like the parent. |
| 1248. | Ọmọ tíò bá gbọ́ Ìtàn ó máa gbọ́ Àróbá; Àróbá dẹ̀ẹ́ rèé, Baba Ìtàn ni | The child who hasn't heard a history narrated may have heard repeated oral legends; and oral legends are in fact the father of all folklore<br>- Looking around you, surely you'll appreciate that what you'd heard for so long is not bulls but the gospel truth. Isn't it time you tied your shoe laces tightly and acted accordingly now? |
| 1249. | Ọmọ t'ó bá fẹ́ jẹ́ Àṣàmú, láti kékeré l'ó ti máa ńṣe shámú-shámúú lọ | A child that wants to be [like] Àṣàmú, it's from youth that he begins to do [shámú-shámú], i.e. he'll start to demonstrate his cleverness. In Yorùbá folklore, Àṣàmú was a very smart and crafty child<br>- Whatever one becomes in later life can actually be traced back to the choices they made early on in life;<br>- You are what you eat;<br>- Make hay while the sun shines. |
| 1250. | Ọmọ t'ó bá ma rìn á dìde, áá ṣubú, áá bó l'órúnkún | A child that is going to walk will stand up, will fall down and will bruise its knees<br>- Don't complain about the teething problems you're experiencing on your way to getting somewhere in life.<br>- Practice makes perfect. |
| 1251. | Ọmọ t'ó bá ṣí'pá l'à ń gbé | A child that opens its arms [and runs towards us] is the child we lift up<br>- He who has made an effort to improve their situation is the one that gets assistance faster;<br>- Heaven helps those who help themselves. |
| 1252. | Ọmọ t'ó ní Bàbá 'un ò là, Ọmọ t'ó ní Bàbá 'un ò l'ówó l'ọ́wọ́, Ẹnu è l'ó kò sí yẹn | The child that claims that his father is not solvent, the child that says his father is not wealthy, he has begun his own journey [of the travails of life, such that made his father to be not so remarkably rich] |

|  |  | - The children that mock their father that he's a loser, it's now their own turn to prove they are not losers as their father;<br>- The new incumbent in a government administration that mocks the outgoing postholder of being ineffective, it's now their turn to demonstrate that they can do better;<br>- The new king or office holder doesn't realize yet that "uneasy lies the head that wears a crown." |
|---|---|---|
| 1253. | Ọmọ t'ó ní kí ìyá òun má sùn, òun nã ò ní f'ojú b'orun | A child that says its mother should not sleep, its own eyes will not feel sleep<br>- A saying that suggests a high tension stand-off between fierce rivals, be it business or personal, to see who blinks first. |
| 1254. | Ọmọ́ tó'yī ò gbọ́n? | A child is this big but lacks common sense?<br>- You have attained this level of knowledge and yet you still haven't improved?<br>- Considering your past experience(s), you still get fooled so easily? |
| 1255. | Ọmọ'lẹ̀ẹ́lẹ̀, t'ọ́n bá gbe s'órí Ẹní, áá yí bọ́ nã ni | An infant of the 'common floor,' if they place it on a mat, it will still fall<br>- No matter what you do to rehabilitate an unrepentant ex-convict, he is likely to revert to his old ways. Like a recidivist. |
| 1256. | Ọmọdé gbọ́n, Àgbá gbọ́n; òun l'a fi dá'lẹ̀ Ifẹ́ | Youth were clever, elders were wise; it was how the land of Ifẹ̀ was founded<br>- Don't leave everything to adults alone; the combined wisdom of both the youth and adults are needed;<br>- We need to pull our brain resources together to get to where we're heading. |
| 1257. | Ọmọdé lí m'ori í jẹ k'ó má yi l'ọ́wọ́ | A child cannot be adept at eating hardened corn-pap enough that it will not soil his hand<br>- No matter how good a child is at something, his juvenile characteristics |

| | | could still surface and disappoint, to the chagrin of everyone;<br>- Could be a pleading by a suppliant on behalf of a youngster to say that the boy might have misused a privilege by his lack of appreciation of that privilege, but had not necessarily intentionally misused it. |
|---|---|---|
| 1258. | Ọmọdé ò m'òògùn, ó ń pèé l'ẹ́fọ́ | A kid fails to identify juju, he calls it spinach<br>- Someone does not recognize the asset he has and regards it as something commonly obtainable as spinach. |
| 1259. | Ọmọdé ṣí'wọ́ lu'gi Ìrókò, ó b'ojú w'ẹ̀hìn; ó rò wípé Ìrókò ń lé òun; kò mọ̀n wípé Ẹ̀ní kọ́ n'ìrókò ó máa jà | A child slaps the Ìrókò tree, he looks back; he thinks Ìrókò is chasing him; he doesn't know it's not today that Ìrókò will fight<br>- You commit a felony against authority and expect an instant arrest but your apprehension might happen at a later date;<br>- You commit an infraction for the first time and you're on probation. |
| 1260. | Ọmọdé t'ó bá m'ọwọ́ ọ́ wẹ̀, á b'ágbà jẹun | A child who knows how to wash hands will dine with adults<br>- Someone who is habitually courteous to those in power or position of authority, he/she typically makes progress in the community. |
| 1261. | Ọ̀nà kan ò w'ọjà | One path does not enter market<br>- Many roads lead to a market;<br>- Becoming successful is not limited to just one business inspiration; there are other business ideas out there;<br>- If you get no joy going one route, why don't you try another? |
| 1262. | Ọ̀nà l'o tọ̀, oò wọ̀'gbẹ́! | You walked the road, you didn't enter bush OR You walked the path, you didn't stray into the bush<br>- You have reasoned well and arrived at the right conclusion;<br>- Ain't that the truth! You're spot on! |
| 1263. | Ọ̀nà l'ó jìn, Ẹrú nã ní Baba | The road [origin] may be far, a slave too |

|       |                                                      |                                                                                                                                                                                                                                 |
|-------|------------------------------------------------------|---------------------------------------------------------------------------------------------------------------------------------------------------------------------------------------------------------------------------------|
|       |                                                      | has a father<br>- Don't be nasty to less-privileged people; they were born just like you.                                                                                                                                       |
| 1264. | Ọ̀nà tí Abẹ́rẹ́ fi j'okùn díẹ̀ lọ, Ọ̀nà gbọọrọ ni    | The 'road' by which a needle is longer than thread is a straight road<br>- The length of the gap between you and I is considerable;<br>- The difference between the entities in the context is like that between chalk and cheese. |
| 1265. | Oníkálukú a bi ti ẹ l'ára                            | Everyone with their own problems.                                                                                                                                                                                               |
| 1266. | Oní-n̄kan ìí kán'gun                                 | The owner is never the last<br>- The celebrant [or beneficiary] is never the last to be acknowledged or celebrated.                                                                                                             |
| 1267. | Oníyàwó kan ṣoṣo ò tíì kúrò l'ápọ̀n                  | A monogamous husband has not left bachelorhood<br>- You haven't reached the economic level you deserve.                                                                                                                         |
| 1268. | Oò fẹ́ d'ẹkùn k'o tó máa fín                         | You don't want to become a tiger before you start to growl<br>- You need to grow up or develop certain habits before you can do certain things.                                                                                 |
| 1269. | Oò tíì m'ẹrú, o ní Aráàlú l'o ma tàá fún             | You have not yet caught a slave, you assumed it's a fellow citizen you will sell him to<br>- You haven't got the essential thing you need most within your grasp, you are already bragging;<br>- Don't count your chickens before they hatch! |
| 1270. | i. Oò tutù dé'bẹ̀<br>ii. Mìò tutù dé'bẹ̀             | i. You are not that quiet [pacifistic]<br>ii. I am not that passive [pacifistic]<br>- That's why no one can walk all over you/me.                                                                                               |
| 1271. | Oókan n'ọ́n ń r'ẹṣin l'ọ́run; aà tíì r'ẹ́ni t'ó gùn-ún wá s'ílé Aiyé | A penny is how much a horse costs in Heaven; we haven't seen anyone yet who has ridden one to Earth<br>- This thing you keep alleging is not new or difficult to get hold of; we are yet to see it happen! Quit mentioning it already! |

| | | |
|---|---|---|
| 1272. | Ọ̀ọ́kán ọ̀ọ́kán l'obìnrín ń gb'óhùn Orò | It's from afar that a female hears the sound of Orò<br>- I think I'll stay away from this; not my business. |
| 1273. | Oore l'ooré ń wọ́ọ́ lé | It's goodness that goodness follows<br>- One good turn deserves another. |
| 1274. | Òòrú Iṣu kán t'ẹní wá fọn'ná | A quarter of a yam [cooked or roasted] is quite enough for someone who came to your farm hut to fetch some embers [to light their own fire in their own hut]<br>- Be appreciative and grateful for what you have been given especially something you haven't earned;<br>- Be thankful that you were at the right place at the right time. |
| 1275. | Òòṣà jẹ́ npé méjì Obìnrin ò sí | A messenger-god that aspires to complete [be] two women does not exist<br>- No wife or lover that wishes for a rival for her man's love and attention exists;<br>- No powerful person relishes sharing his power and influence with another person. |
| 1276. | Oótọ́ Ọ̀rọ́ máa ń dàbí Ìsọkúsọ | The truth always sounds like nonsense<br>- Let me be honest with you; just hear me out. |
| 1277. | Ọpeni níí p'eni í ṣ'ọlá | The Caller is He Who calls one to be in wealth<br>- God is the ultimate Caller who selects those He wants to be in wealth and abundance. |
| 1278. | Ọ̀pọ̀ Ènìà l'ó m'ẹkùn, ṣàṣà Ènìà l'ẹkùn ún mọ̀n | Many people know the tiger, a few people does the tiger know<br>- Everyone may know a famous person, but the celebrity only knows a few. |
| 1279. | Ọ̀pọ̀ Ọ̀rọ̀ ò k'ágbọ̀n, Atẹ́gùn l'ó ń gbé e lọ | Excessive words [pleonasm] cannot fill a [bamboo] basket, it's the wind that blows them away<br>- Don't talk too much; stick to the point. |
| 1280. | Ọ̀pọ̀lọ́ wá'bi t'ó tutù ba sí | The toad looks for a cool place to relax<br>- Said to someone who is always on the lookout for wealthy individuals to befriend or who seeks convenient, no-struggle easy |

| | | |
|---|---|---|
| | | ways out of situations. This type of individual prefers ready-made trouble-free environments. They abhor having to fight for their rights or struggle for their rights or anything. This expression is uttered to rebuke anyone that falls under this category. Sort of a 'happy-go-lucky' person. |
| 1281. | Ọ̀pọ̀lọpọ̀ Aláǹgbá l'ó da'kùn dé'lẹ̀, aò m'èyí t'ínú ń run | Many lizards crawl on their tummies, no one knows which of them have stomach ache<br>- This idiom denotes that although we meet and interact with all kinds of people in our daily lives, we don't know what they think of us;<br>- No one knows the mind of another. |
| 1282. | Ọ̀rẹ́ dà mí, ngó da ọ̀rẹ́ẹ̀ mi padà san; ṣé o mọ̀n p'ọ́dàlẹ́ di méjì? | A friend betrayed me, I'll betray my friend in retaliation; do you realize that there are now two betrayers?<br>- Two wrongs do not make a right. |
| 1283. | Ọrẹ́ ń j'ọ́rẹ, Ọrà ń j'ọ́rà; Ẹnìkan ò kì ń dúpẹ́ẹ "mo t'ọ̀pọ̀" | Gift is gift, buying is buying; no one expresses gratitude for "I sold cheaply"<br>- A kindly person might say this in frustration especially when they get fed up giving handouts to someone who clearly doesn't want to work. |
| 1284. | Ọ̀rẹ́ t'ó bá ti pẹ́ tí a ti rí, k'a má gbára le | An old friend that we have not seen for a long time, we should not trust him |
| 1285. | Orí bíbẹ́ kọ́ l'òògùn Ẹ̀fọ́rí | Decapitation is not the cure for headache<br>- To resolve the matter [at hand] does not necessitate that kind of [drastic] measure, for God's Sake! |
| 1286. | Orí lí f'ájọ, Ẹ̀dọ̀ lí rin Àjọ, bóo bá ti dáa, kóo kóo ni | A joint contribution never has headaches, a joint contribution never has kidney problems, as you have contributed is how you pick it up when it's your turn for collection<br>- You reap exactly what you sow;<br>- No stories or excuses why a contributor will not be paid when it's their turn to collect money. |

| 1287. | Orí kan ṣoṣo l'ejò ń ní t'ó fi ń tú Igba Orí ká | A snake has only one head and yet disperses a gathering of two hundred heads [people]<br>- The fearsome warrior is just one person yet he kills hundreds in battle;<br>- The subject in this context is someone revered or someone that people fear. |
|---|---|---|
| 1288. | Orí l'ẹjá ti ń bàjẹ́ | It's from the head that the fish starts to decay<br>- A community or people cannot move forward if their leaders are corrupt or plain stupid. |
| 1289. | Òrí-má-dé'lé-wí, Olúwa ẹ̀ ò r'íhun t'ó dáa ni | The 'seer' who does not relate a report when he gets home has not seen anything good or remarkable to report about<br>- What I have seen with my own eyes is unbelievable! |
| 1290. | Orí ò r'ẹrù, Ẹnu ò jẹ | The head won't carry/lift loads, the mouth does not feed<br>- In order to eat, one needs to work. |
| 1291. | Orí Òkẹ́rẹ́ kooko l'áwo; báa wí f'ọ́mọ Ẹni, a gbọ́ | The squirrel's head kooko [snug] in the bowl of stew; if we instruct one's child, he ought to listen<br>- This is a sort of lamentation that when one advises a close relative or friend, he should listen; now look at the trouble he's found himself in as a result of not heeding your advice and recommendation. |
| 1292. | Orí Ọmọ l'ó ma ń p'ọmọ w'áiyé | It's the 'heads of children' that call children to the world<br>- The concept of this proverb is the belief that the spirits of newly-born children could influence the fertility of the barren [either the childless woman looks after someone else's child or allowing her husband to impregnate other women]. |
| 1293. | Orí yeye níí m'ògún, t'àìṣẹ̀ l'ó pọ̀ | Numerous heads know Ògún, those who were innocent were many<br>- Innocent people suffer for what they know nothing about. |
| 1294. | Oríburúkú l'ó ń m'ọ́mọdé | Misfortune is what makes the youth |

| | | |
|---|---|---|
| | pín'tan Ewúrẹ́; Àgbàlagbà l'ó ń pín-in | divide and share a goat's thigh; it's the adults that do it<br>- It is improper for the youth to preside over important national matters; it's essentially the remit of elders [governing council]. |
| 1295. | Orin tí kò bá ṣòroó dá, kò yẹ k'ó ṣòroó gbè | A song that is not difficult to begin, should not be hard to chorus and follow<br>- If the foundation was honest and legit, then we should have no issues. |
| 1296. | Orin tí ò ṣòro ó dá ìí ṣòro ó gbè | A song that is not difficult to begin is never hard to chant along in unison<br>- If you start a project that will be beneficial to people in your community, others will gladly join you in harmony. |
| 1297. | Òrìṣà t'ó ní t'Ògún ò sí, yíó f'ẹnu ara ẹ̀ hó'ṣu jẹ | The messenger-god that doesn't put Ògún's into consideration, he'll use his mouth to peel off yam's skin before eating<br>- He who underestimates the powers-that-be will suffer the consequences. |
| 1298. | Oríṣîríṣî Ọ̀bẹ l'à ńrí l'ójọ́ Ikú Erin | We see all sorts of knives on the day of the elephant's death<br>- Everyone is in a frenzy on the day someone falls from grace and his deeds are thrown open for anyone to have their say;<br>- People who hitherto would never have dared say a word against some important public figure when alive are now somewhat emboldened to come forward with scathing accusations, criticism and what not. |
| 1299. | Ọ̀rọ̀ Àròjinlẹ̀ l'ó ń fa Ẹkún àsun-ùn dákẹ́ | A matter that evokes profound thought [reflection] is what causes endless crying<br>- A rueful self-analysis of past good times or halcyon days could trigger ceaseless tears in an emotional person, such as when someone remembers a good instrumental person in their lives who may have passed. |
| 1300. | Ọ̀rọ̀ Àròkàn l'ó ń fa Ẹkún Àsun- | The nostalgic thread of reminiscences / |

|      |                                                                 |                                                                                                                                                                                   |
|------|-----------------------------------------------------------------|---------------------------------------------------------------------------------------------------------------------------------------------------------------------------------|
|      | àìdákẹ́                                                         | memories [of halcyon days gone by] is what causes endless tears.                                                                                                                |
| 1301.| Ọ̀rọ̀ hùn-hùn-hùn, Inú Ẹlẹ́dẹ̀ l'ó ńgbé                         | The grunting of the pig lives inside the pig<br>- Anything you might harbor against (the speaker) will remain in your mind forever;<br>- You will take this secret to your grave. |
| 1302.| Ọ̀rọ̀ ìí dun'ni k'ójú ẹ̀ ó bù                                   | A concern never hurts so much that it leaves a gash in the face<br>- No matter how unpleasant things may look now, time will heal it and it'll soon become a thing of the past.  |
| 1303.| Ọ̀rọ̀ ìí tóbi k'á f'ọ̀bẹ bùú                                    | A problem is never so huge that we cut it up with a knife<br>- A matter is never too unwieldy that you have to slice it up.                                                     |
| 1304.| Ọ̀rọ̀ kékeré l'à ńsọ f'ọmọlúwàbí, t'ó bá dé'nú ẹ̀ á d'odi-ndi    | A few words are enough for the child of Noah; when he has absorbed them, they become whole<br>- A word is enough for the wise.                                                   |
| 1305.| Ọ̀rọ̀ l'ó ńbá mo kó, mo rò wá                                   | It's the discussion in progress that brought up a string of other similar issues, past and present<br>- When there's an issue, there's always a catalyst.                        |
| 1306.| Ọ̀rọ̀ lo sọ, oò purọ́!                                          | What you have spoken is a word, you're not lying!<br>- What someone has just said makes perfect sense!                                                                          |
| 1307.| Ọ̀rọ̀ ǹ bá rò, maa rò'fọ́                                       | Instead of stirring words, I am stirring spinach<br>- Instead of spinning the whole story to you or anyone, I'd better make it short and go straight to the point.               |
| 1308.| Ọ̀rọ̀ nã dà bí Ọ̀rọ̀ Ajá t'ó re'lé Ẹkùn tí ò mú'ra               | The matter is like that of the dog that went to the lair of the tiger unprepared [for any escape route].                                                                        |
| 1309.| Ọ̀rọ̀ nã dàbí Ẹ̀kọ tí ò l'éwé; Adìẹ á shàá jẹ, Pẹ́péiyẹ á jẹ tìẹ; àwọn Ẹiyẹlé nã á f'ẹnu kàn-án | The matter is idiomatically similar to that of hardened corn-pap without leaves [the covering-wrap]; chickens would peck at it, as would ducks; even pigeons will do their own nibbling |

| | | |
|---|---|---|
| | | - The speaker feels they are in a precarious or vulnerable situation where every Tom, Dick and Harry can take advantage of them. |
| 1310. | Ọ̀rọ̀ nã dàbí Ìtàn Ọlọ́dẹ Afàdápakún; Ọdẹ t'ó f'àdá pa'kún tán, tí Ikún lọ, tí Àdá nã sọnù | The matter is like the legend of the hunter that used a cutlass to kill a chipmunk; that after killing the chipmunk, the chipmunk still managed to escape, and the bush hunter also lost the cutlass<br>- The narrative shows the character in the context has lost on two fronts, which is a calamity. |
| 1311. | Ọ̀rọ̀ nã dàbí Òjò Àṣálẹ́ t'ó ń m'óbìnrin-ín ṣ'èkè; Òjò Àṣálẹ́ t'ó ń m'óbìnrin-ín d'ọ̀dàlẹ̀ | The matter is like the evening drizzle that makes a woman beguile and deceive; evening rain that makes a woman become a betrayer<br>- The matter is not really what it appears to be. |
| 1312. | i. Ọ̀rọ̀ ọ fọ́'bí fọ́'ran l'ẹ̀ ń sọ<br>ii. Ọ̀rọ̀ ọ fọ́'bí fọ́'ran l'ò ń sọ<br>iii. Ọ̀rọ̀ ọ fọ́'bí fọ́'ran n'ọ́n ń sọ | The talk that could result in breaking-up of families as well as descendants is what is coming out of your mouth(s)<br>- This kind of rhetoric can tear a family [and lineage] apart, so guard your tongue.<br><br>*For more on the usage of ẹ, è, ẹ́, o, ò, ó, ọ, please consult the "Personal Pronouns" page.* |
| 1313. | Orò ó gb'ádétẹ̀, ẹ ní Ohun burúkú lọ ńlũ; t'ó bá wá gb'ọ́mọ Ọlọ́lá, ẹẹ́ l'óhun burúkú ṣẹ́ yọ | An idol-god snatches a leper, you all chorus that a bad thing has left town; if he next snatches a magnate's child, you will all chant a bad thing has reared its head<br>- It is not possible to satisfy everyone. |
| 1314. | Orò ò gbọdọ̀ t'ojú Obìnrin ké | The Orò idol-god must not squeak in the presence of females<br>- What is certain to happen cannot be allowed to occur in the presence of certain individuals or circumstances. |
| 1315. | Ọ̀rọ̀ ò níí wúwo k'á f'ọ̀bẹ bùú | An issue will not be so heavy that we divide it with a knife<br>- There's always a solution. |
| 1316. | Ọ̀rọ̀ Ọlọgbọ́n bákan nã ni; Ọ̀rọ̀ | The words of the wise men are always |

|  | Àṣiwèrè níí yàtọ̀ | similar; the words of the madmen are those that are commonly different<br>- We have come to the same conclusion! |
|---|---|---|
| 1317. | Ọ̀rọ́ pọ̀ n'ínú Ìwée Kọ́bọ̀ | There is a copious amount of words in a penny book<br>- There is a massive story to narrate;<br>- The story is much more than meets the eye;<br>- The situation is not as simple as it appears to be. |
| 1318. | Ọ̀rọ̀ ṣ'eni wò, k'á lè m'ẹni t'ó fẹ́ ni | Let difficulty happen to somebody, so we know who truly loves them<br>- It's when someone falls on hard times that they'll find out who genuinely cares about them. |
| 1319. | Ọ̀rọ̀ Sùnùkùn kán wà ńlẹ̀ t'a máa f'ojú Sùnùkùn wò | There's a tricky matter on the ground that requires delicate maneuvering to resolve. |
| 1320. | Oró tóo dá mi ni mo dá ẹ | The wrong that you did me is what I did to you<br>- It's tit for tat; payback time. |
| 1321. | Ọ̀rọ̀ t'ọ́lọgbọ́n bá sọ, Ẹnu Aṣiwèrè l'a ti ńgbọ | The words uttered by the wiseman, it's from the mouth of a madman that we hear them<br>- It's beneath someone of your caliber to say such things. |
| 1322. | Ọ̀rọ̀ t'ọ́n bá ní kí Baba má gbọ̀, Baba nã ní ó parí ẹ̀ | The matter they don't want the father to hear about, it's the same father that is going to resolve it<br>- What you're keeping from being discovered will eventually be exposed, possibly by the same person / authority you're keeping them from. |
| 1323. | Ọ̀rọ̀ táà bá fẹ́ k'ó d'ìjà, aò gbọdọ̀ jẹ́ k'ó paruwo | An argument we do not wish to escalate into a physical fight, we should not let it become loud<br>- We should learn to control our temper. |
| 1324. | Ọ̀rọ̀ táa ṣe bí 'õ b'ágbò l'ó b'éwúrẹ́ | A situation that we had expected would birth a goat has [instead] birthed a lamb<br>- A process we had hoped would placate the delicate issue has instead exacerbated it. |

| | | |
|---|---|---|
| 1325. | Ọ̀rọ́ ti dé'bi t'ólõgùn ún ti ń sàá | The matter has progressed to where those who have juju influence will start exercising their supernatural methods<br>- The matter has spiraled out of control. |
| 1326. | Ọ̀rọ̀ t'ó bá dá'ni l'ójú lí kọ'sẹ̀ l'étè Ẹnu | A narrative that one is certain of, flows smoothly out of the lips. |
| 1327. | Ọ̀rọ̀ t'ó dé l'ó ní k'a ma sọ òun | It's the matter that arose that behooves us to discuss it<br>- We are all in discussion/debate because of certain matters arising. |
| 1328. | Ọ̀rọ̀ t'ó ṣ'àkàlàmàgbò t'ó fi d'ẹ́kun Ẹ̀rín rín, b'ó bá ṣe Igúnnugú, yíó wo-nkoko m'órí Ẹyin ni | The problem that stopped the ground hornbill from smiling, if it were the guinea fowl, she would sit tight and brood on her eggs<br>- Those who the matter does not affect do not know the implication of what's going on. |
| 1329. | Ọ̀rọ̀ t'ó wà ńlẹ̀ yī s'òmùgọ̀ kọ́; Ọlọgbọ́n nìkan l'ọ̀rọ̀ ọ̀hún yé | This subject on the ground 'hangs the imbecile up' [confounds those of average intelligence]; the issue is cystal-clear only to the sage<br>- The matter requires the smartest brains in society. |
| 1330. | Ọ̀rọ̀ t'ó wà ńlẹ̀ yī, Àjànàkú ni; kìí ṣe Ẹrú Ọmọdé | This matter on the ground, it's an 'elephant', it's not a load for a child<br>- The matter at hand is enormous and far beyond the remit of the youth to participate in. |
| 1331. | Ọ̀rọ̀ t'ó wà ńlẹ̀ yī, Ọ̀rọ̀ Ojú ni, kìí ṣ'ọ̀rọ̀ Imú | The issue on the ground is a matter for the eyes, not for the nose<br>- Is it not plain to everyone what's going on here and who's responsible?<br>- Look no further for the guilty party. |
| 1332. | Ọ̀rọ̀ tútù a máa yọ Obì l'ápò; bákannáà, Ọ̀rọ̀ kan-ń-bákan a máa yọ Idà l'ápó | Humble words can bring a kolanut from [someone's] pocket; likewise, aggressive words can bring a sword from a sheath. This hyperbolical sentence possibly came into use because of the synonymousness in the meaning of Àpò (pocket) and Apó (sheath) and, of course, the spelling of both words |

|  |  | - Different attitudes produce different results. |
|---|---|---|
| 1333. | Ọ̀rọ̀ yí ní Kọ́lọ́fín ń'nú; ó so Ọlọ́gbọ́n kọ́, ó tún so Wèrè kọ́ | This matter has hidden crannies inside it; it's confounded the wise as well as 'insane' [stupid] thinkers<br>- It's a conundrum basically. |
| 1334. | Ọ̀rọ̀fògànná: wọ́n ń s'ọ̀rọ̀ Ilé kejì í ṣe kàn ẹ́? | Eavesdropper: they're gossiping about [the neighbors] next door, why is that any business of yours?<br>- Mind your business. |
| 1335. | Orogún lè fi Orogùn wó Ilé Ọlá | The wives [in a polygamous marriage] could use a wooden spatula to destroy a house of wealth. This hyperbole resulted from the association of the two rhyming words Orogún (wives in a polygamy) and Orogùn (wooden spatula), differentiated only by the accents on the 'u' in each word, which therefore indicates the pronunciation and thus the meaning of each word<br>- Care should be taken in the current situation for peace to reign. |
| 1336. | Òròmọndìẹ ò m'àwòdì; Ìyá ẹ̀ ló m'àṣá | A chick does not know the eagle; it's its mother that knows the hawk<br>- A youth is being verbally warned by some powerful individual whom he's being rude to; the youngster clearly has zero prior knowledge of what the man can do [with impunity];<br>- Said to someone seen as meddling in delicate but dangerous matters of state where it concerns a certain entity that he has no knowledge of; whereas the leaders and advisers know what this particular entity is capable of. |
| 1337. | Òru ò m'ẹni Ọ̀wọ̀; ó d'ífá ó ní Baba Tanù-hun | Darkness doesn't recognize a person of Ọ̀wọ̀ [reverence]; after divination he asked "whose father is that?"<br>- The night is no respecter of royalty, or anyone for that matter; you've still got to use light to walk through it, whoever you |

| | | |
|---|---|---|
| | | may be. |
| 1338. | Orúkọ Reré sàn ju Wúrà àti Fàdákà lọ | A good name is worth more than gold and silver. |
| 1339. | Orúkọ tí a bá ma sọ Ọmọ Ẹni, Inú Ẹni l'ó ńgbé | The name we're going to give our newborn, resides inside of us<br>- The step you're going to take, you keep it privy and resist the urge to reveal it to anyone. |
| 1340. | Ọsán já, Ọrún d'ọ̀pá | The string snaps, the bow [of an arrow] becomes a walking stick<br>- If the system breaks down, anarchy becomes the rule of the day;<br>- If the bread winner of a family dies, the vacuum can create despondency in the lives of those left behind;<br>- If a business owner/founder dies, the company might cease to exist;<br>- Things fall apart, the center cannot hold. |
| 1341. | Ọsàn t'ó rí Gbajúmọ̀n tí ò bọ́, Ẹiyẹ Oko lásán ní ò fi jẹ | The oranges that see a celebrity and do not fall off, common bush birds are the ones that will eat them<br>- If you are too egotistic or conceited, a lot of good things might pass you by;<br>- Make hay while the sun shines; you won't always be so attractive. |
| 1342. | Òṣìṣẹ́ wà l'óòrùn, Ẹní máa jẹ́ wà n'íbòji | The laborers are in the hot sun, he who is going to eat the fruits of their labor is in the shades. |
| 1343. | Ọ̀tọ̀ l'owó Ẹ̀já, Ọ̀tọ̀ l'owó Ẹja | Variance is the price of Ẹ̀já (medicinal leaves plucked for herbal remedies), variance is the price of Ẹja (fish). Again, this phrase also came about due to the spelling similarity of both words. The different accents placed on a word are indicative of how the word should be pronounced. This in turn would indicate the meaning of the word.<br>- One is not the same as the other. |
| 1344. | Ọ̀tọ̀ n'iṣu Iyán, Ọ̀tọ̀ n'iṣu Ègbodò | The yams for [to make] pounded yam are different from new yams [yet to fully ripen and therefore cannot be boiled to make |

| | | |
|---|---|---|
| | | pounded yam]<br>- Do whatever floats your boat;<br>- People are different. |
| 1345. | Ọ̀tọ̀ nii ti Tọ́lú, Ọ̀tọ̀ nii ti Tọ̀lù | Dissimilarity is that of Tọ́lú, difference is that of Tọ̀lù<br>- There are certain things that belong to me; similarly there are things that belong to other people, therefore why mix things that belong to one with those that belong to another?<br>- What is mine is mine; what is yours is yours;<br>- Give unto Ceasar what is Ceasar's. |
| 1346. | Ọ̀tọ̀ọ̀tọ̀, Àna Ìgbín | "Separately", the inlaw of a snail<br>- That you can do this kind of thing to someone that close to you astounds me, wow!<br>- I thought she was your friend, yet you did this to her?! |
| 1347. | Ọ̀tọ̀ọ̀tọ̀ l'à ń j'ẹpà | Separately is the way we eat groundnuts<br>- Everyone does what they please with their own individual circumstance;<br>- Everybody to his own! |
| 1348. | Ọ̀tún wẹ Òsì, Òsì wẹ Ọ̀tún, òun l'ọwọ́ fi ń mọ́n | The right hand scrubs the left, the left hand washes the right, is how hands get clean<br>- This metaphor suggests having a collaboration that will work well for all concerned. |
| 1349. | Òtútù l'ó ń kìlọ̀ fún Onítòbí, Ooru l'ó ń kìlọ̀ fún Alákàn gb'ẹ̀hìn | The cold is what warns the warm-garment wearer, the heat is what sounds a note of warning to the crab at last [to scurry back into its cool hole]<br>- No one will need to tell you what to do when things get to a head. |
| 1350. | Owó Àbú l'a fi ń ṣ'Àbú l'álejò | It's Àbú's [John Doe's] money we spend to host Àbú<br>- This refers to the scenario where someone is hosting a guest [John Doe] but in fact John Doe the guest is the one who unwittingly is paying for the privilege. |

| | | |
|---|---|---|
| 1351. | Ọwọ́ Epo l'ọmọ ar'áiyé ńbá'ni lá, nwọn ò kì ńbá'ni l'áwọ́ Ẹ̀jẹ̀ | Palm-oily hands are what human beings [might] lick with you; they would not lick bloody hands<br>- It's when you're well-to-do that friends flock to you; when things are hard, they disappear. |
| 1352. | Ọwọ́ kìí pẹ́ n'ísà Àkéekèe | A hand does not stay long in a scorpion's burrow<br>- No one stays too long in an unbearable place. |
| 1353. | Ọwọ́ méjèèjì l'ènìyán fií ja'gun; aìbáãmọ̀n t'íkãn bá gé, ìkan á ṣe é lò | With both hands one fights a battle; just in case one is hacked off, the other will still be useful<br>- You use all the resources you've got to deal with a problem; if one fails, another might work;<br>- Preparedness is everything. |
| 1354. | Ọwọ́ níí ṣ'aájú Ijó; Ọwọ́ níí ṣ'aájú Ìdọ̀bálẹ̀ | It's the hands that initiate a dance step; it's the hands that lead first [outstretched] in a prostration<br>- Whoever is referred to in this metaphor was the precursor that led the way in observance of the traditional rite of passage evident in the context. |
| 1355. | Ọwọ́ ò gbọ́dọ̀ pẹ́ n'ísà Ejò | A hand must not linger in a snake's pit<br>- A very quick decision is of the essence here. |
| 1356. | Owó ò mọn Wèrè | Money does not know a mad person<br>- Wealth does not discriminate. |
| 1357. | Owó ò ń'íran | Wealth has no descendants. |
| 1358. | Ọ̀wọ̀ Ọmọ tuntun ò kì ńjẹ́ k'a f'ọwọ́ gba l'órí | The reverence of a newborn child prohibits us from striking the child on the head<br>- Just as no one can strike a blind person or a physically challenged person, you just grin and bear it if a toddler spits on you or does one of those things toddlers do to annoy adults (if there is);<br>- Don't kill a mockingbird. |
| 1359. | Ọwọ́ Ọmọdé ò tó Pẹẹpẹ, t'àgbàlagbà ò w'akèngbè | A toddler's hand does not reach a shelf, an adult's does not fit inside a gourd |

| | | |
|---|---|---|
| | | - There are things only a child can do and likewise there're things only adults can do that children cannot;<br>- If someone is not useful in one area, they might be useful in another. |
| 1360. | Ọwọ́ t'ó bá d'ilẹ̀ l'èṣú ń rán ńṣẹ́ | The hands that became soil [vulnerable due to inactivity] are those the devil sends on errands<br>- Idle hands are the devil's workshop. |
| 1361. | Ọwọ́ t'ó bá ṣ'ẹ́gũsí, òun l'ó ń jẹẹ́ | The hand that extracts the seeds from Ẹ̀gúsí [melon fruit shells] is the one that eats them<br>- He who labors ought to eat the fruits of his labor. |
| 1362. | Òwú Aláǹtakùn, kò s'ẹ́ni t'ó lè fi rán'ṣọ | The thread of a spider, no one can sew clothes with it<br>- The matter is a moot point;<br>- Whatever you might have heard, you can't take it to the bank. |
| 1363. | Owú jíjẹ, b'ó ti wà l'ọ́kùnrin, bẹ́ẹ̀ l'ó wà l'óbìnrin | Envy, as it is in menfolk, so it is in womenfolk. |
| 1364. | Òwú tí Ìyá gbọ̀n l'ọmọ ń ran | The wool that the mother spuns is what the child will weave<br>- A child is often a chip off the old block;<br>- Sort of "like mother, like daughter". |
| 1365. | Pa mí s'ílé, má pa mí s'íta | Kill me indoors, don't kill me outside<br>- Keep my secret within the family, don't expose it in public. |
| 1366. | Pàkúté t'ó bá m'ámũbọ́, ó kọ́ Ẹranko l'ọ́gbọ́n ni | A trap that failed to catch an animal after snapping shut, has taught the animal a wisdom<br>- If a plot intended to entrap someone came unstuck, then the victim should consider himself lucky and watch out next time. |
| 1367. | Pá-ńsá ò fu'ra, Pá-ńsá jáá'ná; Àjà ò fu'ra, Àjá jìn; b'ónílé ò bá fu'ra, Olè ní ó ko | Pá-ńsá is not wary, it falls into the fire below; the roof is not watchful, it too falls down; if the landlord is not cautious, it's armed robbers that will burgle his house<br>- We need to be mindful and police our communal environments. |

| 1368. | Pàsán t'a fi nà'yáálé ńbẹ l'órí Àjà láti fi na Ìyàwó | The cane [switch] with which we used to whip the first wife is in the attic to whip the new wife with<br>- The unpleasant thing that the person in the narrative is known to have done to the former occupant of a position can be visited on the new entrant as well. This could be in a friendship, relationship, partnership, business etc. You never know, so don't gloat! Similar treatment could be meted out to you as well. |
|---|---|---|
| 1369. | Pèkí n'mo kòó, bàrá n'mo yàá; Onítọ̀ún r'íbi tí ó yà sí ni | Suddenly I met it, quickly I side-stepped it; that's because the person found somewhere to pull into, otherwise it'd be a head-on collision<br>- You are boasting now because you were lucky the first time [to have found a way out]. |
| 1370. | Pèlé-pèlé l'à ń p'àmúkùrù Ẹpọ̀n tàbí…<br>Pèlé l'a fi ń p'àmúkùrùu Pèlé | Slowly and softly does one swat the fly on the testicles<br>- A delicate problem requires a delicate solution. |
| 1371. | Pétẹpẹ̀tẹ̀ l'à ń bá'lée Babaláwo; Babaláwo t'ó bá l'ọ́bùn ni | One always find a Diviner's house in filth; only a Diviner who has inherent squalor<br>- People might have a negative opinion of someone; only if the person truly has the unpleasant bearing attributed to him/her. |
| 1372. | Pírí l'olongó ń jí; a kì ń b'ókùnrùn Ẹiyẹ l'órí Ìtẹ́! | The Olongo bird wakes up sprightly early in the morning; we don't find a sick bird in its nest! (It will usually fly about until it has recuperated)<br>- This is a mantra said to someone who has been taken ill to shake off whatever ails them and get well pretty soon. |
| 1373. | Pètẹpẹ̀tẹ̀ táa nà ní Pọ̀pá, gbogbo Ẹní bá ta bá l'ára, k'ó tún'ra è ṣe ni | The mud that we strike with a stick, all whom it splashes onto should go and clean themselves up<br>- Apologies to those whom the new [severe] law has affected, but there was no alternative. |
| 1374. | Pọ̀n-úh l'àá ṣ'épọ̀n; bí ó ṣ'omi | Swiftly is how we pop a cyst on a testicle; |

| | | |
|---|---|---|
| | k'ó ṣ'omi, bí ó ṣ'ẹ̀jẹ̀, k'ó ṣ'ẹ̀jẹ̀ | if it'll dribble fluid, let it dribble fluid, if it'll seep blood, let it seep blood<br>- Delay may be fatal in this metaphor;<br>- Do what has to be done;<br>- We've got to try and do something - it's now or never! |
| 1375. | Púrọ́ n n'íyì, Ẹ̀tẹ́ ní ń kángun | Lie or deceive to gain fame and prestige, disgrace is the end of it<br>- Lying to save face, it's a definite disgrace that it results in;<br>- He who lies to gain something risks losing everything in the long run. |
| 1376. | Ránti Ọmọ Ẹni tí Ìwọ́ ńṣe | Remember the child of whom you are. This is a word of warning [usually at parting] to someone to be careful and remember why they are doing what they are doing (or why they are where they are)<br>- Remember where you are from;<br>- Never lose your focus, keep your wits about you;<br>- Don't go keeping bad companies. |
| 1377. | Rìkíṣí ò jẹ́ k'ádìyẹ fò | A wicked conspiracy did not make it possible for chickens to fly<br>- An example: a law-making body of a country is trying to enact a law against, say, corruption, and it's apparently not able to execute the legislation. This hiccup could be due to interference from an evil cabal or some secret cult or other entity that is responsible for the stalemate, only it may not be so apparent to the common people;<br>- Another example: a good employee who has been passed for promotion could relate this metaphor that other people who did not like him probably put in a word or two against him to not get the promotion. |
| 1378. | Rírò-rírò l'ọbẹ̀ Gbẹ̀gìrì; bẹ́ẹ̀ bá ròó dáadáa, ṣíṣàn ní ó ṣàn | Stirring-stirring is the [secret of the] soup of toasted beans; if it's not stirred |

| | | |
|---|---|---|
| | | properly, it will be watery<br>- You have to keep an eye out for this [plan] to work. |
| 1379. | Sán'bẹ sùn f'apó rọ'rí; à ṣé Ìwà Ọmọ l'ó ń m'ọ́mọ ṣòògùn Òkígbẹ́ | One who hides a knife under a stool that he's using as a pillow while asleep; so it's a child's character that makes him acquire a juju [protective charm] against knife-stabbing<br>- The speaker is expressing his regrets for his deeds, especially wishing he hadn't exploited his privilege against [poor folks];<br>- It now seems to have dawned on the speaker of this proverb that, "so, this is the way things are with these folks?" |
| 1380. | Ṣe bóo ti mọn, Ẹlẹ́wã Shàpón | Do according to your ability, bean seller of Shàpón. The legend is that of a lady selling delicious beans at Shàpón in Abeokuta in those days. In case someone wanted to buy and pay later or didn't have enough money to buy as much, she would say 'ṣe bí o ti mọn' [do as your condition allows]<br>- Don't live beyond your means;<br>- Cut your coat according to your size;<br>- Don't venture into an activity where you have no experience. |
| 1381. | Ṣé n máa yó kí nmá mọ̀n? | Can I be full up and not know that I am?<br>- I know what I'm doing! |
| 1382. | Ṣé wíwọ́n Eèpo ni k'a wí ni, àbí àìr'ówó ràá? | Are we talking about the expensiveness of shells or not having money to buy them?<br>- What might have dissuaded me from doing the right thing when it's not as if I am so lacking in good judgment to not do the ethical thing? |
| 1383. | Ṣé wọ́n bí Shórin m'éja ni? | Was Shórin born along [together] with the fish?<br>- Are you my identical twin, so that we do things together?<br>- Are you supposed to do everything I do, or have everything I have?<br>- What have we got in common that you |

| | | |
|---|---|---|
| | | keep tailing / hounding me? Leave me alone! |
| 1384. | Ṣókí l'ọbẹ̀ Oge | Little is the stew of Oge [the lady in vogue]<br>- Come straight to the point;<br>- I've said what I wanted to say; a word is enough for the wise. |
| 1385. | Ṣòó báyî òun l'à ń rìn | Straight, narrow and direct is how we walk<br>- We call a spade a spade;<br>- We don't beat about the bush or knowingly mislead others. |
| 1386. | Sùúrù l'a fi ń yọ Òrónro l'ára Ẹran; t'ó bá fọ́ m'ẹran, yíó b'ẹran jẹ́ | With extreme patience do we remove the sac from meat; if it bursts on it, it'll ruin the meat<br>- With extreme caution do we disable a bomb or diffuse a tense stand-off. |
| 1387. | T'a bá f'órìṣà l'ẹ́ran, a máa ń jọ̀wọ́ Okùn-un rẹ̀ ni | If we give a messenger-god a sacrificial animal, we let go of the leash as well<br>- If you give someone a helping hand during their dire straits, you don't gloat about it or continually remind them of what you did. |
| 1388. | T'a bá l'énĩ l'àá mũ, Ọ̀la l'àá mú | If we plan to 'arrest' Today, it's Tomorrow we end up arresting<br>- If anyone plans to harm you or arrest you, it's someone else they'll unwittingly end up with;<br>- If someone proposes to harm us, it's someone else they'll end up hurting.<br>A 'triumphant' boasting really; like saying instead of you being the object of someone's wilful act, someone else will fall victim. |
| 1389. | T'ágbọ́n bá rorò, ó ńb'ónílé gbé ni | If a wasp/hornet is cruel, it [conceivably] lives with a homeowner<br>- The person in question is probably following the footsteps of his parents/peers [likely problematic people]. |
| 1390. | T'áhéré bá ń jó l'ójoojúmọ́n àwọn Àgbà ò kì ń lọ Oko àlọsùn | If a hut [home] burns every day, the elders [of the hut] do not go to the farm and stay the night<br>- There's an unpleasant challenge that |

| | | |
|---|---|---|
| | | someone is facing literally every day that requires attention of the elders [or their personification]. |
| 1391. | T'ápá ò bá ṣeé ṣán, àá ka l'érí ni | If an arm is unstretchable, we fold it over our head<br>- If a log is in our eye, we remove it. |
| 1392. | T'apá t'ẹsẹ̀ l'awún ń wọ'gbá | With arms and legs, the tortoise enters its shell<br>- If you wish to do something, do it with all your energy and personal involvement to demonstrate your commitment. |
| 1393. | T'édìẹ ẹ bá dà mi lóògùn nù, Èmi nã á fọ l'ẹ́yin | If a hen upends my medicine syrup, I too will destroy her eggs [in retaliation]<br>- If someone does me a bad turn, I'll return the favor;<br>- Tit for tat. |
| 1394. | T'ẹléjọ́ bá m'ẹjọ́ ẹ̀ l'ẹ́bi, kò níí pẹ́ ní Ìkúnlẹ̀ | If one who commits an offence admits his culpability, his "sentence" or "judgement" will be short<br>- If you own up to your guilt, your justice might be tempered with a measure of leniency. |
| 1395. | T'ẹlẹ́ṣẹ̀ ẹ bá ń j'ìyà, Olódodó máa ń pín ń'nú ẹ̀ | If a sinner is suffering, the honest one shares in it<br>- For example: if a family man is convicted of a criminal activity and jailed, his family might suffer from his inability to continue to provide for them as before. His family are the "honest ones." |
| 1396. | T'èmí tó mi l'ẹ́rù, má dì kun! | My own issues are abundant as a load, don't top it up!<br>- I have enough problems of my own, don't add to them! |
| 1397. | T'ẹní bẹ́'gi l'ó jù, Igí á rú'wé | He who has cut down a tree is the one with the problem, the tree [stump] will continue to sprout leaves<br>- The COVID-19 is an illustration. We could say that the one with the problem was the coronavirus that made a lot of businesses go under; the government's ambitious new incentives will get everyone back on |

| | | track;<br>- The restoration of the medieval cathedral of Notre-Dame in Paris after fire engulfed it on April 16, 2019 is another example of this proverb that the fire was the one with the problem;<br>- There is hope after all. |
|---|---|---|
| 1398. | T'ẹni t'ó dé l'a rí; t'ẹni t'ó ń bọ̀, aò mọ̀n | We see that of he who just arrived; that of he who is on the way, we do not know<br>- The circumstances of those already here is what we are aware of; the circumstances of those coming are unknown. |
| 1399. | T'ényán bá jẹ Òróǹró m'ẹran, a máa b'ẹran jẹ́ | If one eats the sac attached to meat, it ruins the meat<br>- If one adds the responsibility of another to his own in time of adversity, it complicates things for him. |
| 1400. | T'énìà bá máa j'ọ̀pọ̀lọ́, k'ó kúkú jẹ èyí t'ó l'ẹ́yin | If someone must eat toads, he'd better eat those with eggs<br>- If you've got to do something, better do it well;<br>- If you've got a choice about anything, select the best one. |
| 1401. | T'énìà ò bá ṣ'awun Ọwọ́, Ènìà lí ṣ'awun Ẹnu | If someone doesn't show stinginess to the Hand, the individual won't show parsimony to the Mouth<br>- If people support a cause, those who manage the cause will not cease in their activity [to continue promoting the cause]. |
| 1402. | T'ẹrú bá j'ọba, bí Ìgbẹ́ n'ìlú ń rí | If a slave became king, the city would look like shit<br>- If you installed a corrupt person as your leader, the country would be destitute of common and basic infrastructure before long. |
| 1403. | T'ẹṣín bá da'ni, àa tún-un gùn ni | If a horse upended one from its back, one would still remount the horse<br>- If at first you don't succeed, try, try and try again. |
| 1404. | T'íkú ò bá p'agbe, Aláró á d'áró; | If death doesn't kill the Agbe bird, the tie- |

| | | |
|---|---|---|
| | t'íkú ò bá p'àlùkò, aà lè d'áwọ́ Osùn kíkùn; bí Lékelèké ò bá kú, aà gbọdọ̀ d'árò Oníkẹfun | dyer will continue her tie-dying; if death doesn't kill the Aluko bird, we won't cease camwood painting; if egrets do not die, we mustn't mourn the chalk maker<br>- If the head is stable and secure, things will always run as they always do in society. |
| 1405. | T'ímí bá dé, Fùrọ̀ á là | When it's time for stool to 'arrive', whether it opposes or it's in agreement, the anus must open up<br>- When confronted with overwhelming insurgency, the corrupt government must fall;<br>- When it's time for something to happen, it will happen. |
| 1406. | T'íná bá jó'ni j'ọmọ Ẹni, t'ara Ẹni l'àá 'kọ́ ń gbọ̀n | If fire burns one together with one's child, one extinguishes the flame on their body first<br>- Take care of the most pressing issue at hand before tackling another;<br>- Remove the log [speck] in your eye first. |
| 1407. | T'íwộ bá l'ó máa ya ní Ìbú, t'ó bá lọ ya l'óòró ǹkọ́? | If you figure it would split horizontally, what if the split occurs vertically?<br>- If you think you absolutely want to go this route, what happens if it doesn't pan out the way you expect then?<br>- So you think you've got it all figured out, do you? |
| 1408. | T'o bá máa jẹ Ọ̀ṣáká, k'o jẹ́ Ọ̀ṣáká; t'o bá máa jẹ Òṣoko, k'o jẹ́ Òṣoko; Ọ̀ṣáká-Òṣoko ò jẹ́ ǹkankan | If you want to be Ọ̀ṣáká, be Ọ̀ṣáká; if you want to be Òṣoko, be Òṣoko; you can't be Ọ̀ṣáká-Òṣoko<br>- Choose which side you wish to belong;<br>- Decide what you want to do; don't be two-faced. |
| 1409. | T'ó bá rú'jú tán, Ajá a máa f'aṣọ Ẹkùn ya | If things don't go as planned in the skirmish or things get out of control, a dog could tear off the tiger's cloth [flesh]<br>- If things go awry, the unexpected could happen; you never know;<br>- When push comes to shove, the little guy can do a lot of damage to the big guy. |

| | | |
|---|---|---|
| 1410. | T'Ógūn Ẹní bá dá'ni l'ójú, a ma fi ń gbá'rí ni | If one's sure of his Ògún (the god of iron) one swears by him always<br>- If you're cocksure about some truth, you stand firm and swear by the conviction. |
| 1411. | T'ójú bá yẹ'jú, k'óhùn má yẹ<br>B'ójú bá yẹ'jú, k'óhùn má yẹ | If eyes miss the eyes of others [due to parting], let not our voices follow suit<br>- Though we have parted ways [after our summit], we should not forget what we have agreed on. |
| 1412. | T'ójú ò bá ti Olè, áá ti Olóko | If the eye doesn't 'push' the thief, it will the farmer. (If the thief is unashamed, the farmer will be)<br>- If a convicted individual is not ashamed, members of his family would be;<br>- Expressed as a shock or disappointment: Someone of your status shouldn't be caught dead doing this! |
| 1413. | T'ojú t'ìyẹ l'àparò ó fi ń r'íran | With both eyes and wings is how the bush-fowl sees / watches<br>- Be mindful of those close to you;<br>- One can't be too careful these days. |
| 1414. | T'óke ò bá níí lọ s'ọ́dọ̀ọ Mohammed, Mohammed a dè lọ s'ọ́dọ̀ Òkè | If the mountain won't go to Mohammed, then Mohammed must come to the mountain<br>- Life is a compromise;<br>- If you need to see someone and they are kind of reluctant to come to you, if you can go to them, why not? |
| 1415. | T'ólógìnní bá gun Àjà, Ojú u rẹ̀ ẹ́ máa ń tó'lé t'óko ni | If a cat climbs the roof, its view will extend as far away as the farm as well as the village [far and wide]<br>- If the cat can get to the top, she'll see rats before they hide and prepare her strategy on how to catch her preys;<br>- If you organize your spies strategically and efficiently, coupled with your armed forces, you should win the fight against insecurity and insurgency. |
| 1416. | T'Ọlọ́un ún bá ti f'ọ̀tá Ẹni han'ni, kò leè pa'ni mọ́n | If God Has revealed our enemy to us, he will be incapable of killing us<br>- When we discover |

| | | |
|---|---|---|
| | | • who is working against us,<br>• who doesn't wish us success,<br>• what our stumbling block is or<br>• where and what our source of trouble is, then:<br>we learn to steer clear and find a way past these hindrances. |
| 1417. | T'ọmọ Ẹní bá ń j'aáyán táà ba wí, Hùrù-hẹrẹ ẹ̀ ò níí jẹ́ 'á sùn l'óru | If one's child is eating cockroaches and we don't upbraid him, his guttural hacking sound won't let us sleep at night<br>- If one condones wayward behaviors of his children, sooner or later, they might bring home a problem that could give the parents sleepless nights. |
| 1418. | T'ọmọdé bá dé'bi Ẹ̀rù, Ẹ̀rù á bàá | If a child gets to a place where something scary lurks, he'd be scared<br>- If someone is faced with a sudden huge responsibility, he'd panic. |
| 1419. | T'ọmọdé bá dúpẹ́ Oore Àná, áá tún gbà'mîn si | If a child showed gratitude for yesterday's favor, he would receive more<br>- Always appreciate what someone has done for you; this would encourage them to do more for you and quite possibly others. |
| 1420. | T'ọmọdé bá f'ogún Ọdún jó, t'ó bá w'ẹ̀hìn wò tí ò r'érò l'ẹ́hìn, ó yẹ k'ó p'èrò pọ̀ k'ó gb'oko ibòmîn lọ ni | If a young man dances for twenty years, looks back and not see a crowd behind him, he should gather his wits about him [count his losses] and go in search of another farm<br>- If you have tried a solution and not succeeded, why not try another method to resolve the challenge? Evidently your current strategy is not working. |
| 1421. | T'ọmọdé bá gb'ọ́gbọ́n àti kú l'ẹ̀ẹ̀rùn, àwọn Òbí i rẹ a sì gb'ọ́gbọ́n àti sín s'ípadò | If a child was clever enough to pass away to the netherworld during the heat of summer, the parents would be shrewd enough to bury him in a swamp<br>- You have to find a way to overcome the obstacle in your way. |
| 1422. | T'ọmọdé bá gé'gi n'ígbó, àwọn Àgbà l'ó mọn'bi t'ó ma wó sí | If children are cutting down trees in the forest, it's adults who know which |

| | | direction they'll fall<br>- A great advice for the youth to consult adults before they engage in any activity that might affect the community;<br>- Children sometimes don't know the full consequences of their actions, hence the need for them to consult the elders. |
|---|---|---|
| 1423. | T'ọmọdé bá l'áṣọ bí Àgbà, kò leè l'ákīsà bí Àgbà | If a child had as many clothes as an adult, he could not have rags or hand-me-downs as an adult<br>- If a child had wealth to rival that of an average adult, he would not have as much knowledge as an adult. |
| 1424. | T'ọmọdé bá m'ọwọ́ọ́ wẹ, á b'ágbà jẹun | If a child knows how to wash hands, he/she will eat with adults<br>- If you are respectful to those in power/wealth, you will prosper. |
| 1425. | T'ọmọdé bá ṣu'bú á wo Iwájú; b'ágbàlagbà á bá ṣu'bú a w'ẹ̀hìn wò | If a child tripped and fell, he'd look in front; if an adult fell, he would look behind him<br>- The adult is full of life experiences and experience of course is the best teacher. |
| 1426. | T'ọmọdé bá tóó l'ọ́kọ́, ó máa ń l'ọ́kọ́ ni | If it's time for a child to have a hoe, he gets a hoe<br>- When it's about time an event took place, we should do all we could to allow it to come to fruition. |
| 1427. | T'ọ̀n bá ní Omi l'ó ma se Ẹja j'iná, aá sọ'pé Irọ́ ni | If they said water is what will cook fish till it's well-cooked, we would say it's a lie<br>- This allegory is usually said when a person very close to someone has betrayed them. |
| 1428. | T'ónífá bá da'fáá'lẹ̀, Ẹnìkan l'ó ma ko | After the Ifá diviner has spread his Ifá [on the divination mat], it's someone that will pick them up<br>- You started this; I am ready for you, too, so bring it on! |
| 1429. | T'ónírèsé bá kọ̀ t'ó l'óun ò fín'gbá mọ́n, Èyí t'ó ti fín s'ílẹ̀ yẹn kò níí parun láíláí | If the carver declines to never again etch gourds, those he/she had already hewn would never perish but remain for posterity |

| | | |
|---|---|---|
| | | - If a parent declares they have had enough of looking after their children [who are now adults], the investment they had put in nurturing, raising, and educating the kids should serve them throughout their lifetime.<br>- Someone needs to show some gratitude here. |
| 1430. | T'óo bá t'ìka bọ̀ mí l'ẹ́nu, màá gé ẹ jẹ | If you stick your finger in my mouth, I'll bite you [it]<br>- If you look for a fight with me, I'll oblige you. |
| 1431. | T'órí bá pẹ́ ńlẹ̀, á d'ire | If a head lasts on the 'ground', it becomes "good things"<br>- If one has been toiling for a considerable length of time, he must one day be able to turn the corner and become wealthy. |
| 1432. | T'orí Ìrègún l'énìà án ṣe ń ṣ'oore | Because of the controlling influence over a past favor [that someone has rendered you] is why people do good<br>- Endeavor to always do good unto others;<br>- "Do unto others, as you would have them do unto you." Matthew 7: 12. |
| 1433. | T'oríi Wèrè-ìta l'àá ṣe ń ní t'ilé | It's on account of the external madman that we have one at home<br>- It's precisely because of the threat of attack that could be launched against us without warning that we have an equally-formidable counter-option [as a deterrent] in place. |
| 1434. | T'ọ́rọ̀ ọ́ bá kan Òkè t'ó kan'lẹ̀, ó n'íbìkan t'a ma gbé e lé | If an issue affects both the sky and the ground, there's bound to be somewhere on which we place it<br>- A resolution or a compromise has to be found for the matter on the ground. |
| 1435. | T'ọ́wọ́ Ẹni ò bá tíì tẹ Èkù Idà, a kì ń bèèrè Ikú t'ó pa Baba Ẹni | When a son's hand has not yet felt the handle of a sword, he does not question what kind of death his father died of<br>- When you haven't got the one important thing you desperately need, you act meek/humble and don't ruffle any |

| | | |
|---|---|---|
| | | feathers [of those who would provide it] until you do have it in your hands. |
| 1436. | T'ọ̀wọ̀ t'ọ̀wọ̀ l'à ń w'àfín l'ọ́jà | It's with wonder we stare at an albino in the market<br>- We stare with admiration at someone we know is a special breed who would risk his own life to save others especially when he is not obliged to;<br>- We gape in awe and respect of those whom we feel have earned it. |
| 1437. | Tá kọ́n-ọ́n kọ̀n-ọ̀n kọ́n bí Ọfà Ìmọ̀ndò | Shoot it quickly like the arrow of an Ìmọ̀ndò or Ìmàdò [clumsy man]<br>- Do what you've got to do in good time;<br>- Don't drag your feet about it! |
| 1438. | Ta l'a nà, ta l'ará ń ta? | Whom did we beat, whose body hurts?<br>- What's it got to do with you? |
| 1439. | Ta l'eṣinṣin ì bá gbè bíi bá ṣ'elégbò? | Whom will the fly side with but the man with a sore [open wound]?<br>- Whom will the entity [named or implied in the context] support but their family, relations, friends, cohorts, "partners in crime?" |
| 1440. | Ta l'ó gún'yán fún ẹ t'ó ní t'ọbẹ̀ ò ṣoro? | Who cooked pounded yam for you and said the matter of stew [to eat it with] is not a difficulty?<br>- Who gave you the authority to do what you just did?<br>- What effrontery you exhibit by your conduct, like you were put in the position you hold only to exploit others with impunity?<br>- How dare you? |
| 1441. | Ta l'ó máa ti Ika bọ Iwò Ìdí ẹ tí 'ò níí rùn? | Who will stick a finger into their anus and it will not smell?<br>- Who will use perfumes or deodorants and pass a hornet's nest and not get stung?<br>- Who will dare put his hand into a lion's mouth and not lose it?<br>- Who would do what you did and not [expect to] pay the penalty? |

| | | |
|---|---|---|
| 1442. | Ta l'ó lè wí f'ọ́jà k'ó má p'ariwo, àfí t'ílẹ̀ ẹ́ bá ṣú tí Èró dẹ̀ẹ́ kúrò l'ọ́jà? | Who can tell a market to stop making noise, except it's dusk and the crowd then exit the market?<br>- Who can take it upon himself to stop the protest except when the demands of the protest are met? |
| 1443. | Ta'ní ń jẹun t'ájá ńj'ìrù | Who's eating that the dog is wagging its tail<br>- Who do you think is talking that you want to barge in?<br>- Who is your mate [equal] that is joking with you? |
| 1444. | Táa bá dẹ'jú aá r'îmú | If we slant the eyes, we'll see the nose<br>- If we weigh the matter [at hand] and observe the activity of those in question very carefully, one might glean the truth and/or get to the bottom of the issue. |
| 1445. | Táa bá f'ojúu wíwó w'ogi gbígbẹ, tútùú máa ń wó | If we look at a dry tree and think "uprooted," well, guess what, saplings do uproot, too<br>- This is a cautionary expression to not see and simply accept things at face value;<br>- Do not underestimate. |
| 1446. | Táa bá ń b'ára wa rìn táa lè b'ára wa s'òótọ́, Ọ̀tá araa wa la jẹ́ | If we walk together and we cannot tell each other the truth, then we are enemies to ourselves<br>- This statement is usually said by one friend to another who may need someone to slap them on the wrist and tell them where and how they might have messed up, even if they do not want to hear the bitter truth. |
| 1447. | Táa bá ń rìn ní Póópó, k'a kíyè s'ára, nítorí Gbòngbò; Gbòngbò Àná táa f'ojú fò l'ó wá ń kọ́'ni l'ẹ́sẹ̀ l'énī | When we are walking on the high road, let's pay attention around us, because of roots; the roots of yesterday that we looked down on are now causing us to trip [as they are everywhere]<br>- Those folks are no longer to be toyed with nowadays;<br>- The disenfranchised, under-represented voters of yesterday have now become |

| | | |
|---|---|---|
| | | politicians who are now causing us to lose our constituencies or causing us upsets in the ballot! |
| 1448. | Táa bá ń t'ọmọ l'ọwọ́, aà lè k'órin méjì bọ'ná | If we are raising a child, we cannot put two irons in the fire<br>- We cannot confront challenges at several fronts at the same time;<br>- Face one problem one at a time. |
| 1449. | Táa bá ní k'a di'jú k'ẹni burúkú fi kọjá, tí Ẹni'ré máa fi lọ Ènìà ò níí mọ̀n | If we insist on shutting our eyes till the wicked man has passed, by the time a good person has also passed, we will not know<br>- Don't let bad feelings of yesterday to control your today. |
| 1450. | Táa bá ńw'ówó lọ, táa bá pàdé Iyì l'ọ́nà, ó yẹ k'a mú Iyì ọ̀hún k'a padà s'ílé ni; nítorí táa bá l'ówó ọ̀hún tán, Iyì nã l'a ma kúkú fi rà | If we are looking for Money and meet Dignity along the way, we ought to grab Dignity and return home because when we finally have the Money, it is Dignity we use it to buy after all<br>- If we have been striving for something but halfway during our endeavor, we find something of almost equal value but much easier to attain, the notion is we take it and be grateful for the opportunity that produced it. |
| 1451. | Táà bá r'ẹni bá jà, àá máa fa Ògiri mọ́n'ra ni | If we can't find someone to fight, we draw the wall to oneself<br>- If they can't find someone to intimidate, sometimes bullies turn on the innocent and the weak just for something to do. |
| 1452. | Táa bá ro dídùn Ifọ̀n, àá họ'ra d'éegun | If we considered the painful itching one gets from palm-fronds, we would scratch ourselves to the bone<br>- If we considered the suffering and hardship we endured on our path to get to where we are, we would be mean to everyone. |
| 1453. | Táa bá sọ Abẹ̀bẹ̀ s'ókè nígbà Igba, ibi pẹlẹbẹ nã l'ó máa mú wá'lẹ̀ | If we threw a hand-fan in the air two hundred times, the flat side would always land first, every single time<br>- If a person (or people) have always |

| | | |
|---|---|---|
| | | engaged in egregious activity ever since you knew them, what makes you think they're going to turn a new leaf now? |
| 1454. | Táa bá sọ'kò s'ọ́já, Ará Ẹni níí bà. | If we threw a stone at a [street] market, it usually hits one's relation<br>- This is a warning for those who make draconian laws and/or rules without seriously considering the fallout which might affect their own kith and kin. |
| 1455. | Táa bá t'orí Epo jẹ'ṣu, àá t'orí Iṣu j'epo | If we don't eat yam because of palm oil, we eat palm oil because of yam<br>- If we want to stay clear of something, we get involved because of something else that is equally important. |
| 1456. | T'éníyán bá ń lọ s'óde àlọjù, yíó shi Òde lọ ńjọ́kan | If someone likes going out too frequently, he/she will go to the wrong place one day<br>- Whoever engages in illicit activity with impunity or without control will one day engage in some undertaking that they will live to regret. |
| 1457. | T'éníyán bá ń tọ'pa Odò tí 'ò sẹ'rí padà, yíó b'ólúwẹri pàdé ńjọ́kan | If someone is tracing the source of a river and does not turn back, he will one day come face to face with Olúwẹri [the mermaid]<br>- This is a kind of warning for whosoever is hell-bent or adamant about pursuing a course and refuses to back down. |
| 1458. | T'étí ò bá gbọ́ Yìnkìn, Inú ií bàá jẹ́ | If the ears don't hear an unpalatable gist, the stomach doesn't rotten<br>- One doesn't get sad if one doesn't hear bad news. |
| 1459. | Tí 'ò bá l'ọ́wọ́ Aráa'lé ń'nú, Àlejò kan ò lè wá máa jú'we Sàréè e bàbá Afọ́jú | If it doesn't have the "hand" of relations in it, a stranger cannot come and point out the burial ground of a blind man's father to him<br>- If there are no traitors [within], attackers [or killers] will not be able to find out the weakness of someone or a group, and destroy them. |
| 1460. | Tí 'ò bá s'ígi l'ẹ́hìn Ọgbà, wíwó l'ó ń wó | If there is no tree behind a garden [fence], collapse is what it does |

| | | |
|---|---|---|
| | | - Lack of support results in failure, disintegration and breakdown. |
| 1461. | Tí a bá dé'bi Iṣẹ́, ṣíṣe l'àá ṣe é | When we get to work, we do it. |
| 1462. | Tí a bá f'ọ̀tún b'ọ́mọ wí, àá fi t'òsì fàá mọ́n'ra | If we beat our child with the right hand, we draw him close with the left<br>- If we show our ire against someone, we temper justice with mercy, so to speak. |
| 1463. | Tí a bá gbé Díígí, Ìkejì Ara Ẹni l'àá rí | If we grab a mirror, it's our other self we see<br>- Our life experiences are the same as other human beings, one way or another. |
| 1464. | Tí a bá ńbá Olówó rìn tí aò bá yó, tí a bá f'olówó nã s'ílẹ̀, Ebi ò lè lu'ni pa | If we were buddies with a wealthy person and yet never had much to eat, if we shunned the wealthy man, we could never die of hunger<br>- If you moved with someone who could alleviate your suffering or lighten your load in some way and yet your situation has not improved after a reasonable period of time, if you severed the relationship, you wouldn't miss the affiliation. |
| 1465. | Tí a bá rántíi b'éjõ ṣe gùn tó, àá dá'ná sun'lé | If we recall how long a snake is, we will burn down the house<br>- If we remember the maltreatment or evil that someone has done to us, we won't be able to forgive. |
| 1466. | Tí a ò bá gbàgbé Ọ̀rọ̀ Àná, aà ní r'ẹni bá ṣ'eré | If we don't forget about the falling-out [quarrel, disagreement] of yesterday, we may not have anyone left to play with or talk to<br>- If we keep harbouring past grudges, it might come a point when we would have no one to talk to or do business with. |
| 1467. | Tí Agbọ́n bá mọ̀n'wà á hù, áá bá Onílé gbé | If a hornet knows how to behave, it'll live with the homeowner<br>- If you are well-behaved and do not go beyond your boundary, you can almost survive in any environment. |
| 1468. | Tí Alẹ́ bá lẹ́, aá f'ọmọ Ayò f'áláyò | When it's night time, we give back the pieces of the Ayò game to the Ayò board |

| | | |
|---|---|---|
| | | - After the dust has settled, we should let everything return to normal - no more conflict. |
| 1469. | Tí Awó bá kí fún'ni, a ma ń kí f'Áwo padà | If an oracle priest honors us, we honor the oracle priest in return<br>- Respect is reciprocal. |
| 1470. | Tí Ẹní bá kú, Ẹni nã níí kù | If somebody dies, it's someone that's left<br>- Take comfort in the fact that the situation can be fixed;<br>- Take heart; all hope is not lost. |
| 1471. | Tí Fúlàní bá ńlọ, kò ní gbàgbé Orẹ́ | If a Fúlàní man [cow herder] is leaving town, he never forgets his whip [that he uses to control his cattle]<br>- No one can deny me what belongs to me, so I'm taking it with me if I do leave. |
| 1472. | Tí Ìgànná bá là l'ẹ̀hìn, atẹ́gùn fẹ́ẹ́rẹ́fẹ́ a máa fẹ́ wọ'lé | If the wall had a crack in the back, a soft breeze would find a way in<br>- If you had a weakness in your security, burglars and malicious individuals could always find a way to enter. |
| 1473. | Tí Ìlú ò bá l'ólórí, Ìlú ìí dùn | If a town had no leader, the town would not be much fun<br>- Without a leader, a town would be unruly, lawless and chaotic. |
| 1474. | Tí Iná ò bá tán l'áṣọ, Ẹ̀jẹ̀ ò lè tán l'ëëkánná | If lice are not eradicated from clothes, blood will not be eradicated from nails<br>- If the root cause of a problem is not eliminated, the symptoms will still continue to manifest. |
| 1475. | Tí Iná ò bá tán l'órí, Ẹ̀jẹ̀ ò lè tán l'èèkánná | If lice are not completely exterminated from the head [scalp], blood will not be stamped out from nails<br>- If the root cause of a problem is not eliminated, the symptoms will still continue to manifest. |
| 1476. | Tí Iwájú ò bá ṣeé lọ, Ẹ̀hín á ṣeé padà sí | If we can't go forward, retreat is always possible<br>- If we have begun a project and we don't seem to be making obvious headways, we could abandon this endeavour and start all over again or find another way; OR |

| | | - If the point you're at cannot be sustained, you should be able to double-back to whence you came and check how and where things went wrong. |
|---|---|---|
| 1477. | Tí kòkòró bá ń jẹ Ògọ́mọ̀n, Ìbànújẹ́ gbáà l'ó jẹ́ f'ọ́pẹ | If insects are eating brambles, it's great sadness for the palm tree indeed<br>- If the leader's kin are committing atrocities all over the place, it'll be awkward for him to bring other offenders to justice. |
| 1478. | Tí nbá ní Iná ńjó l'órí Omi, ẹ ní kí n lọ kó Eérú ẹ̀ wá | If I say fire is burning on water, demand of me to go and bring the ash [as proof]<br>- If you feel that I'm lying about what I'm saying, you've only got to ask me to produce the evidence;<br>- Mark my words; I don't make such allegations lightly. |
| 1479. | Tí nbá ní Omí ń jó'ná, ẹ ní kí nlọ kó Eérú ẹ̀ wá | If I say water is burning, just ask me to bring the ash [as evidence]<br>- The story I'm about to narrate, don't take my word for it; ask for proof [which I've got];<br>- It's the gospel truth. |
| 1480. | Tí ò bá ní ìdí, Obìnrin ìí jẹ Kúmólú | Without a reason, a girl is never named Kúmólú<br>- If there's no good valid reason, no one would just wake up and take such a step;<br>- No smoke without fire. |
| 1481. | Tí ò bá ní'un tí Àgbọ̀nrín jẹ tẹ́lẹ̀ Ikùn, kò níí ṣe Ikùn gbẹndu s'ọlọ́dẹ | If it weren't for what a stag had eaten to line its stomach, it would not stick its [bloated] abdomen at the hunter [to aim at]<br>- You know what support [of some higher authority] you've got before challenging a more powerful adversary. |
| 1482. | Tí Ojú bá ti Ìpàkọ́, Iwájú ò n'íyì mọ́n | If the occiput is shamed, the front loses its honor [by default]<br>- If the most influential person in an entity is disgraced, the whole entity will fall into disrepute. |
| 1483. | Tí Olóde ò bá kú, Ojúde ẹ̀ ò kì ń | If he who likes appearances [outings] is |

| | | |
|---|---|---|
| | wu Koríko | not dead, his front yard will never grow weeds<br>- No matter how a man likes to roam about rather than stay at home, he would never leave his home in disarray/decay and allow the overgrowth of grass and weeds to engulf his porch without tending to it;<br>- Except he had been captured, imprisoned or incapacitated by evil government forces, no free leader [agitator, people's champion] would sit still or stand by and let his fellow citizens be slaughtered with impunity by a corrupt and oppressive regime without raising international awareness of the atrocity. |
| 1484. | Tí Òngbìn ò bá gbìn, kín l'Ònká ó kã. | If the planter did not sow, what would the gatherer harvest?<br>- If your parents hadn't put in the investment to educate you, you wouldn't be in your current position;<br>- You reap what you sow [or what someone had sown as your positive right]. |
| 1485. | Tí Onígbá bá pe Igbá è ní "Èkúfó", Yoòbá ma sọ'pé "Pànkàrà" ni | If a calabash seller says her calabashes are second-to-none, her customers will rebut that they are just average<br>- Whoever preens or flaunts himself as the best will be met with derision. |
| 1486. | Tímọ́n tímọ́n l'etí ń mọ́n'rí; tìmọ̀n tìmọ̀n l'alámọ̀n ń d'ámọ̀n | Steadfast is the way the ears are attached to the head; closely and stickily is how the potter molds clay<br>- You have been created well, with all your faculties functioning properly. Be grateful to your Creator. |
| 1487. | Tìt'aruwo l'à ń kọ'là; t'ó bá j'iná tán, t'ẹrú t'ọmọ l'ó ń fẹ́ẹ | Through pain and screaming we get tribal mark incisions; when the marks heal, it is both the house-slaves as well as the children of the house that appreciate them<br>- There's no freedom without spilling of blood; |

| | | |
|---|---|---|
| | | - No pain, no gain. |
| 1488. | Wàá mọ̀n pé Ẹran t'ó fà tíò já n'ọ́n ńpè ní Nọ́nmọ̀n | You'll know that the meat that expands [when pulled with the teeth] and remains intact [unbroken] is what they call tendon<br>- If you attempt what you're threatening to do, you'll know what I'm made of; I'll show you I'm hardcore. |
| 1489. | Wèrè é dùn-ún wò l'ójà; taló fẹ́ bọ́ síta pé òun n'ìyáa Wèrè? | Fun it might be to watch a madman in the market; who could step out and admit she's the mother of the lunatic?<br>- No one would come forward and claim responsibility for this [atrocity]. |
| 1490. | Wèrè l'a fi ń wo Wèrè | We use a mentally-deranged person to cure another<br>- For example, if you have a hangover, try and have the same drink [that you drank so much of and got the hangover from] when you wake up;<br>- If a thug terrorizes a neighborhood, employ the services of another to put him in his place. |
| 1491. | Wèrè níí se'bẹ̀ adùn f'óníbīnú, Ẹran àbámọ̀n n'ọ́n ń jẹ gb'èhìn n'ígbẹ̀hìn Aiyé e wọn | It's a mad person that cooks a delicious stew for an angry individual, the meat of regret is what they typically eat as the last meal of their lives<br>- You shall partake in the comeuppance that the heartless leaders will surely get before the end of their days. |
| 1492. | Wèrè sún Wèrè sún; tí Wèré bá sún t'ó bá k'ògiri, Wèrè á binu | Madman, move a little [to make room for others], madman, move a little; if the madman reached the wall, he would get angry<br>- You can only push someone so much before they reach the end of their tether. |
| 1493. | Wẹ́rẹ́ Wẹ́rẹ́ l'ọtí ń pa'ni; Wàrà Wàrà l'ọmọdé ń t'oko Èèsì í bọ̀ | Leisurely is how alcohol inebriates someone; hurriedly is how a child returns from a poison ivy farm<br>- Let's move quickly;<br>- Get a move on; there's no room for delays. |
| 1494. | Wọ́n l'ẹni à ń wáá lọ, Ọ̀nà l'àá | They say the person we are looking for, |

| | | |
|---|---|---|
| | kòó | we typically run into them on the way<br>- Talk of the devil! |
| 1495. | Wọ́n ní k'ẹran-án kan'ni pa, Ìgbín ń yọ'jú | They said an animal should gore someone to death, a snail appears [throws its hat in the ring]<br>- This allegory is a condescending appraisal of someone that the speaker doesn't seem to think much of;<br>- You are not up to the task, buddy! |
| 1496. | Wọ́n ní kò sí ǹkan; Òhun àti nǹkan n'ọ́n jọ ń rìn | They say there's nothing; it and something are walking together<br>- They may deny it, but something is not quite right here!<br>- No smoke without fire. |
| 1497. | Wọ́n ní k'órò ó má sọ'kò; ó l'éléyìí t'óǔn mú l'ọ́wọ́ yìí ńkọ́? | They beseech the idol-god to not cast a stone. He retorts: how about the one he's holding in his hand?<br>- You should have spoken out before we started on the path we're on now;<br>- There's no turning back;<br>- It's got to happen, once the chain of events has been set in motion;<br>- The epidemic [or justice] has to run its course. |
| 1498. | Wọ̀n-ǹtìrì wọn-ntiri kọ́ l'eyín; bí ò ju méjì tàbí mẹ́ta t'ó bá ti lè gé ẹran | A mouth full of gnashers is not teeth; if no more'n two or three as long as they can cut through meat<br>- For example: Agents dressed in full combat gear such as that of S.W.A.T. are obviously excessive to defuse a domestic argument; a single policeman is quite adequate to accomplish the task;<br>- A little graduation party at home will do to celebrate your child's graduation without the need to be in debt by throwing a lavish party and inviting VIPs in the city;<br>- A little will do without the need to indebt yourself by borrowing so much to buy presents to please others. |
| 1499. | Yin'ni-yin'ni, k'ẹni lè ṣè'mîn ni | Thanking someone [showing gratitude], |

|  |  | it's so that the benefactor might do another<br>- He who thanked you did so to encourage you to do another favor;<br>- Always appreciate what someone has done for you;<br>- Do not deride the assistance someone renders you. |
|---|---|---|
| 1500. | "Yíó ba'lẹ̀", "yíó ba'lẹ̀" ni Labalábá fi ń wọ'gbó | "It'll land", "it'll land" is how the butterfly enters the bush<br>- Little by little, stealth by stealth, what we fear is becoming a reality. |

## Pronunciation guide to alphabets specific to the Yorùbá language

Yorùbá (pronounced Yo-ru-bah) (Re-Do$^1$-Mi) (pronounce the Y as in **Y**oung).

### Yorùbá Alphabets (25)

A B D E Ẹ F G GB H I J K L M N O Ọ P R S Ṣ T U W Y
a b d e ẹ f g gb h i j k l m n o ọ p r s ṣ t u w y

### Yorùbá Vowels (7)

A E Ẹ I O Ọ U
a e ẹ i o ọ u

The Tilde (~) placed over a letter in Yorùbá denotes that the pronunciation of the letter is longer or nasalized.

In this book, though, the Caret (^) and the Diaeresis or Umlaut (¨) placed over any letter should be taken as substitutes for a Tilde (~). They have been used in this book for lack of the right Tilde over the respective letter. Try and pronounce the letters as one might pronounce them in word combination examples in **bold** in the "<u>Sounds like</u>" column.

| Please use the Octet of **Do$^1$ Re Mi Fa So La Ti Do$^2$** | | | |
|---|---|---|---|
| Uppercase | Lowercase | Sounds like | Octet of: |
| A | a | | Re |
| À | à | Dr**a**ma [ə] or **a**t | Do$^1$ |
| Á | á | As in B**a**t /bat/ | Mi |
| Ã (áá) | ã (áá) | As in P**a**rt | Do$^2$ |
| E | e | | Re |
| È | è | | Do$^1$ |
| É | é | As in D**ai**ly /ˈdālē/ | Mi |
| Ê Ë (éé) | ê ë (éé) | | Do$^2$ |
| Ẹ | ẹ | | Re |
| Ẹ̀ | ẹ̀ | | Do$^1$ |
| Ẹ́ | ẹ́ | As in **E**gg | Mi |
| Ệ (ẹ́ẹ́) | ệ (ẹ́ẹ́) | | Do$^2$ |
| GB | gb | As in Ru**gb**y | |
| I | i | | Re |
| Ì | ì | | Do$^1$ |
| Í | í | As in **i**f | Mi |
| Ĩ (íí) | ĩ (íí) | | Do$^2$ |
| J | j | As in **J**oe [dʒ] | |
| Ñ | ñ | | La |

231

| | | | |
|---|---|---|---|
| Ń | ń | | Mi |
| O | o | | Re |
| Ò | ò | | Do¹ |
| Ó | ó | As in **N**o**b**ody | Mi |
| Õ (óó) | õ (óó) | | Do² |
| Ọ | ọ | | Re |
| Ọ̀ | ọ̀ | | Do¹ |
| Ọ́ | ọ́ | As in **O**ff | Mi |
| Ọ̃ (ọ́ọ́) | ọ̃ (ọ́ọ́) | As in **Wh**arf | Do² |
| Ṣ | ṣ | As in **Sh**e | Sh |
| U | u | | Re |
| Ù | ù | | Do¹ |
| Ú | ú | As in P**u**ll | Mi |
| Y | y | | As in **Y**oung |
| Ũ (úú) | ũ (úú) | As in W**oo**l [ʊ] | Do² |

**Do¹** - The first 'Do' sound of the Octet "**Do¹** [low] Re Mi Fa So La Ti **Do²**" [high]
**Do²** - The 2nd 'Do' sound of the Octet "**Do²** [high] Ti La So Fa Mi Re **Do¹**" [low]

The eighth sound of the first Octet Do¹ is high, and sounds like the first sound of **Do²**. Similarly, the beginning of the second Octet Do² sounds like the eighth sound of **Do¹**, which is high. However, the first sound of the first Octet Do¹ is low, and sounds like the eighth sound of **Do²**, which is also low. In other words, the end of Do¹ and the beginning of Do² sound alike. Lastly, the **Do¹** refers to the whole 8 sounds of the first Octet from beginning to the end of it, while **Do²** refers to the whole 8 sounds of the second Octet from beginning to the end of it.

## Personal Pronouns

See the following table for a list of Yorùbá personal pronouns. The table lists the distinctive features for the three forms of you - ìwọ, ẹ̀yin, and ẹ̀yin.

Here's what the abbreviations mean:
s. = singular, pl. = plural, inf. = informal, form. = formal, nom. = nominative, acc. = accusative, dat. = dative.

| Nominative (nom.) | Accusative (acc.) | Dative (dat.) |
|---|---|---|
| èmi (I) | mo (me) | mi (mine) |
| ìwọ (you) (s., inf.) | o (you) (s., inf.), ò (acc.). Example: "o sọ pé **ò** ńbọ̀." - "you said **you** were coming." | ẹ (yours) (s., inf.), o (nom.) |
| ó (he) | ó (him) | è (his) |
| ó (she) | ó (her) | è (hers) |
| ó (it) | ó (it) | è (its) |
| àwa (we) | a (us) | wa (ours), à (acc.) |
| ẹ, ẹ̀yin (you) (pl., inf.) | ẹ (you) (pl., form.) | yín (yours) (pl., inf.), è (acc.) |
| àwọn (they) | nwọ́n, wọ́n (they), nwọn, wọn (they) | wọn (theirs, them) |
|  | nwọ́n mọ̀n (they know) | ti wọn (theirs) |
|  | nwọn ò mọ̀n (they don't know) | fún wọn (for them) |
| ẹ̀yin (you) (pl., form.) | ẹ, ọ (you) (s., pl., form.), è (acc. pl.) | yín (yours) (pl., form.) |

**Usage**

- If you are a young person (teen or younger) you may address others your age or younger in the familiar (ìwọ).

- Adults always address children in the familiar (ìwọ), plural (ẹ̀yin).

- If you are talking to adults irrespective of whether they are strangers or familiar to you, always use the formal (ẹ̀yin) which is also the plural.

- If you are unsure if a person is younger than you, use the formal (ẹ̀yin). Better to err on the side of courtesy than on the side of presumed familiarity.

- Two adults who are strangers to one another (even if one is older) use formal "ẹ̀yin". However, if the other adult is conspicuously older, such as old enough to be your father or mother or aunt or uncle, then the older person may use the familiar "ìwọ," plural "ẹ̀yin" while the younger adult retains the formal "ẹ̀yin" at all times.

- The "ẹ" pronoun is the formal and plural form of "you," as well as "you" for someone you would ordinarily address by name. The absence of "ẹ̀" (with the back slant) means the maxim is directed at a single individual. However, in instances where "ẹ̀" is not suggestive of a formal or plural form, it literally means "of it."

- The pronoun "o" is the informal form of "you" in the singular; the accusative pronoun "ò" or the third-person singular pronoun "ó" are used when addressing someone you would call by name.

**Some Yorùbá Words used in this book that have synonyms:**

| Word | Meaning |
| --- | --- |
| Ahéré, Abà | Hut/farmhouse |
| Akèǹgbè, Kèǹgbè | Gourd |
| Alágẹmọn, Ògà | Chameleon |
| Àmàlà, Ọkà | Doughy pasty food (made out of yam and/or cassava flour, or unripe plantain flour) |
| Àwòdì, Àwòdì-Òkè | Eagle, bush-eagle |
| Ẹdìẹ, Adìẹ | Chicken, hen, rooster |
| Eégún, Egúngún | Masquerades (of ancestral spirits) |
| Ègà, Káàrẹ́ | Songbird |
| Ẹ̀kọ, Ògì | Corn-porridge |
| Ẹ̀kọ, Ori | Hardened corn-pap in its leave-wrap |
| Ènìà, Ènìyàn | Human being |
| Erin, Àjànàkú | Elephant |
| Ìgbálẹ̀, Ọwọ̀ | Broom |
| Igi Ẹyìn, Ọ̀pẹ, Igi Ọ̀pẹ | Palmfruit or palmnut tree |
| Ológbò, Olõgìnní | Cat |
| Ọlọ́run, Ọlọ́un, Olúwa | God Almighty |
| Òrìṣà (Òrìshà), Òòṣà (Òòshà) | Messenger-god |
| Òròmọndìyẹ, Òròmọndìẹ | Chick |
| Ṣàngó, Shàngó | God of thunder and lightning |

# About the author

**Yorùbá**

Táiyé Amọ́lẹ́sẹ̀ ẹ́ jẹ́ oníṣẹ́ ààbò ẹ̀rọ aiyélujára; ó sì ti jẹ́ ọ̀mọ̀wé akẹ́kọ̀ ìjìnlẹ̀ nípa èdèe Yorùbá látìgbà èwe. Ìdánimọ̀n-ọ́n rẹ̀ẹ́ kún nínú àṣàa Yorùbáa rẹ̀, èyí tí ó fi ń yangàn gan-an.

Akẹ́kọ̀ọ́ èdèe Yorùbá yóò ríi pé ìwé yìí wúlò fún ẹ̀kọ́, ó sì n'íye l'órí.

**English**

Táiyé Amọ́lẹ́sẹ̀ is a cybersecurity analyst and web developer and has, from youth, been an avid scholar of Yorùbá. His identity is steeped in his Yorùbá culture, of which he is immensely proud.

The prospective student of Yorùbá will find this book educationally rewarding and invaluable.

---

**French**

Táiyé Amọ́lẹ́sẹ̀ est analyste en cybersécurité et développeur Web et est, depuis sa jeunesse, a été un fervent érudit du yorùbá. Son identité est trempé dans son la culture yoruba, dont il est immensément fier.

Le futur étudiant de Yorùbá trouvera ce livre pédagogiquement enrichissant et inestimable.

---

**Portuguese**

Táiyé Amọ́lẹ́sẹ̀ é analista de segurança cibernética e desenvolvedor web e, desde a juventude, foi um ávido estudioso de Yorùbá. A identidade dele é mergulhado em seu cultura Yorùbá, das quais ele é imensamente orgulhoso.

O futuro aluno de Yorùbá vai encontrar este livro educacionalmente gratificante e inestimável.

---

**Spanish**

Táiyé Amólésè es analista de ciberseguridad y desarrollador web y tiene, desde la juventud, ha sido un ávido erudito de Yorùbá. Su identidad es empapado en su cultura Yorùbá, de los cuales está inmensamente orgulloso.

El futuro estudiante de Yorùbá encontrare este libro educativamente gratificante y inestimable.

www.ingramcontent.com/pod-product-compliance
Lightning Source LLC
Chambersburg PA
CBHW070643160426
43194CB00009B/1556